European Union and its Neighbours in a Globalized World

Volume 21

AF781020

The series publishes monographs and edited volumes in the field of European and international law and policy. A special focus is put on the European neighbourhood policy, current problems in European and international law and policy as well as the role of the European Union as a global actor. The series supports the publishing and distribution of research results of cross-border research consortia. Besides renowned scientists the series is also open for publication projects of young academics. The series emphasizes the interplay of the European Union and its neighbouring countries as well as the important role of the European Union as a key player in the international context of law, economics and politics.

Nasir Muftić

Artificial Intelligence and Tortious Liability

Case Study of Bosnia and Herzegovina

Springer

Nasir Muftić
Faculty of Law
University of Sarajevo
Sarajevo, Bosnia and Herzegovina

ISSN 2524-8928 ISSN 2524-8936 (electronic)
European Union and its Neighbours in a Globalized World
ISBN 978-3-031-86455-1 ISBN 978-3-031-86453-7 (eBook)
https://doi.org/10.1007/978-3-031-86453-7

This Springer imprint is published by the registered company Springer Nature Switzerland AG
The registered company address is: Gewerbestrasse 11, 6330 Cham, Switzerland

To my mentors, my friends, and family who supported me wholeheartedly throughout my journey of life and academia and to Mirha who makes the future seem ever so much more worthwhile.
It goes without saying, all errors and omissions are my responsibility.

Competing Interests The author has no competing interests to declare that are relevant to the content of this manuscript.

Contents

Chapter 1
Introduction

Hardly can any discussion about the future occur without reference to digital technologies. Whether seen as a utopian vision or a dystopian concern, nearly everyone has thoughts on the impact of digital technologies on our lives. Among digital technologies, artificial intelligence (hereinafter: AI) is the one that captures the most attention and raises eyebrows. Often described as unprecedented and groundbreaking, it bears the potential to change the way we interact with one another, do every day simple and complex tasks, and, eventually, how we perceive the world. AI would be able to incrementally replace humans in their jobs and probably so in an unmistakable fashion. If AI replaces human jobs, what would be the fate of the vast workforce left jobless? Can we already now predict who are going to be victims of the change and do something to enhance their position? Historian of technology Carl Benedikt Frey in his book "The technology trap"[1] suggests that we have seen this before and that inequalities in wealth caused by the emergence of groundbreaking technology were a realistic scenario in the past. The rise of inequality therefore appears as a recurring pattern in technological revolutions. Addressing the breadth of potential problems in this work would be overly ambitious. Rather, I will focus on the responses of the tortious liability system of Bosnia and Herzegovina (hereinafter: B&H) to accidents involving AI.

This, too, is a question which, in my opinion, deserves the attention of not only lawyers. The practical implications of having AI involved in potentially harmful events have broader societal importance. Reduction of human involvement in accidents caused by human errors, such as fatigue or stress requires rethinking legal standards with characteristics of humans in focus. Technology, unlike humans, doesn't experience fatigue or stress. It does not have a sick child due to which it would lose focus or simply have a bad day. Research suggests that a great number of motor vehicle accidents occur due to human errors, such as speeding, driving under the influence of alcohol and other psychoactive substances, nonuse of motorcycle

[1] See Frey (2019).

N. Muftić, *Artificial Intelligence and Tortious Liability*, European Union and its Neighbours in a Globalized World 21, https://doi.org/10.1007/978-3-031-86453-7_1

helmets, seatbelts, child restraints, and distractions such as mobile phones.[2] None of these problems may exist if we exclude humans as the operators of vehicles. However, implementing AI in activities requires rethinking how tort law systems work. Challenges within the system exist on both broad and specific levels. On the broad level, for example, it is hard at the outset to formulate what is AI in an operable legal definition. There is no consensus among scientists on what is AI due to its changing and unpredictable nature. Definitions typically describe it through terms such as autonomy, intelligence, and opacity, but even these can be vague. What is autonomy or intelligence exactly? If an acceptable scholarly definition of this phenomenon may be hard to fathom, so is a legal one. Answers to many questions should not be a matter of exclusive deliberation of lawyers but of a broader population. For example, whether AI should be allowed in every field of our lives, or certain parts of it are simply too vulnerable or sensitive. This has been debated in the EU institutions as a part of the broader discussion about the legal instrument titled AI Act. While such questions do not strictly fit under the work on civil liability, they certainly cannot be divorced from it. They will be at least mentioned in this work, as well as their importance for the regulation of liability. Another set of questions that can be described as broad has to be addressed with a clear opinion of their author, however. Those are broad questions that act as a basis for any further deliberations on the regulation of liability for AI. In this work, such questions are provided with a clear understanding and proposed solutions. The examples would be understanding of product under the regulation of product liability and which of the potential addressees of liability deserves to bear the ultimate burden of remuneration.

Despite the title puts Bosnia and Herzegovina in focus, this work relies on the work of scholars from different countries. There are two reasons why this approach is not only justified but only possible. First, as far as I am aware, jurisdictions around the world are still developing their approaches to the regulation of AI liability. The non-existence of specific rules on AI liability does not mean that there are no rules on liability at all. A decision to treat AI with general rules of liability, such as the ones found in civil codes and statutes, is also a regulatory choice. General rules are designed to be future-proof and technology-neutral in order to be flexible and therefore applicable to a range of accidents. While general rules around Europe differ from one another, they are typically based on the same foundations and principles. These similarities allow for drawing comparisons. Second, scholarship in Bosnia and Herzegovina (hereinafter: B&H) on legal aspects of AI is almost non-existent. It would be impossible to use the opinions of local experts since they are unavailable in written form so far. B&H is not the only country in which liability law succeeded Yugoslavia's law. Other state successors also apply the same statute—Law of Obligation from 1978, in original or amended versions. Unfortunately, a scholarship that would deal with the issue of liability for AI is also very limited. The work also relies on the findings of lawmakers from various

[2]Road traffic injuries, available at: https://www.who.int/news-room/fact-sheets/detail/road-traffic-injuries.

jurisdictions, especially the European Union (hereinafter: EU). As I will elaborate in Chap. 2, the pertinence of the EU's acquis communautaire is high for B&H. Domestic legislators, especially when it comes to the regulation of technology, model their instruments after the EU ones. B&H has a goal of becoming a Member State of this supranational organization, which is why its behavior is not supported only by the soft power of the EU but also by the legal duty the state has under the Stabilisation and Association Agreement which entered into force in 2015. Furthermore, the EU and its institutions became unofficially one of the main forums for the regulation of AI worldwide. This organization is a platform where the main debates and exchanges of arguments concerning AI take place. At the time of writing this work, the EU has adopted the AI Act, a comprehensive regulatory instrument that provides a classification of different AI systems based on the risk they generate and affords various duties accordingly. This is not a liability instrument as it concerns ex ante mitigation of AI harms, but it is nonetheless important for the regulation of liability. The approach to liability in the EU law has changed a couple of times in the last decade. The EU Parliament introduced the idea of treating AI as a person in 2017. In 2020, it gave up on it and introduced a new idea whereby backend and frontend operators should be liable jointly and severally for harm caused by AI. Lastly, the EU Commission stepped in and introduced a third approach: updates to the Product Liability Directive, a legal instrument from 1985 that has been partly obsolete due to technological advancements, and an AI Liability Directive, a new piece of legislation. The two major changes in the EU approach to the regulation of liability for AI suggest that this issue is rather complex. In comparison, the AI Act of the EU, arguably the most famous piece of AI legislation in the world currently, had not been subject to such radical change in the approach by the EU. While its provision had been heavily debated and criticized, the main approach behind it had remained untouched from the beginning.

To write about how a relatively small jurisdiction such as Bosnia and Herzegovina deals with novel technological challenges is unusual. Arguably, its power to regulate is limited as it may follow an approach established by the EU or other major jurisdictions that have the capacity to regulate AI. However, the approach of any of the major jurisdictions will not take into account the peculiar characteristics of the national legal system of a small country as well as its enforcement capacities. It will be left to deal with it alone. After all, even in the EU, the question of liability is mainly regulated by the national laws of the Member States and they are left to regulate liability for AI. Even though a country may be small, the interconnectedness of the modern world and the rapid development of digital technologies guarantee that it will not be bypassed by its impact. Dealing with the challenges of AI is inevitable notwithstanding the size of the population or GDP of a country.

Moreover, this work is an attempt to contribute to the democratization of AI regulation. The voices of the major digital companies equipped with substantial regulatory resources and influence, as well as of the developed states with significant regulatory capacities dominate the discourse on AI governance. Their voices shape the standards and policies that govern AI on a global scale. The voices from the other states are not heard so much. This work aims to amplify the perspectives of states that are often overlooked in global regulatory discussions. Just like the users fight for empowerment and a seat at the table, so should the states as they will be exposed to the risks of AI, These states, like their citizens, deserve meaningful participation in shaping the rules that will ultimately impact them. This is especially crucial as these states face the risks associated with AI systems that are typically developed, owned, and operated by private companies headquartered in foreign countries. This work aims to contribute to a more inclusive and equitable discourse on AI regulation—one that reflects the diverse needs and circumstances of all stakeholders, including smaller jurisdictions and their citizens.

Reference

Books

Frey CB (2019) The technology trap. Princeton University Press

Chapter 2
Understanding AI and the Current Legal Landscape

2.1 Introduction

AI is widely recognized a technology with the potential to undermine various domains of human life. It has the potential to change the way we commute, labor, create and consume media, and interact. The fields which it can reform are unlimited. For the law, it brings many challenges. These problems, even if dealt with by other fields of law, necessarily impact how parties interact in their civil law relationships. For example, if a company employs AI to draft a contract it offers its consumers, it may reduce its transaction costs. It may need fewer employees to perform these tasks. By using appropriate prompts, it's AI can not only provide a standard form of contract, but it can create terms that are more favorable for the company, based on the analysis of the customer's data. Or, more radically, it may decide not to consider the credit application submitted by an applicant based on the analysis of their data. As evidence suggests, AI is prone to making mistakes in such contexts and even to making decisions based on the applicant's race, gender, or other identity markers. A company that uses AI may therefore reduce its transactional costs and potentially expose its customers to unfair and biased treatment.

Understanding AI requires understanding its characteristics. This is a rather challenging task. Due to the noise surrounding this technology, many of its characteristics are exaggerated or misinterpreted. AI is often seen as omnipotent and without a clear background structure and set of rules governing it. Moreover, the field itself is very technical and prone to innovations. In reality, AI is a highly technical field, grounded in complex mathematical and engineering principles. There is no single method used in the field of development or deployment of AI, but rather many. These methods are not static as designers and engineers constantly improve them or adapt them to new circumstances. The evolution of technology and the way it is created is hard to capture in a moment, and it is even harder to come up with predictions that will certainly be correct in the future.

N. Muftić, *Artificial Intelligence and Tortious Liability*, European Union and its Neighbours in a Globalized World 21, https://doi.org/10.1007/978-3-031-86453-7_2

For the goal of this book, it is useful to discern characteristics of this technology that have the most significant impact on civil law and especially tort law. The sheer task of deriving the most significant characteristics is not easy due to the current stage of development of AI as well as due to its diversity. AI is currently in its infancy, and it is projected to be developed significantly in the future. It is therefore hard to predict characteristics of technology which is potentially going to evolve. Even in the current stage of development, AI exists in various forms and performs many different tasks. Moreover, the techniques used to develop it are manyfold, halting the task of generalizing its abilities. To prevent this problem, this book presents those characteristics widely recognized by policymakers and scholarship.

The chapter presents the basic characteristics of the laws of B&H and the European Union law. B&H law had been adopted after the civil law codifications in Europe and it is based on Roman law. Despite the time distance, its understanding is linked to the understanding of civil law in Europe. The similarities between the challenges it faces are similar to those faced by other legal systems in Europe. Second, the EU is at the forefront of AI regulation globally. Although it is not a Member state, the significance of the EU and its Member States' national laws is undeniable for B&H. There is a legal duty for B&H as a candidate state to implement the EU law as its national law. Also, due to proximity and reliance on economic activity, compliance with the EU law is a priority. Lastly, even Member States of the EU have to apply their national law to tort law accidents. The role of the EU law is limited only to a few issues in this area, leaving the majority of power in the hands of Member States to develop and apply their national law. Consequently, the treatment of AI accidents by any national legal system in Europe is educational for other legal systems.

2.2 Origins of AI

The idea that human creations can become thinking beings is not new. History offers many examples of oral and written accounts where the inanimate objects turn out to be alive or thinking beings. Turner notices that such ideas permeate ancient societies and religious doctrines and offers many examples.[1] For instance, the ancient Sumer, Chinese, and Greek mythologies attest to the existence of tales about the servants of Gods made of clay and other natural materials. Hephaestus, the god of blacksmith from Greek mythology, could create his own servants made of gold, as Homer noted in Iliad. A similar understanding of human creation is present in Judeo-Christian and Islamic doctrines, where God created humans from clay.[2] Further history is replete

[1] Turner (2019), p. 4.

[2] Genesis 2:7, King James Bible: "And the Lord God formed man of the dust of the ground and breathed into his nostrils the breath of life; and man became a living soul."; Quran: "We created man from sounding clay, from mud moulded into shape…" (15:26). "He began the creation of man from clay and made his progeny from a quintessence of fluid" (32:7–8).

with stories and myths about beings whose intelligence is undisputed. The beings in these narratives often have similar features—they were created by an external force from the Earthly materials and they are self-thinking or self-acting entities.

Some versions of these narratives have a twist. It concerns the creator of such beings. The following stories and myths did not consider God as the only one capable of the creation of intelligent entities. Humans became capable of it too. For instance, the creation of Golem, a non-human being whose existence is part of the traditional Jewish folklore, is often connected to remarkable Rabbis who were able to create them for the purpose of protecting Jews from pogroms but also for other reasons such as providing help with the housework or even for sexual relations. The narrative became a part of the common practices after Rabbi Eleazer of Worms, an early German Kabbalist in the thirteenth century, created a manuscript that provided "detailed instructions for how to create a golem; by the end of that century, summoning golems was a common part of Kabbalistic practice."[3]

History does not offer only examples related to gods or superhumans or the use of methods involving some sort of magic or divinity. Humans throughout history have been trying to create methods to increase the speed of labor or render it easier by using a scientific approach. The inventions that automated human activities were great engineering achievements of societies where they occurred. The ancient Greeks' construction of water mills, and the Antikythera, "perhaps even the world's first mechanical computer used to predict astrological movements"[4] were landmark inventions at the time. "Pneumatica", a treatise on the use of air, steam, and water written by the Roman engineer Hero of Alexandria is another example of it.[5] The inventions or blueprints of Leonardo da Vinci and the likes fit into this category too.

The idea of intelligent creations of humans was popularized by the nineteenth-century novel Frankenstein's monster written by Mary Shelley. The Frankenstein used scientific method he discovered to create a being who is not only intelligent but also resembles humans as it has emotions and personality. It is hard to say whether the fact that humans created intelligent units was more appealing to the audience than the human characteristics of the creation. The writer Karel Čapek in 1920 published a play R.U.R. [R.U.R. stands for *Rossumovi Univerzální Roboti* (Rossum's Universal Robots)], where he further popularized the idea. The play is considered important in popular culture especially because it introduced the term "robot". One of the most prominent writers who further developed human understanding of AI is Isaac Asimov, a science fiction and fantasy writer who dealt with issues such as the rules of ethics pertaining governance of AI.[6]

---

[3]Marilyn Cooper, Jewish Word | Golem, available at: https://momentmag.com/jewish-word-golem/.

[4]Abbot (2020), p. 19.

[5]Ibid.

[6]The "Three laws of robotics" are a part of his short story "Runaround": "(1) A robot may not injure a human being or, through inaction, allow a human being to come to harm. (2) A robot must obey orders given it by human beings except where such orders would conflict with the First Law. (3) A robot must protect its own existence as long as such protection does not conflict with the First or

The popularization of AI is not divorced from its development, although this chapter does not attempt to offer a complete account of any of these issues. Notwithstanding the intention of humans to create intelligent beings in order to achieve various goals is not new and does not have a single origin or the way in which it was supposed to materialize. AI can be understood as the closest endeavor of people to do so, provided we do not believe in the previous accounts of successful attempts mentioned in mythology and religion due to the lack of scientific evidence.

2.3 Modern AI

What we call AI has a foundation in modern times. It is related to the improved abilities of humans to conduct complex calculations and the high state of the art in the technology. John McCarthy, a computer scientist, organized the workshop at the Dartmouth Summer Research Project on Artificial Intelligence in 1956, the event in many accounts recognized as giving birth to the scientific discipline of AI.[7] McCarthy saw the research field as follows: "For the present purpose the artificial intelligence problem is taken to be that of making a machine behave in ways that would be called intelligent if a human were so behaving."[8] Even before this event, several thinkers produced a significant amount of work on intelligent creations of humans capable of performing cognitive processes. Some of the most notable are Charles Babbage, Ada Lovelace, and Alan Turing. Turing had, in his seminal work of 1950, attempted to establish the understanding of machine intelligence through human intelligence.[9]

He adopted the so-called Turing test that determines whether a machine can think. It can be deemed intelligent if a person cannot discern whether it interacts with a human or a machine. Details of this test suggest that intelligence exists if a machine meets the following conditions: (1) natural language processing; (2) knowledge representation (to store what it knows); (3) automated reasoning (to employ stored information to answer questions and to draw new conclusions); and (4) machine learning (to adapt to new circumstances and to detect and extrapolate patterns).

Increasing attention to the development of AI and the recognition of its commercial potential has marked recent history, driven by established and new businesses.[10] The private sector is, in fact, the frontrunner in the development and deployment of

Second Law." He later added the Zeroth law: "A robot may not harm humanity, or, by inaction, allow humanity to come to harm."

[7] Kovac (2020), p. 51.

[8] Proposal for the Dartmouth summer research project on artificial intelligence, available at: http://www-formal.stanford.edu/jmc/history/dartmouth/dartmouth.html.

[9] Turing (1950), p. 460.

[10] Tracking AI Investment Initial Findings From the Private Markets, available at: https://cset.georgetown.edu/publication/tracking-ai-investment/.

this technology. AI is increasingly used in employment,[11] assessment of creditworthiness,[12] tackling misinformation,[13] and many other fields. While companies are competing in who is going to have more developed AI, jurisdictions compete in who is going to provide more favorable conditions to them thereby attracting investment.[14] AI has become a buzzword nowadays and even mainstream media is loaded with reports on it. The momentum of this technology continues to grow daily. The World Economic Forum projected that AI is going to be at the forefront of the Fourth Industrial Revolution, a set of events that will change the way we labor, pay taxes, and live.[15] PricewaterhouseCoopers predicts that the contribution of AI to the global economy by 2030 might be $15.7 trillion to the global economy, of which $6.6 trillion could come from increased productivity and $9.1 trillion from consumption-side effects.[16] Its potential has been recognized by governments and international organizations[17] that are developing or enforcing strategies on its development and management.

Although we can hear it daily in our lives, the term is often used with a different range of meanings. Some use AI to speculate about the future, often attributing it to the possibility of a technological utopia or a fear of an impending dystopia. These interpretations are frequently driven by futurological hopes or anxieties about scenarios that are unlikely to materialize within our lifetimes. This lack of clarity highlights the importance of delving deeper into the true substance of this concept to better understand its implications and avoid being swayed by vague or sensationalist narratives.

[11] Amazon scraps secret AI recruiting tool that showed bias against women, available at: https://www.reuters.com/article/us-amazon-com-jobs-automation-insight-idUSKCN1MK08G.

[12] Bias isn't the only problem with credit scores—and no, AI can't help, available at: https://www.technologyreview.com/2021/06/17/1026519/racial-bias-noisy-data-credit-scores-mortgage-loans-fairness-machine-learning/.

[13] Fake News Is Rampant, Here Is How Artificial Intelligence Can Help, available at: https://www.forbes.com/sites/bernardmarr/2021/01/25/fake-news-is-rampant-here-is-how-artificial-intelligence-can-help/?sh=3abf5c7d48e4.

[14] Microsoft wants to stop AI's 'Race to the Bottom', available at: https://www.wired.com/story/microsoft-wants-stop-ai-facial-recognition-bottom/.

[15] Klaus Schwab, The Fourth Industrial Revolution: what it means, how to respond, available at: https://www.weforum.org/agenda/2016/01/the-fourth-industrial-revolution-what-it-means-and-how-to-respond/.

[16] PricewaterhouseCoopers Global Artificial Intelligence Study: Exploiting the AI Revolution, available at: https://www.pwc.com/gx/en/issues/data-and-analytics/publications/artificial-intelligence-study.html.

[17] For example: The EU Parliament. What is artificial intelligence and how is it used?, available at: https://www.europarl.europa.eu/news/en/headlines/society/20200827STO85804/what-is-artificial-intelligence-and-how-is-it-used; The Council of Europe, Artificial intelligence and human rights, available at: https://www.coe.int/en/web/artificial-intelligence/secretary-general-marija-pejcinovic-buric.

2.4 Understanding AI

AI is a multi-purpose technology. It is based on various techniques and it can perform different tasks. Its surprising growth in some fields, such as the relatively recent rise in popularity of large language models, can change the public perception of its capabilities. Furthermore, typical educational programs often do know include AI as a subject. Individuals are left to obtain information about it individually through various sources. These factors contribute to a diverse and often inconsistent understanding of AI by the general population. Scholars are also struggling to reach a consensus on what constitutes AI.

There is not a single universally accepted definition of AI. Nilsson defines it as an "activity devoted to making machines intelligent, and intelligence is that quality that enables an entity to function appropriately and with foresight in its environment".[18] Calo argues that it is "a set of techniques aimed at approximating some aspect of human or animal cognition using machines".[19] In the definition used by the EU Commission, AI "refers to systems that display intelligent behavior by analyzing their environment and taking actions – with some degree of autonomy – to achieve specific goals. AI-based systems can be purely software-based, acting in the virtual world (e.g. voice assistants, image analysis software, search engines, speech and face recognition systems) or AI can be embedded in hardware devices (e.g. advanced robots, autonomous cars, drones, or Internet of Things applications)".[20] The common denominator of the majority of definitions includes the term intelligence or cognition as an ability of this technology. Intelligence itself can be understood very differently as it is a notion employed in various scientific fields. As AI changes (or improves) over time, a lack of its static nature hinders consensus on the definition.

Rationality has been recognized as a word that depicts the intelligence this technology yields.[21] An entity can be considered intelligent if it has the capacity to make rational decisions based on the inputs from the environment. Intelligence, thus, does not mean the presence of cognition which expands on other fields from the ones in which the system is supposed to express it. In that sense, AI does not need to have a universal rationality in order to be perceived as intelligent. Rather, its role can be constrained to a limited set of tasks or even a single task where it behaves rationally. For instance, the fact that some AI systems might outperform humans in translating words does not mean their ability to understand the context behind the speech is supreme and even less that it is able to perform other tasks such as solving complex mathematical equations. Also, intelligence does not mean consciousness.

[18] Nilsson (2010).

[19] Calo (2017).

[20] Communication from the Commission to the European Parliament, the European Council, the Council, the European Economic and Social Committee and the Committee of the Regions on Artificial Intelligence for Europe, Brussels, 25.4.2018 COM(2018) 237 final.

[21] Russell and Norvig (2009).

Consciousness is very hard to define and usually entails moral, ethical or philosophical considerations. It refers to an "the perception of what passes in a man's own mind".[22] Notwithstanding the lack of consensus,[23] the resolution of this problem is not essential for determining tort liability. It might appear so in the question of the appropriateness of holding the AI itself liable, but as it will be demonstrated, other considerations such as its existence of funds to compensate the injured party are more important, or at least have more direct and tangible impact.

AI can observe environment, process the inputs, and decide how to act accordingly. However, the ability to perform tasks that is not what makes it different from other human inventions. Such understanding would not separate a traditional cuckoo clock from the Tesla self-driving car as each perform the allocated actions. The supreme potential of AI lies in the ways in which it perceives and perform those tasks. As it will be demonstrated below, there are various techniques, systems, and method used in to render the algorithms behave intelligently. This is what separates it from the traditional technologies. I will refer to the specific characteristics of AI in the following sections.

The number of differences understood under the term AI does not allow one to easily provide a definition of this technology. The lack of clarity has caused occasional failures of optimism in the technology, backed by the lack of funding, often referred to as AI winter.[24] On the other hand, a lack of definition is not necessarily bad: "Curiously, the lack of a precise, universally accepted definition of AI probably has helped the field to grow, blossom, and advance at an ever-accelerating pace. Practitioners, researchers, and developers of AI are instead guided by a rough sense of direction and an imperative to "get on with it"."[25] To define what is AI would be to limit it, to paraphrase Oscar Wilde in his book the Picture of Dorian Gray. Exactly the diversity of approaches could be one of the reasons for the flourishment of AI, as the expectations one a single, universally accepted definition, has not curtailed researchers.

2.4.1 Reasoning, Decision-Making, and Learning

Compared to other technologies, AI has an exquisite power of computing its environments. After it percepts the exterior signals, it transforms them into understandable information upon which it designs and executes its action. The supreme

[22] Encyclopædia Britannica consciousness, available at: https://www.britannica.com/topic/consciousness.

[23] For example Reggia et al. (2015).

[24] What should we learn from past AI forecasts?, available at: https://www.openphilanthropy.org/focus/global-catastrophic-risks/potential-risks-advanced-artificial-intelligence/what-should-we-learn-past-ai-forecasts.

[25] Stone et al. (2016).

capacity to conduct this process is what makes AI transformative technology. Steps employed in this process, as described by the High-Level Expert Group on Artificial Intelligence set up by the European Commission, include knowledge representation and reasoning, planning, scheduling, search, and optimization.[26]

To be able to do this, one needs to transform data into knowledge, so one area of AI has to do with how best to model such knowledge (knowledge representation). Once knowledge has been modeled, the next step is to reason with it (knowledge reasoning), which includes making inferences through symbolic rules, planning, and scheduling activities, searching through a large solution set, and optimizing among all possible solutions to a problem. The final step is to decide what action to take. The reasoning and decision-making part of an AI system can be complex and opaque.[27]

What renders AI a groundbreaking technology is a set of techniques that enable the decision-making and execution process to become better over time. Based on previous experiences, AI can improve its decisions in the future. Listing a set of these techniques is hard as various authors designate different ones. Notwithstanding, some of the techniques undisputedly fit this category. These are speech and language understanding, computer vision or behaviour prediction, machine learning and deep learning.[28] One of the most renowned among them is machine learning, a "capacity of a system to improve its performance at a task over time".[29] Within machine learning there, again many techniques, of which the main ones are supervised learning, unsupervised learning, and reinforcement learning.[30] Supervised learning entails providing the AI with examples of input-output behavior and allowing it to create general rules from them which would be useful for future encounters with similar situations. Unsupervised learning involves "finding clusters of observation that are similar in terms of their covariates—dimensionality reduction; also, matrix factorization, regularization, and neuro-networks".[31] Reinforcement learning refers to rewarding AI's decisions with positive or negative signals, thereby allowing it to learn from them on a trial-and-error method.[32] Some other notable machine learning techniques include neural networks and deep learning.

Naturally, for AI to become better at decision-making, it needs data to process as it learns based on previous experiences. In fact, the availability of data is one of the

[26] High-Level Expert Group on Artificial Intelligence set up by the European Commission, A definition of AI: Main capabilities and scientific disciplines, available at: https://www.aepd.es/sites/default/files/2019-12/ai-definition.pdf.

[27] Ibid, 3.

[28] Ibid.

[29] Surden (2014).

[30] Apart from these techniques, the EU's AI Act proposal in Annex I lists also: Logic and knowledge-based approaches, including knowledge representation, inductive (logic) programming, knowledge bases, inference and deductive engines, (symbolic) reasoning and expert systems; Statistical approaches, Bayesian estimation, search and optimization methods.

[31] Varian (2014).

[32] Nilsson (2009).

most important factors for the rapid development of AI globally.[33] However, providing the systems with data is not an easy task. On the example of facial recognition, Kate Crawford explains the importance of the internet in this respect: "The internet, in so many ways, changed everything; it came to be seen in the AI research field as something akin to a natural resource, there for the taking. As more people began to upload their images to websites, to photo-sharing services, and ultimately to social media platforms, the pillaging began in earnest. Suddenly, training sets could reach a size that scientists in the 1980s could never have imagined."[34] Naturally, apart from the emergence of the internet, the improvement of hardware used for sensing, perception, and object recognition has additionally enhanced data collection and processing.[35] Despite the world-wide presence of the internet and modern hardware, not all parts of the world follow the same policy concerning the data. Some parts of the world set up rules on data protection that limit the availability of data for AI to use unconditionally. Such policies curtail the growth of AI by reducing the amounts of trial-error attempts AI can render, but at the same time protect other interests deemed important too. The most prominent is the data privacy of individuals.

However, the AI's ability to analyse the environment and adopt a decision accordingly is not equal to its understanding of the environment. Understanding is a deeper process that involves the ability of an entity to outline the context from a myriad of information present in the environment as well as from the previous experiences and values in force. This is one of the potential problems of AI. The words of Isiah Berlin reflect this point:

> [Mathematics] did not, as they supposed, correspond to an objective structure of reality; it was a method and not a body of truths; with its help, we could plot regularities—the occurrence of phenomena in the external world—but not discover why they occurred as they did, or to what end.[36]

This problem is not a central one in the domain of tort law as its primary focus is not on the cognition of AI. Its decision-making, as is the case with other technology, is in orthodox tort law understanding always attributable to humans behind. Notwithstanding, when an autonomous action of AI creates a consequence sanctioned by law, one should be aware that the cognition behind it does not replicate the human thought process. Computation does have its limits despite the hardship in defining them, especially in grasping the more abstract concepts. For example, the inclusion of AI and other automated means of decision-making in legal decision-making is heavily debated as it requires "the translation of the linguistic categories used by the

---

[33] Who Is Winning the AI Race: China, the EU or the United States? available at: https://datainnovation.org/2019/08/who-is-winning-the-ai-race-china-the-eu-or-the-united-states/.

[34] Crawford (2021), p. 106.

[35] Peter Stone (2018).

[36] Berlin (1973).

law into mathematical functions".[37] Such a task attempts to equalize mathematical formulas with natural language semantic, grounding AI's decisions only on "deterministic or probabilistic outputs, produced on the basis of static or unambiguous legal rules, in a societal vacuum".[38] Even if AI manages to understand the rules, the decisions would need to be transparent and explainable to humans, especially taking into account potential problems such as bias or fatigue. The supreme computational power thus does not mean understanding the context or abstract concepts, especially when AI cannot fathom them by recognizing patterns on the basis of the trial-error method.

2.4.2 AI, Algorithms, and Autonomous Systems

AI and other software are predicated on algorithms—instructions in the form of rules or principles that define the modus operandi of software. The algorithms, therefore, act as an alphabet used to program software. In the study about the impact of AI on human rights, democracy, and the rule of law, published by the Council of Europe, an algorithm is defined as: "A computational process or set of rules that are performed to solve some problem. A computer is typically used to carry out complex algorithms, but a human could also follow an algorithmic process, such as by following a recipe or using a mathematical formula to solve an equation."[39]

Autonomous systems is another umbrella term often used as a synonym for AI. It presupposes a software, embodied or not, which is capable of conducting a certain degree of independent decision-making process and therefore influencing its environment. Again, the term itself includes various techniques of algorithm design and deployment. The term autonomous system is not a synonym for automated decision-making[40] as the latter might also include more than that, depending on the interpretation. Automated decision-making does not necessarily mean that the autonomous system has made a certain decision. First, automated decision-making might mean a decision made by a machine that is not autonomous, but it occurs without any human involvement. An example would be a vending machine where one can buy a can of soda or candy. Although it executes decisions without supervision or direct involvement of humans, it follows clear instructions and does not depart. In fact, any departure from them would be considered problematic it was not intended by the manufacturers. Second, automated decision-making might mean a decision involving humans who decide by routinely applying automatically generated profiles to

[37] Markou and Deakin (2020), p. 33.

[38] Markou and Deakin (2020), p. 7.

[39] Artificial intelligence, human rights, democracy, and the rule of law—a primer, available at: https://rm.coe.int/primer-en-new-cover-pages-coe-english-compressed-2754-7186-0228-v-1/1680a2fd4a.

[40] This is the term used in the Article 22 of the EU General Data Protection Regulation.

individuals without any actual influence on the result.[41] For instance, an algorithm used by a bank suggests an interest rate based on the personal data of clients and the bank employee adopts it without any further assessment.

The terms AI, algorithm, and autonomous systems appear in the depiction of what we consider AI in this work. Literature also uses self-learning, intelligent/smart/thinking/autonomous, and/or robotic systems/machines. For purposes of this work, all these terms would be considered functionally equivalent and the content they label would be referred to as AI.

2.4.3 Robots and AI

In a common parlance, robots are often used to describe AI and *vice versa*. However, the two terms are not synonyms but the two separate phenomena which occasionally overlap. Robots denote AI which has a manifestation in the physical world. They can be described as machines programmable for autonomous or semi-autonomous decision-making in the dynamics, the uncertainties and the complexity of a physical world.[42] In order to do so, robots are equipped with sensors, cameras and lasers to and others means used to measure and assess the environment. Not all software embodied in a hardware can be considered robots. In order to qualify as such, a machine has to possess some characteristics. Although there is a lack of consensus about which characteristics precisely those are, a description of Ryan Calo[43] is often used in scholarship. He argues that robots possess at least three qualities: "embodiment," "emergence," and "social valence" and that "robots are best thought of as artificial objects or systems that sense, process, and act upon the world to at least some degree".[44]

Just like in the case of defining AI, the hardship to define a robot exists mainly due to technology which escapes to be confined to the galloped speed of its advancement as well as the great diversity between existing robots. A robot must certainly exercise a degree of autonomy, i.e. capacity to conduct a decision-making

---

[41] Sancho (2020), p. 143.

[42] High-Level Expert Group on Artificial Intelligence set up by the European Commission, A definition of AI: Main capabilities and scientific disciplines, 4, available at: https://www.aepd.es/sites/default/files/2019-12/ai-definition.pdf.

[43] Calo (2015).

[44] More recent literature though often does not use robots as to mean only embodied AI. For example, Mark A. Lemley and Bryan Casey argue, while acknowledging Calo's definition of robot: "Today, the terms "robotics" and "artificial intelligence" are often used interchangeably, referring to both embodied and disembodied systems that affect the physical and digital worlds alike. And while there are important technical distinctions to be made between the two concepts, we adopt the convention of construing "robot" to encompass both robots in Calo's "essentialist" sense and artificially intelligent systems embodied only in software. Our goal is to include any hardware or software system exhibiting intelligent behavior." See Lemley and Casey (2019), p. 1320.

process.[45] For this reason, robotic prostheses that a person can carry, or devices that are controlled remotely are not robots. Examples would be self-driving vehicles or autonomous drones. The existing definitions demonstrate that robots are seen more from such, a functional perspective, rather than from the technological perspective, i.e. the technology upon which they are based. The International Standards Organization defines a robot as an "actuated mechanism programmable in two or more axes with a degree of autonomy, moving within its environment, to perform intended tasks."[46] Susana Navas argues that the EU Parliament's understanding of robots can be subsumed under the five characteristics which derive from the EU Parliament Resolution of 16 February 2017 on Civil Law Rules on Robotics, 2015/2103 INL. Those are: (1) acquisition of autonomy through sensors or by exchanging data with the environment (inter-connectivity) as well as the trading and analysis of such data; (2) ability to learn (self-learning) from experience and by interaction with other robots (M2M); (3) a minor physical presence, to distinguish it from a virtual robot; (4) adaptation of its behaviour and actions to the environment; and (5) absence of biological life. This is not a legally binding definition though. It has only been used in the invitation made by the EU Parliament to the EU Commission for the submission of legislative proposals. On the other hand, AI does not always appear as a robot as it does not have to be embodied. It can be software without a body, acting as part of a greater system that does not necessarily have a physical presence. Such manifestation is often described as "stand-alone", depicting "software that runs on computer systems but is not embedded in them".[47] The examples would be AI investment advisors or the aforementioned hiring AI. Classification of AI based on the criterion of the existence of physicality is legally relevant. For instance, the rules on health and safety may differ for the embodied AI such as "machinery" and the one which does not have a physical component. The notion of product, as defined under the Product Liability Directive[48] until the amendments from 2024, covered only movable property, leading to the conclusion that this regime would not be applicable in the case of stand-alone AI.

[45] Navas (2020), p. 161.

[46] ISO 8373, 2012, available at: www.iso.org/obp/ui/#iso:std:iso:8373:ed-2:v1:en.

[47] Wagner (2021), p. 548.

[48] Council Directive 85/374/EEC of 25 July 1985 on the approximation of the laws, regulations and administrative provisions of the Member States concerning liability for defective products [1985] OJ L210/29, as amended by Directive 1999/34/EC of the European Parliament and of the Council of 10 May 1999 [1999] OJ L141/20.

2.5 AI Characteristics Important for Tort Law

There is no single universally accepted definition of AI in science. Questions about the appropriateness of any definition stem from the lack of understanding of the technology, its diversity and often unpredictable development. It may also be hard to distinct between the impact the digital technologies make when they act together. Due to the interconnectedness of digital technologies and the expectation that their impact will be joint, it might be hard to assess the specific characteristics of each of them without risking omitting their behavior when they interact with other technologies. Here, I refer to an umbrella term of "emerging digital technologies", a broader term that captures various digital technologies with the likes of AI, the Internet of Things and Services or distributed ledger technologies.

Although hitherto legislative activities of the EU will be described below, it is important to briefly introduce the work of the European Commission at this point. In 2018, it established the Expert Group on Liability and New Technologies—New Technologies Formation Complexity (hereinafter: the Expert Group)[49] for the purposes of providing an opinion of the suitability of the current liability framework, in light of the challenges of emerging digital technologies. The New Technologies Formation of the Expert Group in 2019 published a Report on Liability for Artificial Intelligence and other emerging technologies[50] (hereinafter: Report). The Report does not only focus on AI. Rather, it provides an assessment of digital emerging technologies that "have extraordinary potential to transform products, services and activities, procedures and practices, in a multitude of economic sectors and in relation to many aspects of society".[51] AI is treated only as one of the technologies taken into consideration. Such subject matter definition made by the Expert Group is in line with the previous approach of the European Commission which used the notion of "emerging digital technologies" to encompass AI and related technologies. Such an approach recognizes the close connection of digital technologies and/or their impact. Another characteristic of the Expert Group's approach is that it avoided the hard task of defining emerging digital technologies in general, especially beyond addressing their impact or current liability regimes. The Report mentions characteristics of emerging digital technologies that require consideration since they bear the potential to cause disruption. Those characteristics are complexity, opacity, openness, autonomy, predictability, data-drivenness, and vulnerability. The Report does not distinguish between digital technologies it concerns and does not attribute the abovementioned characteristics specifically to AI.

[49]Expert Group on liability and new technologies, available at: https://ec.europa.eu/transparency/expert-groups-register/screen/expert-groups/consult?do=groupDetail.groupDetail&groupID=3592.

[50]European Commission's Expert Group on Liability and New Technologies—New Technologies Formation Report on Liability for Artificial Intelligence and other emerging technologies, 2019.

[51]Ibid, 11.

Out of all the characteristics addressed in the Report, autonomy, opacity, and vulnerability will be described in more detail. Some of these characteristics described cannot always be attributed to AI but rather to other emerging digital technologies, or they refer to the characteristics of AI only when it is part of a broader digital ecosystem. Furthermore, some of the characteristics mentioned in the Report will be jointly presented under the same term for the sake of clarity. For instance, the opacity will be explained through the complexity of AI and lack of predictability.

Categorization of AI characteristics might create a false image of the clear separation among them. Although they might be labeled differently and described separately, they are highly intertwined and often mutually causal. For example, opacity leads to vulnerability, but also vulnerability can cause opacity. Also, both characteristics can be described through the openness of AI. Therefore, the outlined characteristics should not be understood as strictly separate.

2.5.1 Autonomy

AI has capacity to conduct the process of decision-making on its own or with little human involvement. So far, human creations have acted as instructed by their manufacturers or operators, regardless of the level of sophistication of instructions that are required. AI is peculiar in the sense that it does not strictly follow the instructions of humans, especially in situations that have not occurred before. The system reacts to the external outputs in order to reach the goals set by humans, in the way it considers the most appropriate within the defined parameters. Autonomy is achieved through machine learning, a set of techniques described in previous sections. The autonomy is predicated on the availability of data, external outputs as well as great processing power of such data. Thus, AI as autonomous as it currently exists emerged with the availability of data and "when computers – or better, their processors and data storage devices – became fast and powerful enough to process the vast quantities of data required for machine learning".[52]

The term autonomy might not be the most appropriate as it suggests the existence of free will, which is not accurate in the case of AI. Rather, it should suggest that AI does not strictly follow the rules (especially when they are not provided for new situations), but it obeys the principles set by humans. This process has been described in the Report as an ability of AI to alter "the initial algorithms due to self-learning capabilities that process external data collected in the course of the operation."

Autonomy has already been addressed in previous sections as one of the foundational features of AI which is typically used in various definitions of it. Thus, it will not be elaborated further at this point.

[52] Kirchberger (2017).

2.5.2 *Opacity*

Opacity refers to a lack of understandability of the decision-making process of AI. The process of learning from previous experience is conducted in a fashion that might not be discernible to people. It does not mean that the outcome of the decisions is wrong or harmful. Opacity does not refer to any unpredictability that can be attributed to technology, as traditional software can behave unpredictably.[53] This characteristic refers to a "black-box", a concept closely related to the feature of AI that renders its decision-making process often untransparent and hardly explainable. Even the programmers who wrote the code might not be able to understand and even less able to predict the decision-making process of AI. Due to this characteristic, the term often used to describe it is "unpredictable by design".[54]

The first reason for opacity lies in the application of various self-learning techniques which *modus operandi* varies. Although humans can set the goals AI has to reach and provide it with data, it very often cannot understand the patterns it recognizes. AI has a supreme computational power which allows it to recognize what humans cannot. The lack of explainability of AI is more likely in the case of AI which learns from data. Opacity can also be attributed to the complexity of AI. Not only robots which consist of various parts, but also stand-alone AI are increasingly sophisticated. In both cases, there are various components of either hardware or an algorithm which might contribute to the harm.[55] Moreover, as AI requires vast amounts of data in order to operate and improve, the data itself can lead to harmful actions. For instance, datasets might be corrupted or there might be errors in labelling in the process of training data.

The complexity of AI can also refer to the interconnectedness of digital technologies. This will be elaborated in the following section.

2.5.3 *Vulnerability*

Vulnerability reflects the potential risks generated by the exposure to external data. The data might arrive from various parts within a specific AI or other components of a digital ecosystem, as well as from the data it processes in its environment.

As mentioned above, more than one actor might participate in the production of an AI as they might contribute to different parts of the process or jointly work in any of them. For instance, in the case of a robot, some producers can provide sensors and other receptors used for data collection, while others might provide an algorithm for processing the data in order for a robot to act. A different scenario would exist in case of a variety of interconnected components of a digital ecosystem that interact, but

[53] Wendehorst (2020), p. 152.

[54] Chagal-Feferkorn (2020), p. 143.

[55] Koch (2020), p. 120.

where each of them constitutes a separate unit. An example would be a smart fridge and other related devices that interact within a household. In both situations, several different actors who produce or maintain digital devices come into play. Such complexity is additionally enhanced by the openness of parts of components of an ecosystem. It is not uncommon that AI and other digital products are in the phase of production even after they leave the factory in a sense that manufacturers can provide impact on their performance through updates which are done completely remotely. For example, it is common to have a digital device and to receive a notification about available updates which should improve its performance. It is also possible that a product has components created by different manufacturers. The may not be static but "subject to frequent or even continuous change. It is in particular through the provision of over-the-air (OTA) updates for embedded or accessory software as well as through a variety of different data feeds and cloud-based digital services that products change their safety-relevant features after the product has been put into circulation".[56] Digital products remain under the influence of their manufacturers even if they are used by their owners. From the perspective of liability, this is an important point as it continuously enables owners to fix bugs and make products better and safer since their relationship with the product does not end once it has been deployed.

As it has already been mentioned, AI is so-called data-intensive technology. Its prime potential can be achieved only if it is provided with data that can be analyzed. Its decision-making process is being improved dependent on the availability of data that enables it to "learn" from. Due to the need for constant interaction with outside information, there is an increased exposure. The availability and quality of data is not only relevant for the advancement of AI, but also for the accuracy of the results it produces and, consequently, its performance. "Even the smartest algorithm does not deliver usable results, if the underlying data (structure) quality is poor".[57] AI is therefore vulnerable as it depends on the externally provided data.

Cybersecurity breaches are a potential threat too. As modern technologies typically operate in an interconnected fashion, potential breaches to any component of a digital ecosystem might generate a threat to others, including AI.[58]

2.6 Toward a Legal Definition of AI

In previous sections, we have seen that there is not universally accepted definition of AI in the scholarship. It is very hard to define it as it is an umbrella term for set of techniques which provide for the intelligent creation based on algorithm which is capable of conducting cognitive tasks. Having a legal definition of this technology is

[56] Ibid, 153.

[57] Steinrötter (2020), p. 270.

[58] Rodríguez de las Heras Ballell (2019), p. 308.

even harder, especially since it has not yet reached its potential or a definite of forms of manifestation. This is a growing field where the boundaries are still not determined. Moreover, quest for a comprehensive AI legal definition is additionally troubled by the multitude of differences between currently existing AI applications, rendering the common denominators hard to discern. "For example, an autonomous weapon system can hardly be compared to a spam filter, even though both are based on an AI system. Indeed, this example alone illustrates the futility of lawmakers considering a general Artificial Intelligence Act that would regulate the whole phenomenon top down…".[59]

Legal definitions differ from academic or any other definitions. They require clarity in understanding the specific characteristics of the object of definition since the rights and duties depend on it. However, as law provides a sanction, consequences for potential deficiencies of a definition are inevitably higher than in academia. Opposite views are emphasized in the scholarship about this issue.[60] Some argue that a common definition of the term AI is necessary, while others believe that the law can operate without one-size-fits-all terminology. The latter approach leads to a number of different policy choices, the main one being the preference of sector-specific regulation over general regulation of AI.[61] Legal definition of AI is important for many reasons. Jurisdictions seeking to attract AI investments need to provide clarity and foreseeability, hallmarks of which a vague definition certainly is not. If a definition is too broad, it might attract technologies disguised as AI, relying on its popularity in the investment circles and among regulators in order to yield benefits of favorable regulatory policies and investment climate.

It is possible that AI would be defined differently for purposes of liability than for other purposes. AI might not need a definition which is universally applicable. As a sensitive field which development lawmakers would not like to halt, clear-cut measures in certain aspects might be exactly what is required. AI brings lawmakers' attention in various fields such as tax law, judiciary, intellectual property law, competition law etc. Some of these fields still cannot be properly addressed at the moment or even may not need any modifications of the law at all. It is also possible that only particular applications within these sectors require intervention.[62] However, a consensus on the definition of AI has been reached within the Organisation for Economic Co-operation and Development (OECD). AI is defined as "a machine-based system that can, for a given set of humandefined objectives, make predictions, recommendations, or decisions influencing real or virtual environments."[63] This definition became a basis for the EU lawmakers and it became a legally binding

[59] Ebers (2020), p. 42.

[60] Ibid, 3.

[61] See Chap. 3.

[62] Smuha (2021).

[63] OECD, "Recommendation of the Council on Artificial Intelligence" (2019) Available at: https://legalinstruments.oecd.org/en/instruments/OECD-LEGAL-0449.

definition within AI Act, a first comprehensive legal instrument on AI of its kind. Article 3 of the AI Act defines AI as "a machine-based system that is designed to operate with varying levels of autonomy and that may exhibit adaptiveness after deployment, and that, for explicit or implicit objectives, infers, from the input it receives, how to generate outputs such as predictions, content, recommendations, or decisions that can influence physical or virtual environments".[64] This definition employs terms that may seem overly technical or vague. In order to clarify the main component of the definition, Recital 12 states that "a key characteristic of AI systems is their capability to infer. This capability to infer refers to the process of obtaining the outputs, such as predictions, content, recommendations, or decisions, which can influence physical and virtual environments, and to a capability of AI systems to derive models or algorithms, or both, from inputs or data."

Defining AI for purposes of civil liability, and more specifically tort liability is one of the options. That would mean adoption of the definition not applicable in other fields of law. Such definition needs to capture all important characteristics of AI for tort law as well as to distinguish it from other actors who might appear as tortfeasors or on their behalf. While AI definition cannot be completely technology-neutral, it can strive to generalize specific characteristics until the point where it remains distinguished from other terms used in tort law jargon. The threats of wrong definitions are manyfold. For instance, the state might favor one developer over another only due to the narrow or too specific definition of AI by providing subsidies to the former and not to the latter. Also, the definition itself should not contradict definitions used in other fields of law in order to provide foreseeability in a legal order. While AI definition cannot be completely technology-neutral, it can strive to generalize specific characteristics until the point where it remains distinguished from other terms used in tort law jargon.

Due to the lack of agreement on what constitutes AI as well as due to the change of this technology, the definition should describe distinguishing elements of this technology from other actors but remain open-ended to be applicable to future developments. For example, the Alan Turing Institute defines it as "the design and study of machines that can perform tasks that would previously have required human (or other biological) brainpower to accomplish."[65] AI Act also offers a definition of the "AI system", as it names this technology. It designates a software that is developed with one or more of the techniques and approaches listed in Annex I and can, for a given set of human-defined objectives, generate outputs such as content, predictions, recommendations, or decisions influencing the environments they interact with.[66] Annex I lists the following techniques: "Machine learning

[64] AI Act, Article 3.

[65] The Alan Turing Institute (online). Data science and AI glossary, available at: https://www.turing.ac.uk/news/data-science-and-ai-glossary.

[66] Proposal for a Regulation of the European Parliament and of the Council laying down harmonised rules on artificial intelligence (artificial intelligence act) and amending certain union legislative acts, available at: https://eur-lex.europa.eu/legal-content/EN/TXT/?uri=CELEX%3A52021PC0206.

approaches, including supervised, unsupervised and reinforcement learning, using a wide variety of methods including deep learning; (b) Logic- and knowledge-based approaches, including knowledge representation, inductive (logic) programming, knowledge bases, inference and deductive engines, (symbolic) reasoning and expert systems; (c) Statistical approaches, Bayesian estimation, search and optimization methods." In order to update the list of techniques, the Commission is empowered to adopt delegated acts and therefore avoid potentially long-lasting amending procedure that would involve cooperation with other EU bodies.

Definition in AI Act, however, is not designed (solely) to address the question of liability but it is pertinent as currently the only non-sector-specific definition of AI offered in a formal legislative proposal. In the Resolution of 2020, which addresses only civil liability, EU Parliament offers a definition of AI too. This document defines it as "a system that is either software-based or embedded in hardware devices, and that displays behavior simulating intelligence by, inter alia, collecting and processing data, analyzing, and interpreting its environment, and by taking action, with some degree of autonomy, to achieve specific goals".[67] AI Liability Directive and the updated Product Liability Directive refer to the definition in the AI Act, thereby departing from the previous understanding of the problem by the EU Parliament and aligning with the definition of AI which seem to be acceptable for purposes broader than the regulation of liability.

The task of finding appropriate definition of has been demonstrably difficult, but necessary in order to limit the applicability of specific legal rules only to the desired domain. Along with defining AI, another important task is to address the risks it bears. The following sections will expound on that issue.

2.7 AI Undermines Civil Law Principles

AI bear characteristics which potential is a challenge to various fields of law, especially so when it acts in concert with other emerging technologies. In fact, it can be purposed that the rule of law, a fundamental concept of a legal order requires rethinking. If it is understood in line with the classic definition, rule of law is "the mechanism, process, institution, practice, or norm that supports the equality of all citizens before the law, secures a nonarbitrary form of government, and more generally prevents the arbitrary use of power".[68] Across various sectors of interaction between the state and an individual, the latter has a lower level of access to law as the technological complexity associated with AI prevents it from understanding the rules one must follow.[69] Governments increasingly employ AI[70] in order to

[67] See Article 3.

[68] Choi (2021).

[69] See Greenstein (2021).

[70] "The digital welfare state is either already a reality or emerging in many countries across the globe. In these states, systems of social protection and assistance are increasingly driven by digital

assess citizens' behavior,[71] track their movement,[72] and punish them for socially unacceptable actions. All these developments bear different characteristics and produce impact in different fields of civil law. Civil law is characterized by the freedom of parties to enter a transaction without coercion and to define the terms of it. Or if there is a lack of freedom of entering into a transaction, such as there is in the tort law, they are still free to negotiate and rearrange it. They can forgive one another, allow for delay of payment or for replacement of payment with another duty. Disruptions caused by technological developments are dealt with by various means. Sometimes a body of law is left to courts to be shaped through interpretation, while in other cases new rules are adopted. These new rules can be so diverse and specific that they may fail to interact. This is especially the case with administrative agencies that create and enforce rules in specific realms. As Edward L. Rubin puts it, "standard for judging the value of law is not whether it is coherent but rather whether it is effective, that is, effective in establishing and implementing the policy goals of the modern state".[73]

Coherent or not, it can be argued that the new set of rules has a goal of enhancing principles of civil law. In the case of AI, as Chap. 3 will demonstrate, there is a high likelihood that a technically complex and vast number of legal rules devoted specifically to AI can be expected soon. They may not all be devoted to the question of liability, nor may they be coherent with the general standards that embody civil law principles.

AI creates unique problems in interactions between private actors too. In the field of civil law, it creates problems with its fundamental underlying principles. An involvement of AI presupposes an impact of autonomous intelligent actors on civil law relationships of private actors.

The public has only relatively recently become aware of the ways in which their fortunes may be governed by systems they do not understand and feel they cannot control; and they do not like it. Hopes of feeling in control of these systems are dashed by their hiddenness, their ubiquity, their opacity, and the lack of an obvious

data and technologies that are used to automate, predict, identify, surveil, detect, target and punish. In the present report, the irresistible attractions for Governments to move in this direction are acknowledged, but the grave risk of stumbling, zombie-like, into a digital welfare dystopia is highlighted. It is argued that big technology companies (frequently referred to as "big tech") operate in an almost human rights-free zone, and that this is especially problematic when the private sector is taking a leading role in designing, constructing and even operating significant parts of the digital welfare state. It is recommended in the report that, instead of obsessing about fraud, cost savings, sanctions, and market-driven definitions of efficiency, the starting point should be on how welfare budgets could be transformed through technology to ensure a higher standard of living for the vulnerable and disadvantaged", United Nations General Assembly, Report of the Special Rapporteur on extreme poverty and human rights, 2019, available at: A/74/493—E—A/74/493—Desktop (undocs.org).

[71] An example is the parole assessment AI used in the United States—Correctional Offender Management Profiling for Alternative Sanctions (COMPAS).

[72] An example is SyRI Act used to detect welfare fraud in Netherlands.

[73] Rubin (2017), p. 311.

means to challenge them when they produce unexpected, damaging, unfair or discriminatory results. Once, people talked in hushed tones about "the market" and how its "invisible hand" governed and judged their lives in impenetrable ways: now it is observable that there is similar talk about "the algorithm," as in: "I don't know why the algorithm sent me these adverts" or "I hate that algorithm."[74]

Its ability to act independently, along with its self-learning capacity in an unpredictable and unexplainable fashion creates a potential for the agency problem. An agency can be understood as "a form of contract between a company's owners and its managers, where the owners (as principal) appoint an agent (the managers) to manage the company on their behalf".[75] The problem arises when an agent has different interests from the principal. The problem is a traditional one as hierarchical labor structures have existed for a long time it usually includes the calculation of costs the principal might incur in supervising the agent. If we place AI in the position of an agent, the problem becomes different.[76] Instead of a human agent, a "digital" one does not act in accordance with human perception, nor does it conduct the thinking process in the same way. Monitoring of humans is therefore very different from monitoring AI. Due to AI's opacity, the owner might not be able to fathom the reasoning behind decisions, regardless of the favorability of its outcome to the owners.

However, the opacity does not necessarily mean there will be a lack of congruity between the interests of the principal and the agent. In order to prevent such situations from occurring, scholarship widely recognizes that the design of AI has to reflect it. Even early scholarship argued that ethical values built into the design ought to act as a barrier.[77] A lack of congruity between the interests of human owners and AI agents is not the only potential reason behind the undesirable behavior of AI. Civil law principles can also be undermined even if all precautionary measures have been undertaken by designers, for instance by the great variety of potential uses and contexts in which the consumers can deploy AI, which designers and engineers will not be able to predict in order or due to the vulnerability of AI. Therefore, the agency problem coupled with opacity has the potential to provide parties with uncertainty.

These characteristics affect principles of party equality and party autonomy. It impacts the information asymmetry. This term designates a lack of information on a certain subject matter which impairs a person's ability to make decisions of the fully rational premises. Therefore, a person in such a situation faces uncertainty.[78]

[74] Edwards and Veale (2017), p. 19.

[75] Moloi and Marwala (2020), p. 96.

[76] Agency, as used in this example, is not a legal agency. Some authors use term legal agency as to mean legal personality and/or legal responsibility, which is not intended here. Rather, it should be understood as factual agency, a de facto relation of master-agent in which the latter performs tasks assigned by the former. See Brozek and Jakubiec (2017).

[77] For example Mitchell Waldrop in the 1987 AI Magazine article "A Question of Responsibility" champions this position.

[78] See, for example: Mackaay (1982).

Consider a consumer who visits an online store to purchase a product. The company operates an AI-driven dynamic pricing system that adjusts prices based on the consumer's browsing behavior, purchase history, and even real-time factors like demand and supply. AI allows for great amounts of data to be sorted, linked, and analyzed in a way that would otherwise be impossible. Industry is the front-runner in the development and use of AI. Therefore, the already existing imbalance of power in corporation-to-human interactions can be even higher if corporations are equipped with such a supreme tool.

On the other hand, AI can also enhance the party equality. Consumer protection law aims at providing consumers with various devices in order to equal their position with the positions of their contracting parties, typically highly sophisticated companies. While the latter are very well versed in a business, consumers are usually lay. While many potential reasons can be identified behind the imbalance of their positions, one of them is the impossibility of consumers to make an informed choice. If consumers are employed with AI or if it is possible to employ AI to prevent unfair practices, however, their position might be enhanced as it might enable consumers to make decisions on the basis of near-complete information.

The previous only reflects the clear situations where one is aware they have upcoming contract negotiations. AI impacts the availability of information even before that. For example, targeted online advertisement[79] and echo chambers,[80] coupled with the so-called "confirmation bias"[81] distorts one's possibility to view all available options. It might potentially reduce the market to only those products and services determined by AI as desirable, perhaps based solely on the commercial interests of advertisers. "Thanks to big data and AI, traders may come to know what may influence particular consumers or groups of them one way or the other. More generally, a personal data economy is emerging where all kinds of personal data are collected and exchanged, their value consisting in their possible uses to anticipate and modify the behavior of people."[82] The impact on party equality and party autonomy goes way beyond and they cannot be comprehended. One of the pertinent ways private relationships may be reshaped is by the use of AI that can read and understand human emotions.

This is not science fiction, as the French robot Pepper[83] attests. As a humanoid robot, it can interact with humans by imitating human behavior and reactions. It is

---

[79] For example, see Boerman et al. (2017).

[80] For example, see Bandy and Diakopoulos, More Accounts, Fewer Links: How Algorithmic Curation Impacts Media Exposure in Twitter Timelines, available at: http://www.nickdiakopoulos.com/wp-content/uploads/2021/04/more-accounts-fewer-links.pdf.

[81] "Many psychologists have proposed that human reasoning is subject to positive confirmation bias. This is a tendency, when testing an existing belief, to search for evidence which could confirm that belief, rather than for evidence which could disconfirm it." See Jones and Sugden (2001), p. 59.

[82] New aspects and challenges in consumer protection, available at: https://www.europarl.europa.eu/RegData/etudes/STUD/2020/648790/IPOL_STU(2020)648790_EN.pdf.

[83] Pepper the humanoid robot debuts in France, available at: https://www.cnet.com/tech/computing/pepper-the-popular-humanoid-robot-debuts-in-france/.

capable of performing dance and playing games with their owners. It can do way more than a traditional household machine. It follows its owners and charges itself independently, but most importantly, it can read emotions. It recognises smiles, sadness, anger, and other emotions by analyzing the facial expressions of its owner. It also listens to the intonation of human voices to learn their emotions. Over time, it is becoming better at assessing the emotional condition due to its previous history. As consumers, we may think of having a companion who understands us and tailors their interactions in accordance with our needs. Pepper is hardly the only robot with the ability to read human emotions and improve over time in order to provide adequate reactions. As Nathalie Rébé notes: "Robots can now vacuum your carpet, mow your lawn, and drive cars. Soon, the average robots bought in retail will be capable of sensing our desires and satisfying them. We will start to see them as companions; they will no longer be simply machines to us."[84] This is a promising industry with a growing potential. Understanding human emotions and reacting accordingly is likely to be a cornerstone of interactions between humans and AI. Already, sex workers are being replaced by humanoid robots who can be shaped and designed to meet their owners' desires. Along with its physical appearance, owners can select the types of behavior they prefer their robot to possess. However, they are yet not capable of learning over time, according to what was available for this research.[85] From the perspective of civil, there are several potential problems with this development. If a human interacts with a non-human entity that can understand its emotions and learn from its behavior to become better for future interactions, is that an interaction between persons? As we are unaware of the AI's potential development in recognizing emotions, we are unable to assess what is it capable of doing. Due to the black-box effect, we may be in a position to only react *ex post,* after an undesired consequence has already occurred. Problems may be also framed within the civil law discourse as a debate on whether particular sectors should be protected from AI applications. In other words, if it is treated as a thing rather than a person, when should AI be considered as res extra commercium. This is a pending debate with a set of open questions. "The use of robots for sex is only justified on the basis that they are not real entities; they are things. As they become increasingly aware of emotions, pain and their surroundings, should robots have their word to say in the relationships they are involved in and give consent to marry or engage into sexual relationships with humans or one another? Aren't relationships about the free will of romantic partners? In the not too distant future, the issue will arise of robots needing to understand the notion of giving consent in these sexual relationships?"[86]

When employed in different contexts, AI's supreme ability to recognise human emotions may constitute a threat on its own. If it is used in communication with consumers as a sales agent, it may be able to see what suits us and provide a tailored

[84] Rébé (2021), p. 53.

[85] Ibid, 54–58.

[86] Ibid, 56.

offer. But what if it can understand our fears, traumas, and other weaknesses it can exploit in order to achieve benefits for the persons who hired them? Essentially, this is one of the fundamental problems of facial recognition. While Pepper seems closer due to its humanoid characteristics, AI can pierce through a veil of mystery too in much less attractive forms, such as a set of cameras installed in a workplace or a street.

Furthermore, it can be argued that AI is different from other human creations to the extent it does merit having certain rights. Understanding of agency is predicated on the free will, reason, and self-awareness of agents. They do not act merely as non-thinking tools in the hands of their principals. The idea of divorcing the concept of persons from humans is not very novel. J.-R. Trahan notes that Hugo Grotius in his Introduction to Dutch Jurisprudence already argued against applying the concept of persons exclusively to humans.[87] Rather, collectivities should also have such status, in his opinion. Other authors claim that this idea precedes Grotius. As Kurki argues, Grotius was a commentator of Hugues Doneau's work Commentarii in iure civili.[88] Around three decades before Grotius, Doneau argued that the term person should not be understood strictly to designate humans but rather a set of functions one performs in society.

Most modern societies envisage that a person can be either natural or legal. Without exception, humans nowadays have a status of persons, although this process was long and painstaking as excluded some categories of humans such as slaves and women. Legal persons are a category of non-humans who receive the status of persons typically recognized by legal systems. This dichotomy and the impact of AI on it will be discussed in Chap. 5. At this point, we can note that AI may undermine how we perceive persons.

In the field of intellectual property law, authors are traditionally considered to be only natural persons. Law in B&H provides for this very rule too in Article 9 of Law on authorship and related rights.[89] However, it is not unusual to have an algorithm that can produce a prosaic text. Already in 1984, a book titled "The Policeman's Beard is Half Constructed: Computer Prose and Poetry", was created by an algorithm named Racter. While human programmers provided inputs of grammar rules and vocabulary, the work was produced by the algorithm. The question of who should claim the authorship arose.[90] Ever since, many texts in both fiction and non-fiction genres have been produced by AI. This remarkable development was not limited to texts only. AI managed to compose music and generate drawings and paintings and works that come under copyright protection. It inevitably expresses creativity as a characteristic intellectual property law ought to protect. It has not only combined available inputs provided by programmers but also behaved unpredictably. In 1843, Ada Lovelace questioned the meaning of creativity in

[87] Trahan (2008), p. 11.

[88] Kurki (2019), p. 35.

[89] Official Gazette B&H 63/10.

[90] Butler (1981–1982).

automated engines. That is, automated agents can do only as much as their programmers allow it to. Humans set the framework where it can operate, while, as she claims, creativity requires leaving the realm of known and predictable. The scholarship questions this paradigm.[91]

In the field of law of obligations, the nature of the entity behind the action determines its legal duties. In the case of tort law, a centerpiece of this work, this problem is materialized in the following question: what happens when AI causes harmful action? The problem of non-human agents or entities who cause harm is not a new one. Law has previously established rules on the allocation of liability in the case of legal persons. Even if harm has been caused by entities without legal personality, such as animals, there is a long-lasting understanding that persons who were in charge of the animals should be liable. When it comes to contract law, first, the way contracts are negotiated and drafted has been changed by AI. As we mentioned before, the positions of parties who can use AI for these purposes impact the principle of party equality.

But what happens when AI is used by all involved parties in the negotiation and conclusion of a contract? For example, what if one party's AI drafts a contract and the other one accepts it? There are offer and acceptance, two necessary elements of contract conclusion in B&H law. If there is a meeting of minds of AI, whether there is a contract or not? This is a different situation from a situation where people use digital means of communication. Here, they outsource powers of negotiation and conclusion of a contract to AI. This conundrum, again, is not the new one. Tom Allen and Robin Widdison in their 1974 paper argued that "if a person can be bound by signing an unread contract, then it seems reasonable to say that by making the computer available, the human operator should be bound by the agreements it generates."[92] A number of further extensions of this basic problem can be imagined. For instance, what if a contract is concluded in a language non-discernible to one or two persons whose AI participated in the process, or what if both AIs understood the meaning of terms used in the contract differently from the persons on whose behalf they act?

Beyond doubt, it can be stated that AI brings a tremendous change to how we perceive civil law relationships. It is hard to present the overall impact of AI on civil law without reference to specific problems. The following section will thus provide a specific impact on tortious liability, the central aspect of this work.

[91] Bridy (2012).

[92] Allen and Widdison (1996), p. 44.

2.7.1 Understanding the Risks

Regulation of risk requires understanding the nature of the threat as the proper way to address it. Risk can be understood as:

1. A potential of harm arising from an activity.
2. A situation of imperfect information.[93]

AI certainly fits both definitions. Some predictions still remain in the realm of science fiction. Naturally, attempts to anticipate the development path of such unpredictable technology are very hard, especially when it is coupled with the high expectations humans have. The most widespread expectations concerning AI are the ones most radical. They capture the attention of film directors, dystopian novelists, and conspiracy theorists. AI is represented in various shapes and pursues various goals, and it usually bears two characteristics each time—it is more powerful than humans (sometimes even when humans act jointly against it) and humans can hardly control it, if at all. It can be depicted as positive or negative (or even more precise, human-friendly or non-human-friendly). It appears as an incredibly powerful killing device embodied in artificial soldiers[94] or a robot scientist[95] but also as self-aware beings willing to take over the Earth from humans.[96] However, law should not deal with unforeseeable phenomena until their existence becomes plausible.[97] Currently, the scope of application of AI is limited as well as its potential to become akin to what it represents in popular culture. Law, therefore, does not have a task to deal with what is not there and what is likely not going to emerge soon. However, some risks fall within the legal domain. Some of them are not even legal categories but rather broader political and sociological phenomena. Stuart and Norwig identify six potential threats that might arise from AI and other related technologies: "1. people might lose their jobs to automation; 2. people might have too much (or too little) leisure time; 3. people might lose their sense of being unique; 4. AI systems might be used toward undesirable ends; 5. the use of AI systems might result in a loss of accountability; 6. the success of AI might mean the end of the human race".[98]

In the case of tort law, specific risks brought by AI disrupt some of the fundamental underlying concepts. Some of them have been in force for centuries and are

[93] van Zeben (2018), p. 84.

[94] For example, a 1987 movie RoboCop.

[95] For example, a character of Data from the movie Star Trek.

[96] For example, the enemies of the main character in the movie Terminator.

[97] Steven Hawing, a world-renowned physicist, does not exclude this option. He pointed out that "there is no physical law precluding particles from being organised in ways that perform even more advanced computations than the arrangements of particles in human brains". Available at: https://www.independent.co.uk/news/science/stephen-hawking-transcendence-looks-implications-artificial-intelligence-are-we-taking-ai-seriously-enough-9313474.html.

[98] Russell and Norvig (2016).

shared as underlying principles of the tortious liability architecture. AI raises questions in at least four domains of interest of tortious liability:

1. proper regulatory approach
2. allocation of liability
3. appropriate basis of liability
4. position of an injured party

These exact questions are very broad and presuppose a comprehensive understanding of the rules of a legal system in order to be addressed. Application of current rules might lead to unfavorable outcomes for various reasons. Therefore, this work follows the structure of these questions. The Report has recognized that it is "necessary to consider adaptations and amendments to existing liability regimes, bearing in mind that, given the diversity of emerging digital technologies and the correspondingly diverse range of risks these may pose, it is impossible to come up with a single solution suitable for the entire spectrum of risks".[99] In line with this observation, the question of proper regulatory approach examines the suitability of current general terms pervasive in tort law for dealing with challenges related to AI. Premised on the understanding that it might not be the case, it questions the appropriate level of regulation, the time of adopting the new rules, and whether general or sector-specific rules would be more suitable. It also addresses the question of coherence in the overall regulation of AI by connecting tort law with auxiliary mechanisms such as safety rules and insurance and compensation funds. In a sense, it sets the scene for other, more specific, questions within tort law. Without having an entire approach in mind, it is impossible to understand the connection between various components of tort law and how a change in any of them might impact the entire system.

Allocation of liability is undermined as finding the most appropriate party to be held liable is not as easy as with traditional tools. Traditional criteria of control over technology, benefits of using technology, whose behavior caused harm, and who is the cheapest cost avoider or insurance taker do not lead to the appropriate outcomes.[100] Moreover, the question of holding AI itself in various forms is another option. Which of the potentially liable parties ought to bear the costs of negative externalities and if a balance between them is required, how it should be achieved?

Determining the proper basis of liability entails a rethinking of the traditional basis of liability and its scope of applicability. Whether strict liability, fault liability, vicarious liability, and defect liability would be an apt solution is debatable. These notions are impacted by AI. For example, the concept of negligence is impaired "due to the lack of comprehensive understanding of proper functioning of AI and its self-learning ability".[101] Also, there might be an issue with an understanding of what

[99] Report, 34.
[100] Report, 34.
[101] Muftić (2021).

would constitute fault as the rules regarding safety standards one might expect from AI have not been established yet.

The last set of questions concerns the position of the injured party. The basic understanding is that the complexity of technology, coupled with current rules of substantive and procedural law is likely to put a victim in a harder position to achieve compensation than usual. For instance, it might be hard to even determine who the responsible party is due to the multiple potential tortfeasors who participated in the development, deployment, and operation of AI. The likes of standard and burden of proof, causation, increment of expertise, and costs related to achieving the compensation fall within this question.

None of these questions should be treated in isolation as they all create connected parts of a liability system that utilizes their individual value. Without understanding their role and what any change might bring to the functioning of the entire system, an avenue to be pursued is hard to fathom. Treatment of the injured party, for instance, cannot be seen as separate from the questions of the basis of liability or who should be liable. While strict liability is more favorable from its position, the lack of easily identifiable tortfeasor might halt the compensation. Even if this latter impediment is removed, it is hard to determine whether all potentially liable parties should be held to the same standard as their power to control the behavior of AI could significantly vary. Hence, answers to the questions presented in this work should be seen as intertwined and co-dependent.

2.7.2 Sources of Harm

In the domain of tort law, there might be many reasons why harm occurs when AI is involved. According to Muehlhauser and Salamon,[102] the following factors that determine the occurrence of damage (resulting in damage) can be identified:

1. The objective of AI to preserve itself in order to maximize the satisfaction of its present final goals;
2. The objective of AI to preserve the content of its current final goals; otherwise, if the content of its final goals is changed, it will be less likely to act in the future to maximize the satisfaction of its present final goals;
3. The objective of AI to improve its own rationality and intelligence in order to improve its decision-making, and thereby increase its capacity to achieve its final goals;
4. The objective of AI to acquire as many resources as possible, so that these resources can be transformed and put to work for the satisfaction of AI's final goals.[103]

[102] Muehlhauser and Salamon (2012).

[103] Ibid, 383.

The commonality in all four principles is the existence of the goals. From that perspective, AI can be understood as a goal-oriented technology that uses its environment only as a proxy. Even if harm occurs as a consequence of AI's endeavor to achieve its goals, this explanation does not cover all potential situations involving AI that generate recoverable harm. First, AI might have wrongly assessed the environment due to erroneous observation of the environment. For instance, a self-driving car can hit a pedestrian at the pedestrian crossing, or a military system might wrongly detect and attack and launch its missiles and kill many people.[104] Second, designers might not be able to adequately provide instructions on risk-utility in order to maximize its goals. An example is the overly aggressive behavior of AI as a consequence of design.[105] Third, AI might be trained by damaged data and consequently make wrong decisions. An example is an online AI which failed to recognize black and female people as the data it was trained on data mainly consisted of images of white people and predominantly white males.[106] Fourth, AI might cause harm without errors in design, data, and the ways it has been operated. An example would be the COMPAS model for recidivism prediction in the United States, AI that evolved into a system with unintended behavior.[107]

The list above does not attempt to outline all potential situations leading to harm. It would be hard to fathom all due to the opacity of technology as well as a myriad of potential factual settings. It only describes some situations as examples of possible situations. All of them, however, are not scientifically interesting to the same extent. Some of them are more traditional, such as the misuse of technology or an error in design. They might require certain adaptations of currently existing rules. The others might require more than that, such as the situations involving black-box where liability cannot be instantly attributed to any person related to accidents. Naturally, such cases would therefore be the primary concern of this work. This does not mean, however, that other situations will not be covered. If for nothing else, due to the complexity of the problem, it might be hard in reality to determine whether a situation involving accidents clearly fits into any of the situations described above.

2.8 Regulatory Landscape

This section will provide a brief overview of the state of play in the field of tortious liability law in Europe and governmental responses and deliberations in relation to AI. As it will be demonstrated throughout this work, there is no consensus on what a

[104] Russell and Norvig (2016), p. 39.

[105] Ibid.

[106] Gender Shades: Intersectional Accuracy Disparities in Commercial Gender Classification, available at: http://proceedings.mlr.press/v81/buolamwini18a/buolamwini18a.pdf.

[107] Rudin and Radin (2019).

proper response of a legal system should be, and national legal orders in Europe have already responded to challenges to tort law differently.

In order to set the scene for the following chapters, it is necessary to display the regulation of tort law in Europe and the EU. The longevity of tort law in Europe is impressive as the main concepts survived throughout centuries with mild adaptation to various social circumstances and evolving technological landscape. Thus, the effort to provide a proper response to new phenomena should not be understood as novel, despite the peculiar characteristics of AI.

2.8.1 *Tort Law in Europe*

2.8.1.1 Common Principles of Tort Law in Europe

Tort law in Europe is mainly regulated by national legal systems. Although the differences among them are manyfold, the available studies demonstrate that European tort law regimes share the same principles. The examples in this respect are Book VI of the Draft Common Frame of Reference[108] as well as the 'Principles of European Tort Law', compiled by the European Group on Tort Law.[109] The idea of shared principles and origins of tort law is not a new one. Greatly inspired by the discovery and reception of Roman law, the idea received an impetus in the second half of the twentieth century in Europe, as a part of the movement for unification of Europe. Roman law has exactly served as a basis of various national legal systems, especially norms of private law including tort law:

> Roman legal learning soon formed a major component of what has come to be known as the Roman-Canon ius commune. Law, in the Middle Ages, was not conceived of as a system of rules enacted for, and exclusively applicable within, a specific territory, and thus the ius commune provided the cornerstone for the emergence of an essentially unified, European legal tradition.[110]

The idea of a European community in the second part of the twentieth century brought optimism and the hope that European legal tradition could aid in the creation of a common identity. A single European Civil Code as a distant and as it turned out, a utopian idea, represented a symbol of unity and identity.[111] A more practical consideration had been also behind such reasoning. Having diverse rules of private created a diversity of legal systems in Europe which could be seen as red tape for doing business. The costs of having to adjust to specific standards in each jurisdiction effectively put a tax on undertakings that operate across the EU.[112] The idea of

[108] von Bar and Clive (2009).

[109] European Group on Tort Law (2005).

[110] Zimmermann (2005). See also: Zimmermann (1996).

[111] Van Dam (2013), p. 128.

[112] Wagner (2005), p. 653.

unification has never lived up to the expectations for various reasons. Some claim that differences in private law, including tort law, in Europe are too great and point to unsurmountable conceptual differences between common and civil law.[113] As van Dam points out, there are differences in the general approach towards tort law between the United Kingdom, France, and Germany, as probably the leading political actors in the European Union (until Brexit) as well as the jurisdictions with the most influential private law internationally. While Germany has a tort law codified in a rule-based system, the French Code Civil contains more legislatively established principles applied by a judge in a specific case. The United Kingdom, as an extreme on this spectrum, does not have a systematized law in the form of codification.[114] On a more specific level, differences are manyfold and stem from the understanding of fault and strict liability, the role of courts in applying the law, causation etc.[115]

Notwithstanding the peculiarities of any jurisdictions, the shared principles and basic settings of tort laws in Europe lead to the same problems in the context of the application of the current body of tort law to AI. Legal systems throughout Europe had differently reacted to challenges put before them, which is exactly why certain avenues some of them took before could help in overcoming current hurdles. As the starting point of this work is tort law in B&H, experiences and specific solutions found around Europe might be helpful due to the common underlying principles.

2.8.1.2 Basic Characteristics of Tort Law in Bosnia and Herzegovina

In B&H, tort law is a part of the Law on Obligations (hereinafter also as: LO). Although it lacks a comprehensive codification of civil law, B&H has the law of obligations and tort law regulated in this statute. LO was adopted in Yugoslavia, a former state of which B&H was a part, along with Croatia, Montenegro, Slovenia, Serbia, and Northern Macedonia. According to the Constitution of Yugoslavia from 1974, the power to adopt the binding legal instrument in the field of law of obligations was held by the federal state of Yugoslavia. It had adopted LO in 1978 and ever since, LO remained almost unaltered in B&H. In fact, even after the dissolution of Yugoslavia, this statute remained a core building block of private law in all its former states.[116] This is very curious given that LO was brought during the socialist reign. Despite its status as one of the fundamental laws on private relationships in a socialist country, its applicability in successor states can be marked as successful. Unlike many former socialist countries, the more-less successful transition of B&H to a market-based economy was not halted by its civil law

[113] Legrand (1996).

[114] von Bar and Clive (2009).

[115] Ibid.

[116] Accordingly, even the new case law in former Yugoslavian states can be used as a persuasive informal source of interpretation of B&H's LO and vice versa.

rules. New civil procedural laws had been adopted, but the substantive rules remained to the greatest extent untouched. The reasons were up-to-date provisions of civil law at the time placed in the text, drafted by the students of modern European codifications.

After the dissolution of Yugoslavia and the war in the 1990s, B&H changed its constitutional structure. The Dayton Peace Agreement of 1995, an agreement made to end the war in B&H, had one of its Annexes devoted to the governmental structure of the country after the war. Annex 4 is a constitution of B&H. B&H, as one of the successor states of Yugoslavia, continued to exist but under radically different interior structures. Instead of the central government being entitled to adopt the most important rules, the new constitution provides different power-sharing mechanisms and new actors. B&H consists of two entities—the Federation of B&H and Republika Srpska as well as a third part—Brcko District. In the purview of the central government lies a limited number of areas where it can exercise power. Instead, entities and the Brcko District are entitled to regulate private relationships, including civil law. There are some exceptions to this rule, such as a set of intellectual property laws and the Consumer Protection Law, all of which had been adopted on the state level. However, the vast majority of private law as well as a majority of other areas fall within the purview of lower-level governments.

In the beginning, immediately after the dissolution of Yugoslavia, the new state faced a lacuna in the most fundamental question regulated by law until that point. In order to overcome it, many laws which had been in force in Yugoslavia were transposed into the B&H legal system. Entities and Brcko District have adopted the Yugoslavian LO into their legal systems, effectively providing for the continuity of well-known and deeply grounded rules that governed their society for decades. Ever since 1995, the civil law in entities and Brcko have departed from one another due to the mainly diverse legislative activities of their respective bodies. This inevitably led to fragmentation to a certain extent. However, luckily for this thesis, LO remained almost untouched in all three jurisdictions and in most cases remains an apt solution to a myriad of new problems that appeared in the last 25 years. For this reason, when it refers to the law of obligation of B&H, this work will refer to LO as there is no relevant difference within B&H's jurisdictions.

LO is a long text consisting of 1109 articles. Its structure consists of four parts: The first part concerns the general provisions applicable to all obligations. The second part lists rules on specific contracts.[117] The third part contains a conflict of laws rules. The fourth part contains transitional and final provisions. The first part of LO is the most interesting for tort liability as it sets out detailed rules on damages. It posits torts as one of the sources of obligation, along with contracts, unjust enrichment, unilateral expression of will, and negotiorum gestio. In the first part—general provisions, the text lists principles that are applicable in all law of obligation transactions, including tort law. Those are:

[117] Perović (2010), p. 53.

- party autonomy;
- equality of parties;
- the principle of good faith;
- prohibition of misuse of rights;
- prohibition of the creation and misuse of a monopoly position;
- the principle of equal consideration;
- prohibition of causing damage;
- conduct in carrying out obligations and realizing rights.

Yugoslavia did not impose a special commercial law on obligations. As Đurović points out, "after the adoption of the last Constitution of the Socialistic Federal Republic of Yugoslavia in 1974, there was no more constitutional basis for the adoption of a unique Yugoslav Civil Code. This is because the regulation of the entire family and inheritance law became the exclusive competence of the federal units."[118] LO applies to all obligations involving citizens and enterprises, as well as when the state itself is a party to the obligation law relationship. However, LO itself does contain specific provisions applicable only to commercial relationships, thereby differentiating the rules of B-B obligations from the rest of the provisions. An example would be shorter statute of limitation periods in commercial relationships compared to civil law relationships. The opening provisions list a number of principles applicable to all legal relationships regulated by this law. Those are party autonomy, party equality, good faith, and honesty, prohibition of misuse of rights, prohibition of the creation and misuse of a monopoly position, the principle of equal consideration, *neminem laedere*, responsibilities in performing obligations, a duty of care in carrying out his obligation, settling disputes peacefully, self-regulating character of the provisions of the present law, the dispositive character of LO, the applicability of fair trade custom and usage, and proceeding in accordance to general acts. Having the character of omnipresent, these principles also apply in the case of torts. Naturally, not all of them apply to the same degree as their impact differs depending on the type of obligation.

There was no official declaration of the influences on the drafters of the LO. However, Mihailo Konstantinović, the main academic drafter of the text, emphasized a comparative approach and foreign influences in his publication.[119] The scholarship has recognized that the main influences came from the Swiss Code of Obligations and French Code Civil, but the impacts of the Austrian Allgemeines bürgerliches Gesetzbuch, Italian Codice civile, German jurisprudence, the Hague Uniform Sales Law and other international soft law existing at the time of adoption.[120] The Swiss nomotechnic influence is noticeable through the structure and specific contracts with the LO, a monistic approach towards civil and commercial transactions, as well as in the linguistic style of having one-sentence subparagraphs

[118] Đurović (2011), p. 68.
[119] Konstantinović (1969a, b).
[120] Nikšić (2014), p. 188.

within a paragraph. The same is visible in the choices of terminology such as the use of the term "contract" instead of "legal transaction". The impact of French law is seen in the field of contract law through the notion of *la cause* as a condition for the validity of a contract.[121] Austrian law influenced the adoption of *laesio enormis*, the ultra alterum tantum prohibition, and the regulation of lease contracts. German law, along with Swiss and Austrian law, impacted the trade usages adopted in Yugoslavia in 1954 which were applicable also after the adoption of LO in 1978. It also influenced the regulation of permanent obligations as the notion of Dauerschuldverhältnis was looked upon.[122]

LO was a remarkable piece of legislation not only due to the well-rounded partial codification of the existing law but also due to the successful combining approaches of the aforementioned foreign influences. After its adoption, it became a cornerstone of the economy and a modern framework for transactions. As Ratomir M. Slijepcevic describes, the success of LO can be summed up in the following:

1. It is a collective interdisciplinary product of a high number of experts from different institutions.
2. It is a unified synthesis of civil and commercial law as it applies to both types of transactions, with some exceptions.
3. It has a universal application, as it is applied subsidiarily to all legal transactions in the legal order.
4. It has a special legislative and legal quality due to the language used, fitness of phrasing, style, and legislative technique.
5. It predominantly acts as a code of dispositive legal rules.
6. It acts as a lex generali to all matters of obligation relationships.
7. It is a functional legislative act as it is an optimal synthesis of legal principles and flexible standards.
8. It is as creative codification act as it does not blindly replicate any foreign legal text.

Torts are regulated in the first part of LO, along with contracts and other extra-contractual sources of obligations. In the field of tort law, commentators recognized that the strongest influence arrived from the French Code Civil. It is most obviously displayed through the adoption of *neminem laedere* as a fundamental principle.[123] This influence can be noticed also in the stipulation of LO in Article 154: "Whoever causes injury or loss to another shall be liable to redress it, unless he proves that the harm was caused without his fault." As Baretic noticed,[124] many influential European civil law codifications in the equivalent stipulation require that the harm

[121] Ibid.

[122] Tot (2018), p. 1171.

[123] Slakoper and Tot (2021), p. 8.

[124] Baretić (2020), p. 598.

is unlawful,[125] whereas Code Civil in Article 1240, in a similar fashion to LO, stipulates: “Tout fait quelconque de l’homme, qui cause à autrui un dommage, oblige celui par la faute duquel il est arrivé, à le réparer.”

After the dissolution of Yugoslavia, successor states amended their law of obligation statute, but the main pillars set in LO remained. As Drago Divljak[126] notes, there are two main directions. First, new contracts and institutions were added. The second direction concerned modifications that aimed at harmonizing LO with the EU *acquis*. B&H was an exception as it has not amended LO but it remains to be in force in an unchanged version to this day. While LO provides an operable framework, the same was not the case with the Yugoslavian property law, which was a subject of fundamental and long-lasting changes in B&H after 1992.[127]

Throughout the work, specific details about the regulation of tort law devices in LO will be elaborated in the appropriate sections.

2.8.1.3 Regulation of Tort Law in the European Union

In the EU, extracontractual liability, including tort law, remains within the purview of Member States, with some exceptions. Tort law is hence divergent throughout the national legal systems within this supranational organization. A notable exception, relevant to the deliberation of AI is product liability. In 1985, the EU law adopted the Product Liability Directive[128] (hereinafter also as: PLD), which harmonized this field. Other exceptions include liability for violation of data protection law (Article

[125] For example: The German Bürgerliches Gesetzbuch in Article 823(1): “(1) Wer vorsätzlich oder fahrlässig das Leben, den Körper, die Gesundheit, die Freiheit, das Eigentum oder ein sonstiges Recht eines anderen widerrechtlich verletzt, ist dem anderen zum Ersatz des daraus entstehenden Schadens verpflichtet.”; The Austrian Allgemeines bürgerliches Gesetzbuch in Article 1294: “Quellen der Beschädigung Der Schade entspringt entweder aus einer widerrechtlichen Handlung, oder Unterlassung eines Anderen; oder aus einem Zufalle. Die widerrechtliche Beschädigung wird entweder willkührlich, oder unwillkührlich zugefügt. Die willkührliche Beschädigung aber gründet sich theils in einer bösen Absicht, wenn der Schade mit Wissen und Willen; theils in einem Versehen, wenn er aus schuldbarer Unwissenheit, oder aus Mangel der gehörigen Aufmerksamkeit, oder des gehörigen Fleißes verursachet worden ist. Beydes wird ein Verschulden genannt.”; Swiss Code of Obligations in Article 41: “A. Haftung im Allgemeinen I. Voraussetzungen der Haftung 1. Wer einem andern widerrechtlich Schaden zufügt, sei es mit Absicht, sei es aus Fahrlässigkeit, wird ihm zum Ersatze verpflichtet. 2. Ebenso ist zum Ersatze verpflichtet, wer einem andern in einer gegen die guten Sitten verstossenden Weise absichtlich Schaden zufügt.”; Italian Codice Civile in Article 2043: “(Risarcimento per fatto illecito) – Qualunque fatto doloso o colposo, che cagiona ad altri un dano ingiusto, obbliga colui che ha commesso il fatto a risarciare il danno.”

[126] Divljak (2008).

[127] See Povlakić (2010).

[128] Council Directive 85/374/EEC of 25 July 1985 on the approximation of the laws, regulations and administrative provisions of the Member States concerning liability for defective products [1985] OJ L210/29, as amended by Directive 1999/34/EC of the European Parliament and of the Council of 10 May 1999 [1999] OJ L141/20.

82 of the General Data Protection Regulation[129]) and competition law (Directive 2014/104/EU[130]). In 2024, the amendments to the PLD had been passed. They focused on the expansion of the notion of a product to cover software and AI, expansion of the notion of harm, establishing mandatory disclosures of certain evidence from the defendant to the claimant, and introducing a rebuttable presumption of defectiveness in certain cases. There has also been an attempt at the EU level to harmonize liability for services, along with liability for products.[131] However, it has never become a binding instrument. Furthermore, although not an instrument that strictly regulates liability, the EU harmonized an instrument on insurance against civil liability concerning the use of motor vehicles.[132] Tortious liability in the EU is thus characterized by the fragmentation and coexistence of several legal regimes. Even though the EU regulates product liability, the jurisdiction in this matter remains to a major extent within the scope of the national legal systems of every Member State. Directive, as a type of legal instrument, allows Member States to transpose the rules to a certain degree in accordance with their understanding and specific rules a respective legal system, effectively leading to different implementations. In the case of González Sánchez,[133] the European Court of Justice stated that Article 13 of PLD does not bar a Member State from applying national rules of tort law in finding a producer liable.

A lack of a single set of EU rules in the context of AI brings additional challenges. First, the technology itself should not be limited to national borders in order to reach its potential. AI requires vast amounts of data and a single set of rules on the EU market is helpful. The EU generally seeks to create harmonized safety rules and many other market conditions and such endeavour has historically created a single market for many products and services. An example is the AI Act, which in a way ought to replicate this approach. Lawmakers are facing this dilemma regarding the regulation of liability, as a single set of tort law rules would be better for AI development as it would create a single set of rules and enhance the number of cases from which AI can learn. The position of an injured party would be deemed more predictable as well.

---

[129] Regulation (EU) 2016/679 of the European Parliament and of the Council of 27 April 2016 on the protection of natural persons with regard to the processing of personal data and on the free movement of such data, and repealing Directive 95/46/EC (General Data Protection Regulation) [2016] OJ L119/1.

[130] Directive 2014/104/EU of the European Parliament and of the Council of 26 November 2014 on certain rules governing actions for damages under national law for infringements of the competition law provisions of the Member States and of the European Union [2014] OJ L349/1.

[131] European Commission, 'Proposal for a Council Directive on the liability of suppliers of services' COM (90) 482 final [1991] OJ C12/8.

[132] Directive 2009/103/EC of the European Parliament and of the Council of 16 September 2009 relating to insurance against civil liability in respect of the use of motor vehicles, and the enforcement of the obligation to insure against such liability [2009] OJ L263/11 (Motor Insurance Directive).

[133] Case C-183/00, González Sánchez v Medicina Asturiana SA, [2002] ECR I-3901.

2.8.2 *What Has Been Done so far in the Lawmaking?*

Liability for AI as well as any specific rules concerning this technology has been seldom a subject of legislative acts throughout the European Member states. Some governments are preparing strategies for AI, thereby displaying an understanding of the potential of this technology.[134] Member states of the EU often halt any rule-making activities presumably due to hitherto EU's activities in this field. Exceptions to this rule are France and Germany. The both states adopted in 2021. French law regulates autonomous vehicles with various degrees of autonomy and contains liability rules whereby a victim can refer to an insurer to be compensated.[135] Germany adopted the Act on Autonomous Driving in order to amend the Road Traffic Act and the Compulsory Insurance Act.[136] It provides for level 4 automation autonomous vehicles to operate, regulating mainly safety requirements. When it comes to liability, the German Act extends the current road traffic liability framework to new technology. States that are not Member states will, naturally, have to rely on their own rule-making and will be therefore in a different situation. Due to the influence proximity of the EU, as well as due to a general lack of consensus, there are not so many rules concerning specifically AI in force. The UK has already in 2018 adopted a law regulating autonomous vehicles—the Automated and Electric Vehicles Act.[137] It contains specific rules for liability for accidents caused by automated vehicles as well as provisions on compulsory insurance.

In B&H AI is not in focus. Emerging technologies are seen as something distant and there is no belief that the state might be a winner of the Fourth Industrial Revolution. As the media reported,[138] the Federation of B&H, an entity within B&H, plans to adopt a strategy on AI development. So far, any documents or public discussions have not taken place, and this is the only available piece of information.

Regulation of AI is a popular topic in academic and regulatory circles nowadays, and a number of technological novelties are followed by an increasing number of regulatory initiatives. It can be stated, however, that as sectoral and national legislation, the new laws mentioned in this section have limited reach. Traffic road liability has previously too been a subject of specific rules of liability. The new legislation thus does not attempt to provide for general rules but rather sector-specific ones, which is not the main concern of this work. Apart from regulation of

[134] German strategy is available at: https://knowledge4policy.ec.europa.eu/ai-watch/germany-ai-strategy-report_en; French strategy is available at: See https://knowledge4policy.ec.europa.eu/ai-watch/france-ai-strategy-report_en.

[135] See a newspaper article about it: https://www.rtl.fr/actu/sciences-tech/comment-le-code-de-la-route-s-adapte-a-la-voiture-autonome-7900052176.

[136] Bundestag nimmt Gesetz zum au-tonomen Fahren an, available at: https://www.bundestag.de/dokumente/textarchiv/2021/kw20-de-autonomes-fahren-840196.

[137] Automated and Electric Vehicles Act 2018, available at: https://www.legislation.gov.uk/ukpga/2018/18/contents/enacted.

[138] Federacija BiH namjerava razvijati umjetnu inteligenciju, available at: https://www.klix.ba/scitech/tehnologija/federacija-bih-namjerava-razvijati-umjetnu-inteligenciju/210308082.

liability, the Commission adopted a plan of activities within the "AI Package"[139] published in April 2021. It consists of three documents: Communication on Fostering a European Approach to Artificial Intelligence,[140] Coordinated plan on AI 2021 review,[141] and the Proposal for the so-called "AI Act",[142] which was adopted on 13 June 2024.[143] The Commission announced the publication of a proposal to regulate civil liability in 2022.[144] The intention of the Commission is, as it appears, to first focus on safety standards and then the question of liability. The AI Act, although not a part of the liability framework, offers interesting insights into the Commission's reasoning for AI. It does not focus on AI as a static category but attempts to capture its evolution. Based on that premise, it attempts to provide a regulation of risks it is projected to generate with ex ante measures aimed at preventing and reducing it when it is deemed justifiable. It reflects a continuation of a risk-based approach of the Commission, as envisaged previously in the Commission Staff Working document.

Regulation of liability for AI has gained the attention of the lawmakers in the EU. The European Commission published a Data Economy Communication of January 2017[145] and the accompanying Commission Staff Working Document on the free flow of data and emerging issues of the European data economy.[146] New technologies became the subject of the EU Commission's interest, and the matter of liability is one of the central topics. The EU Parliament adopted a Resolution on

---

[139] A European approach to artificial intelligence, available at: https://digital-strategy.ec.europa.eu/en/policies/european-approach-artificial-intelligence.

[140] Communication on Fostering a European approach to Artificial Intelligence, available at: https://digital-strategy.ec.europa.eu/en/library/communication-fostering-european-approach-artificial-intelligence.

[141] Coordinated Plan on Artificial Intelligence 2021 Review, available at: https://digital-strategy.ec.europa.eu/en/library/coordinated-plan-artificial-intelligence-2021-review.

[142] Proposal for a Regulation of the European Parliament and of the Council laying down harmonised rules on artificial intelligence (Artificial Intelligence Act) and amending certain union legislative acts.

COM/2021/206 final, available at: https://eur-lex.europa.eu/legal-content/EN/TXT/?qid=1623335154975&uri=CELEX%3A52021PC0206.

[143] Regulation (EU) 2024/1689 of the European Parliament and of the Council of 13 June 2024 laying down harmonised rules on artificial intelligence and amending Regulations (EC) No 300/2008, (EU) No 167/2013, (EU) No 168/2013, (EU) 2018/858, (EU) 2018/1139 and (EU) 2019/2144 and Directives 2014/90/EU, (EU) 2016/797 and (EU) 2020/1828 (Artificial Intelligence Act) (Text with EEA relevance) PE/24/2024/REV/1.

OJ L, 2024/1689, 12.7.2024, ELI: http://data.europa.eu/eli/reg/2024/1689/oj (BG, ES, CS, DA, DE, ET, EL, EN, FR, GA, HR, IT, LV, LT, HU, MT, NL, PL, PT, RO, SK, SL, FI, SV).

[144] Liability Rules for Artificial Intelligence, available at: https://commission.europa.eu/business-economy-euro/doing-business-eu/contract-rules/digital-contracts/liability-rules-artificial-intelligence_en.

[145] European Commission, Building a European Data Economy (Communication) COM (2017) 9 final, 13ff.

[146] Commission, 'Commission Staff Working Document on the free flow of data and emerging issues of the European data economy' SWD (2017) 2 final, 40ff.

Civil Law Rules on Robotics[147] in February 2017 which initiated action of the Commission. It invited the Commission to propose an instrument regarding civil liability for harm caused by AI as well as other emerging technologies. In line with the Data Economy Communication of January 2017[148] and the accompanying Commission Staff Working Document, the Resolution discusses two regimes for AI: the first was labeled as 'risk management'[149] and the second as 'strict liability'.[150] Furthermore, this document envisages the introduction of mandatory liability insurance[151] and the idea of attributing AI with legal personhood.[152] The Commission established an Expert Group on liability and new technologies[153] with the goal of the revision of current product liability regime and its applicability to new technologies such as AI, as well as developing principles for possible adaptations if needed. The Expert Group operates in two formations—the Product Liability Directive Formation and the New Technologies Formation.[154] On 21 November 2019, the New Technologies Formation published the aforementioned Report, where it presented its findings and recommendations.

On 20 October 2020, along with the resolutions on ethics[155] and intellectual property rights,[156] the European Parliament issued a Resolution with recommendations to the Commission on a civil liability regime for artificial intelligence [2020/2014(INL)]. This document addresses liability for AI based on risk. It differentiates between those "high-risk AI-systems", as it names the technology, and the ones which do not pose such risk. This differentiation is important as high-risk AI would be subject to strict liability, whereas fault-based liability would remain a default rule. The remuneration provided by the proposal would be capped at 2 million Euros. Furthermore, it introduces new terminology for potentially liable parties—backend and frontend operators as well as the limits of compensation by excluding moral

[147] European Parliament resolution of 16 February 2017 with recommendations to the Commission on Civil Law Rules on Robotics [2015/2103(INL)] [2018] OJ C252/239 (Resolution), paras 49ff.

[148] COM (2017) 9 final, 13ff.

[149] Risk-management approach entails that liability is assigned to the market actor which is best placed to minimize or avoid the realization of the risk or to amortize the costs in relation to those risks: SWD (2017) 2 final, 45.

[150] The Resolution omitted to mention risk-generating approach as one of the proposals contained in the Commission Staff Working document.

[151] Ibid, para 57.

[152] Ibid, para 59.

[153] See group details at European Commission, 'Register of Commission expert groups and other similar entities', available at, available at: https://ec.europa.eu/transparency/regexpert/.

[154] The difference in the roles of two formations is in that the one is 'looking at the interpretation and possible revision of the PLD and the other one at liability for new technologies from a holistic point of view'. See Lohsse et al. (2019a, b), p. 17.

[155] European Parliament, Resolution on a framework of ethical aspects of artificial intelligence, robotics and related technologies, 2020/2012 (INL).

[156] European Parliament, Resolution on intellectual property rights for the development of artificial intelligence technologies 2020/2015 (INI).

damage. The document abandons the ground-breaking idea of assigning AI with legal personality which was a part of this body's Resolution from February 2017.

Departing from the EU Parliament envisioned approaches in Resolution 2017 and Resolution 2020, the Commission published a "White Paper on Artificial Intelligence: a European Approach to Excellence and Trust" on 19 February 2020, announcing its vision of how the liability regime should be changed. The Commission's conclusion regarding the safety and liability is that "in addition to the possible adjustments to existing legislation – a new legislation specifically on AI may be needed in order to make the EU legal framework fit for the current and anticipated technological and commercial developments."[157] Accordingly, on 28 September 2022, it published two proposals: AI Liability Directive[158] as a completely new legislative instrument, and the updated Product Liability Directive.[159] While the latter is still in the legislative process, the updated Product Liability Directive was adopted on 10 October 2024 in the EU legislative process.[160] As the main legislative instruments of the EU in this field, they deserve to be more elaborated.

AI Liability Directive

The AI Liability Directive is a new proposal aimed at adding to the landscape of the EU liability law as it addresses the question of fault-based liability. Essentially, it is a relatively modest legal instrument, compared to the previous initiatives articulated by the EU Parliament in the Resolution of 2017 and the Resolution of 2020.[161] A key aspect of the AI Liability Directive is its emphasis on disclosure. It imposes a duty on defendants to disclose evidence, but this obligation is limited to high-risk AI systems. If a defendant fails to comply, national courts are instructed to assume the defendant's non-compliance with a relevant duty of care. The Directive also provides rules for courts to infer causality between a defendant's actions and resulting harm, specifically for operators of high-risk AI systems that have breached obligations under Chapters 2 and 3 of Title III of the AI Act. For non-high-risk AI systems, the presumption of causality applies only in cases where national courts deem it excessively difficult for claimants to prove a causal link. Moreover, while the Directive incorporates risk management measures outlined in Article 9 of the AI Act, the precise significance of these measures remains ambiguous beyond the listed obligations.[162]

---

[157] European Commission, White Paper on Artificial Intelligence: a European approach to excellence and trust, 16.

[158] Proposal for a Directive of the European Parliament and of the Council on adapting non-contractual civil liability rules to artificial intelligence (AI Liability Directive) COM/2022/496 final.

[159] Proposal for a Directive of the European Parliament and of the Council on liability for defective products COM/2022/495 final.

[160] See https://www.consilium.europa.eu/en/press/press-releases/2024/10/10/eu-brings-product-liability-rules-in-line-with-digital-age-and-circular-economy/pdf/.

[161] Muftić (2023).

[162] See Hacker (2023).

As Wagner observes, "its provisions remain rudimentary, as they are closely tied to the definitions and framework established by the proposed AI Regulation, known as the Artificial Intelligence Act".[163] Unlike the approach suggested in the EU Parliament's 2017 Resolution, it does not establish a legal personhood for AI, and unlike the 2020 Resolution, it does not establish strict liability or distinguish between operators and backend operators. Instead, its focus lies on addressing the issue of information asymmetry stemming from AI usage.[164]

Many objections have been made to this proposal. It fails to adequately cover general-purpose AI systems, which can lead to significant harm, particularly in non-discrimination and personality rights areas.[165] It does not ensure coherence and legal clarity as it refers to the AI Act but fails to consistently use its terminology. In case of liability for discrimination, it does not solve enforcement challenges. It only applies to fundamental rights harms when allowed by Member States' traditions,[166] limiting its scope primarily to public sector AI.[167] The scope of harms covered is not complete and fails to include certain types of material and immaterial harm. It does not apply to contractual liability or certain other legal fields. The burden born by the injured party may be excessively hard as it has to prove the defendant's fault, establish a causal link between the fault and the produced output, and prove that the outputs caused the damage.[168] Although the legal disclosure mechanisms are envisaged, they are available only if the AI system has been classified as high-risk by the AI Act, thereby leaving an injured person with an additional duty in order to have a successful claim. Moreover, it exclusively addresses the harm caused by fully automated systems, excluding cases where a human was involved in the decision-making process, therefore providing that a "token "human in the loop" will avoid liability".[169]

The legislative process for the AI Liability Directive has been stalled at the time of writing. However, since the updates of the Product Liability Directive have been adopted, and the idea is to have the AI Liability Directive as its complementary instrument, the current text will likely change to tackle the main objections, but its main characteristics will remain. It should be noted that the final shape of the fault-based liability will not be provided by this Directive. While the PLD prohibits EU Member States from enacting national laws that are either more or less restrictive than those specified in the Directive (Art. 3)[1], the AILD generally permits them to introduce stricter national laws addressing non-contractual liability for AI-induced damages outside the PLD's scope [Art. 1(4), Recital 11][2]. Also, the AILD does not alter national definitions of fault, standards of care, burdens or standards of proof,

163 Wagner (2023), p. 11.

164 Spindler (2023), p. 30.

165 Hacker (2024).

166 Wachter et al. (2024).

167 Wachter (2024).

168 Ibid.

169 Ibid.

concepts of remoteness of damage, or approaches to multiple tortfeasors and contributory conduct, among other aspects. National definitions of causality remain unchanged as well, rendering that litigation outcomes are likely to vary across Member States. Consequently, EU Member States retain significant discretion in shaping national rules governing liability for harm caused by AI systems.[170]

Updated Product Liability Directive

Unlike the AILD, the updated PLD has been adopted and became the binding law in the EU at the time of writing this book. The update seeks to address errors and inconsistencies identified over decades of implementation in Member States while modernizing the framework to align with emerging digital technologies. The main features of the new PLD are that it broadens the definition of a product to include software, extends liability to product components or services connected to the product, and expands the scope of recognized damages—most notably to encompass data loss or corruption. Furthermore, the updates adapt the defectiveness test for digital technologies, address the impact of updates and machine learning on product liability, and revise the list of liable parties to include "fulfillment providers" and, under certain conditions, online marketplaces. To tackle information asymmetry and the weakened position of injured parties, it introduces disclosure obligations for potential tortfeasors and establishes a rebuttable presumption of product defectiveness if the defendant fails to provide relevant documents. Additionally, it creates a rebuttable presumption of causality between a product's defectiveness and the resulting damage if defectiveness is proven and the damage aligns with typical outcomes. Finally, the proposal removes the existing €500 liability threshold from the current framework.

There are many differences between the AI Liability Directive, despite the idea that they should be complementary. While the PLD is rooted in EU law and addresses both material and procedural aspects of product liability for physical products, software, and AI systems, the AILD focuses solely on AI systems, covering procedural aspects of non-contractual civil liability rooted in Member State law. The PLD relies on strict liability, whereas the AILD adopts a fault-based liability approach. The scope of claims under the PLD includes manufacturers and entities in the supply chain, while the AILD expands this to include professional users and consumers. Eligible damages under the PLD are limited to privately used property, death or personal injury, and data loss, whereas the AILD includes professional property, fundamental rights violations, and primary financial losses. Finally, the PLD mandates full harmonization across the EU, while the AILD requires only minimum harmonization.[171]

As Wachter notes, the limitations of the updated PLD and the AILD can be summarized in three key points. First, the complaint-based systems rely on claimants' awareness of the harm caused by AI to initiate legal action. However,

[170] Nunez Duffourc and Gerke (2023).

[171] Hacker (2023), p. 7.

immaterial harms, such as discrimination, often occur without individuals realizing it. For example, AI systems may exclude individuals from viewing advertisements for jobs, housing, or financial services, or offer higher-priced products without their knowledge. This lack of awareness undermines the effectiveness of complaint-based mechanisms in addressing such harms. Second, much of the harm caused by AI is intangible, and both directives lack clear protections for immaterial harms. These types of harm are difficult to quantify in monetary terms, or even to measure at all. Additionally, compensation for immaterial and material harm in the EU has traditionally been relatively low, further limiting the remedies available to claimants. Third, the evidentiary standards set by the PLD and AILD pose significant challenges for claimants, particularly for those without specialized knowledge or access to legal representation. As liability under these frameworks is addressed through civil court procedures, the burden of litigation—including its risks and costs—rests entirely on the claimant. Furthermore, certain AI-driven harms, such as slightly elevated prices, may be dismissed as trivial, discouraging individuals from pursuing claims. These factors raise doubts about whether individuals will have the time, resources, and expertise necessary to effectively utilize the legal remedies offered by the directives.[172]

References

Books

Abbot R (2020) Reasonable robot. Cambridge University Press
Berlin I (1973) Counter enlightenment. In: Wiener PP (ed) Dictionary of the history of ideas
Chagal-Feferkorn K (2020) Tort law: applying a “reasonableness” standard. In: The Cambridge handbook on the law of algorithms. Cambridge University Press, p 504
Choi N, Encyclopædia Britannica 2021., available at: https://www.britannica.com/topic/rule-of-law
Crawford K (2021) Atlas of AI: power, politics, and the planetary costs of artificial intelligence. Yale University Press
Ebers M (2020) Regulating AI and robotics: ethical and legal challenges. In: Ebers M, Navas S (eds) Algorithms and law. Cambridge University Press, Cambridge, p 42
Jones M, Sugden R (2001) Confirmation bias in the acquisition of information. Theory Decis 50: 59–99
Koch AB (2020) Liability for emerging digital technologies: an overview. J Eur Tort Law 11(2)
Konstantinović M (1969a) Obligacije i ugovori: skica za zakonik o obligacijama i ugovorima. Pravni fakultet u Beogradu
Konstantinović M (1969b) Obligaciono pravo. Beleške sa predavanja
Kovac M (2020) Judgement-proof robots and artificial intelligence a comparative law and economics approach. Palgrave Macmillan
Kurki AJV (2019) A theory of legal personhood. Oxford University Press
Legrand P (1996) European legal systems are not converging. ICLQ 45

[172] Wachter (2024).

Lohsse S, Schulze R, Staudenmayer D (2019a) Liability for artificial intelligence. In: Lohsee S, Schulze R, Staudenmayer D (eds) Liability for artificial intelligence and the internet of things: Münster Colloquia on EU law and the digital economy IV. Nomos
Lohsse S, Schulze R, Staudenmayer D (2019b) Liability for artificial intelligence and the internet of things. Nomos
Mackaay E (1982) Economics of information and law. Kluwer Nijhoff Publishing, Boston
Moloi T, Marwala T (2020) Artificial intelligence in economics and finance theories. Springer Nature Switzerland
Muehlhauser L, Salamon A (2012) Intelligence explosion: evidence and import. In: Eden A, Søraker J, Moor HJ, Steinhart E (eds) Singularity hypotheses: a scientific and philosophical assessment. Springer
Navas S (2020) Robot machines and civil liability. In: Ebers M, Navas S (eds) Algorithms and law. Cambridge University Press, Cambridge
Nikšić S (2014) Nekoliko napomena o nomotehničkom materijalu Zakona o Obligacionim odnosima. In: Slakoper Z (ed) Liber amicorum in honorem Vilim Gorenc (Pravni fakultet Sveučilišta u Rijeci)
Nilsson JN (2009) The quest for artificial intelligence: a history of ideas and achievement. Cambridge University Press, Cambridge
Perović J (2010) Contract law in Serbia. In: Christa J-H et al (eds) Private law in Eastern Europe. Mohr Siebeck
Povlakić M (2010) Property law in Bosnia and Herzegovina. In: Jessel-Hols C et al (eds) Private law in Eastern Europe. Mohr Siebeck
Rébé N (2021) Artificial intelligence robot law, policy and ethics. Brill/Nijhoff
Rubin EL (2017) From coherence to effectiveness. In: van Gestel R, Micklitz H-W, Rubin EL (eds) Rethinking legal scholarship. Cambridge University Press, New York
Russell S, Norvig P (2009) Artificial intelligence: a modern approach, 3rd edn. Prentice Hall
Russell S, Norvig P (2016) Artificial intelligence: a modern approach, 3rd edn. Pearson, Harlow
Sancho D (2020) Automated decision-making under Article 22 GDPR: towards a more substantial regime for solely automated decision-making. In: Ebers M, Navas S (eds) Algorithms and law. Cambridge University Press, Cambridge, p 143
Slakoper Z, Tot I (2021) Contract and tort law in the digital age: contemporary challenges to the law of obligations. In: Slakoper Z, Tot I (eds) Digital technologies and the law of obligations. Routledge
Steinrötter B (2020) The (envisaged) legal framework for commercialisation of digital data within the EU: data protection law and data economic law as a conflicted basis for algorithm-based products and services. In: Ebers M, Navas S (eds) Algorithms and law. Cambridge University Press, Cambridge
Stone P et al (2018) Artificial intelligence and life in 2030 – the report of the 2015 study panel 50. Stanford University
Turner J (2019) Robot rules: regulating artificial intelligence. Palgrave Macmillan
Van Dam C (2013) European tort law, 2nd edn. Oxford University Press
von Bar C, Clive E (eds) (2009) Principles, definitions and model rules of European private law, Draft Common Frame of Reference, vol 4. Sellier
Wagner G (2021) Haftung für Künstliche Intelligenz – Eine Gesetzesinitiative des Europäischen Parlaments. ZEuP 545, 556, available at: https://beck-online.beck.de/Dokument?vpath=bibdata%2Fzeits%2Fzeup%2F2021%2Fcont%2Fzeup.2021.545.1.htm&anchor=Y-300-Z-ZEUP-B-2021-S-550#FNA32
Zimmermann R (1996) Savigny's legacy: legal history, comparative law, and the emergence of a European legal science. LQR 112
Zimmermann R (2005) Characteristic aspects of German legal culture. In: Reimann M, Zekoll J (eds) Introduction to German law, 2nd edn. Kluwer Law International, Hague/Munich/Frederick

Articles

Allen T, Widdison R (1996) Can computers make contracts? Harv J Law Technol 9(1):25

Baretić M (2020) Protupravnost kao pretpostavka odštetnopravne odgovornosti u hrvatskom pravu. Zbornik Pravnog fakulteta u Zagrebu 70(5)

Boerman CS, Kruikemeier S, Zuiderveen Borgesius JF (2017) Online behavioral advertising: a literature review and research agenda. J Advert 46(3):363–376

Bridy A (2012) Coding creativity: copyright and the artificially intelligent author (July 18, 2011). Stanford Technol Law Rev 5:1–28 (Spring 2012). U. of Pittsburgh Legal Studies Research Paper No. 2011-25

Brozek B, Jakubiec M (2017) On the legal responsibility of autonomous machines. Artif Intell Law 25:293–304

Butler T (1981–1982) Can a computer be an author? Copyright aspects of artificial intelligence. Comm/Ent L.S. 4

Calo R (2015) Robotics and the lessons of cyberlaw. Cal Law Rev 103:513

Calo R (2017) Artificial intelligence policy: a primer and roadmap. UC Davis Law Rev 51:399–435

Divljak D (2008) Law on obligations and development of obligation codes in the countries of former Yugoslavia. In: Thirty years of the law on obligations – de lege lata and de lege ferenda, Kragujevac

Đurović M (2011) Serbian contract law: its development and the new Serbian Civil Code. Eur Rev Contract Law 7(1)

Edwards L, Veale M (2017) Slave to the algorithm? Why a right to an explanation' is probably not the remedy you are looking for. Duke Law Technol Rev 16:18

Greenstein S (2021) Preserving the rule of law in the era of artificial intelligence (AI). Artif Intell Law

Hacker P (2023) The European AI Liability Directives - critique of a half-hearted approach and lessons for the future. Comput Law Secur Rev 51, Article 105871

Hacker P (2024) Proposal for a Directive on adapting non-contractual civil liability rules to artificial intelligence: complementary impact assessment

Kirchberger T (2017) European Union policy-making on robotics and artificial intelligence. CYELP 13:191–214

Lemley AM, Casey B (2019) The University of Chicago Law Review, Remedies for Robots

Markou C, Deakin FS (2020) Is law computable? From rule of law to legal singularity. University of Cambridge Faculty of Law Research Paper

Muftić N (2021) Liability for artificial intelligence. In: Slakoper Z, Tot I (eds) Digital technologies and the law of obligations. Routledge

Muftić N (2023) Understanding the risks of artificial intelligence as a precondition for sound liability regulation. In: Artificial intelligence and normative challenges law, governance and technology series, 2023, pp 85–105

Nilsson JN (2010) The quest for artificial intelligence: a history of ideas and achievements. Cambridge University Press, Cambridge

Nunez Duffourc M, Gerke S (2023) The proposed EU directives for AI liability leave worrying gaps likely to impact medical AI, 6 NPJ DIGIT. MED., no. 77

Reggia J, Huang D-W, Katz G (2015) Beliefs concerning the nature of consciousness. J. Conscious Stud 22:146–171

Rodríguez de las Heras Ballell T (2019) Legal challenges of artificial intelligence: modelling the disruptive features of emerging technologies and assessing their possible legal impact. Uniform Law Rev 24(2)

Rudin C, Radin J (2019) Why are we using black box models in AI when we don't need to? A lesson from an explainable AI competition. Harv Data Sci Rev 1(2)., available at: https://hdsr.mitpress.mit.edu/pub/f9kuryi8/release/6

Smuha AN (2021) From a 'Race to AI' to a 'Race to AI Regulation' - regulatory competition for artificial intelligence. Law Innov Technol 13(1)

Spindler G (2023) Different approaches for liability of artificial intelligence – Pros and Cons – the New Proposal of the EU Commission on Liability for Defective Products and AI Systems. Available at SSRN: https://ssrn.com/abstract=4354468 or https://doi.org/10.2139/ssrn.4354468
Surden H (2014) Machine learning and law. Wash Law Rev 89(1):87–115
Tot I (2018) Prestanak trajnih obveznih odnosa. Zbornik Pravni fakultet Rijeka 39
Trahan JR (2008) The distinction between persons and things: an historical perspective. J Civil Law Stud 1:9
Turing MA (1950) Computing machinery and intelligence. Mind: Q Rev Psychol Philos 59(236): 433–460
van Zeben J (2018) A law and economics perspective on judicial risk regulation. Eur J Risk Regul
Varian RH (2014) Big data: new tricks for econometrics. J Econ Perspect 28(3):3–27
Wachter S et al (2024) Do large language models have a legal duty to tell the truth? R Soc Open Sci 22–23:11240197
Wagner G (2005) The project of harmonizing European tort law. Common Market Law Rev
Wagner G (2023) Liability rules for the digital age - aiming for the Brussels Effect, available at SSRN: https://ssrn.com/abstract=4320285 or https://doi.org/10.2139/ssrn.4320285
Wendehorst C (2020) Strict liability for AI and other emerging technologies. J Eur Tort Law 11(2)

Chapter 3
Liability Within the Wider Framework

3.1 Introduction

Regulation of technology is not what preoccupied B&H in the previous decades. Ever since the end of the war in 1990, the public has been focused on establishing a framework whereby the coexistence of dominant diverse ethnopolitical groups might be possible. The agenda was focused on the most elementary issues such as free and fair elections and establishing a single market within B&H. Although the majority of powers remained vested in the entities, several laws had been adopted on the state level, such as the Law on Competition,[1] a set of intellectual property laws,[2] the Law on Protection of Personal Data,[3] and the Law on Consumer Protection.[4]

However, the degree of cooperation on the state level has been reduced for some time. Questions that would entail political agreement remain unaddressed. One of them is the question of digital transformation. B&H 2021 the Report of the EU Commission states that:

> Bosnia and Herzegovina made limited or no progress in most areas of competitiveness and inclusive growth (information society and media, taxation, economic and monetary policy, enterprise and industrial policy, education and culture, and the customs union), where it is at an early stage or has some level of preparation.[5]

[1] Official Gazette B&H 48/05, 76/07, 80/09.

[2] Law on Patents (Official Gazette B&H 53/10); Law on Trademarks (Official Gazette B&H 53/10); Law on Industrial Designs (Official Gazette B&H 53/10); Law on the Protection of Indications of Geographical Origin (Official Gazette B&H 53/10); Law on the Protection of Topographies of Integrated Circuits (Official Gazette B&H 53/10); Law on Copyright and Related Rights (Official Gazette B&H 63/10); Law on the Collective Management of Copyright and Related Rights (Official Gazette B&H 63/10).

[3] Official Gazette B&H 49/2006, 76/2011, 89/2011.

[4] Official Gazette B&H 25/2006, 88/2015.

[5] European Commission, Communication from the Commission to the European Parliament, the Council, the European Economic and Social Committee and the Committee of the Region, 2021

N. Muftić, *Artificial Intelligence and Tortious Liability*, European Union and its Neighbours in a Globalized World 21, https://doi.org/10.1007/978-3-031-86453-7_3

In fact, emerging digital technologies, B&H has not even held a comprehensive public discussion about emerging digital technologies and their significance for society's future. The rules already in place often do not meet technological and regulatory trends. For instance, data protection legislation has not been updated to reflect the latest findings of the EU's data protection law, although the Law on Personal Data in BiH was adopted in 2006 (and amended in 2011) after the previous Data Protection Directive. When it comes specifically to AI, the situation is the same. So far, the only public authority that announced its willingness to deal with the challenges of AI is the government of the Federation of B&H.[6] Its contents remain unknown, but even at the outset, some problems are apparent. First, the counterparts of the Federation of B&H, Republika Srpska, and Brcko District, have not announced such a strategy. Moreover, a regulation that might regulate AI is significantly made on the state level (e.g. data protection legislation and the intellectual property legislation). The existing laws on state-level preempt entities' power to adopt laws that would contradict them. In such a context, it is impossible to refer to B&H's specific regulatory approach to AI or emerging digital technologies. Therefore, the majority of the discussion in this chapter will build on the findings of the EU as well as authors from other jurisdictions.

Rules of liability do not exist in a lacuna. Rather, the broader policy and legal framework is important for achieving any goals liability law should achieve. These goals depend on the contents of rules which rely on the underlying policy choices. However, they also depend on the regulatory approach. This includes a set of choices such as level of regulation, timeliness of new rules, understanding and classifying risks arising from AI, and the interaction of liability rules with other legal rules. Only after they had been addressed, the following chapters can answer the specific and usually central questions of tort law—who should be responsible for the harm and under what circumstances.

The following chapter introduces the context surrounding the regulation of liability for AI. Tort law is displayed as a piece of mosaic in a legal framework. As such, its impact and goals cannot be determined in isolation, but rather in concert with other applicable rules. The adoption of proper measures should strive to provide equilibrium between fair and timely allocation of losses without disincentivizing innovations, on the one hand, and ensuring that a victim has a sound chance of being compensated on the other. Accordingly, several questions emerge.

Selecting a proper level to adopt new rules is important as it impacts the predictability of the legal framework. Such rules of liability, with a couple of exceptions, do not exist on the EU level. In B&H, the liability framework is de facto almost the same throughout the entire state, but the entities retain the power to

---

Communication on EU Enlargement Policy, 6, available at: https://ec.europa.eu/neighbourhood-enlargement/bosnia-and-herzegovina-report-2021_en.

[6]Development strategy for Federation FB&H 2021–2027 (Strategija razvoja Federacije BiH 2021–2027), available at: https://fzzpr.gov.ba/files/Strategije/Strategija%20razvoja%20FBiH%202021.-2027.pdf.

change it. The current lack of fragmentation exists due to the reception of Yugoslavian law which has not been changed significantly ever since. Just like in the EU, discussion regarding the level of regulation is not conducted only on the expert level, but also on a political one. Furthermore, the proper time to adopt new rules, if they are necessary, is also a sensitive question as it needs to take into account our current capability to assess the risks generated by the use of AI as well as to fathom general rules apply for this technology in general. Regulation of particular sectors instead of having general rules might aid as it would require addressing the aforementioned question only concerning a limited application of AI. The next set of questions concerns the design of liability rules. Many authors suggest a targeted approach to the changes in the current liability rules to avoid disruption. A targeted approach does not mean necessarily limiting the scope of new rules to specific sectors. It can also mean recognition of specific risks and attribution of tailored rules to them. A champion of such an approach has, however, to determine whether it will limit the new rules to AI or for all emerging digital technologies. While the choice is not easy, a technology-specific approach is preferable if it takes into account the specific risks of technology as well as its joint impact with other emerging digital technologies. A targeted approach should address specific risks stemming from AI. However, classifying risks is not an easy task.

Lastly, to regulate liability for AI, one should consider safety standards and insurance and compensation funds. Among various tools which go hand-in-hand with liability, questions of ex ante measures that ought to ensure safety and certainty of payment are some of the most relevant for AI.

3.2 Understanding Tort Law in Light of Principles of Civil Law

To grasp the desired approach towards the regulation of tortious liability for AI, it is necessary to address what is the role of this field of law in the first place. As various branches of law govern AI, rules interact and act in concert, creating a regulatory framework that in theory ought to navigate the object of regulation in a socially desirable way.

Tort law is not an overarching field of law designated to cover all potential accidents. H. L.A. Hart stated: "in relation to maintenance of any social institution, it is necessary to recognize the goals it ought to achieve and then to identify whether any considerations limit the pursue them".[7] Seen through the prism of this statement, tort law can be understood as an instrument for achieving certain goals. While recognizing the importance of Kant's understanding of undoing the wrongs as *per se* value worth protecting,[8] the instrumental character of tort law puts in focus

[7] Hart (1968), p. 10.

[8] Immanuel Kant, The Metaphysics of Morals, 1: "Nothing can possibly be conceived in the world, or even out of it, which can be called good without qualification, except a Good Will."

specific and material interests. Undoing the wrongs might occur beyond the realm of tort law or law in general, as well as along with it. Therefore, certain wrongs might not be treated by legal sanction, other types of social norms might enter for justice to be served.

Provided that the liability regime pursues utilitarian goals, the question is how to identify them. Bentham considered that individual interests should be in focus,[9] but utilitarianism can put in focus the benefit of society over the protection of individuals whose rights are concerned. Jhering argued that individuals ought to pursue their interests because of the utility for society, regardless of their personal preferences:

> However, while the realization in practice of public law and of criminal law is assured because it is imposed as a duty on public officials, the realization in practice of private law is presented to individuals under the form of their legal rights; that is, it is left exclusively to them to take the initiative in its realization, left exclusively to their action. In the former case, its practical realization depends on the performance of their duty by the authorities and public officials, and, in this latter case, on the assertion by individuals of their legal rights. If the latter, for any reason, neglect to assert their rights, permanently and generally, be it from ignorance, love of ease, or fear, the consequence is that the principles of right lose their vigor.[10]

In his understanding, society relies on citizens who protect the public interest through pursuing individual rights.[11] Claiming damage for the caused harm would signal the wrongdoer that what he is doing is inadequate, but more importantly, it would enable people to express their moral identity and link them to a broader community. Jhering saw the protection of personal rights as bear vitalizing function and perpetuating social unity. The purpose of the law as an aim to facilitate social interactions by integrating individuals into a culture, as Jhering claims, had been disputed. Max Webber claims that the maintenance of metaphysical values is not the main purpose of the law.[12] Rather, it aims to provide "the routine, often largely passionless, structuring of a 'disenchanted' existence, not the vibrant, rich moral life that Jhering apparently thought it might facilitate".[13] In short, the law provides a procedure in which social interactions occur, potentially without any hidden moral background. Notwithstanding the differences, the commonality between the authors is the recognition of a broader societal utility of law.

In his work, Hart mainly considered criminal law and attributed a set of questions toward understanding its purpose. Based on Hart's questions and due to the similar purpose of dealing with socially undesirable behavior, Honore states[14] that corresponding questions might be posed in order to understand the purpose of tort law:

---

[9] Stanford Encyclopedia of Philosophy, available at: https://plato.stanford.edu/entries/bentham/#CivLawPolEco.

[10] Rudolf von Jhering (2008), pp. 71–72.

[11] Ibid, 32.

[12] Weber (1948).

[13] Ibid. p. 139, in Cotterrell (2008), pp. 373–384.

[14] Honore (1995).

1. Why are certain types of behavior made tortious?
2. What is the definition of tort liability?
3. What general aims justify the state of maintaining a system of tort law?
4. What justifies the person whose rights have been infringed in claiming compensation by the wrongdoer?
5. Subject to what conditions may one who by their conduct has infringed the rights of another be required to pay compensation?
6. What limits should be placed on the extent of the duty to compensate?

The following subsections will group and address these questions in three parts. The first part will outline the aims of tort law. The second part will elaborate on the question of the distribution of liability. The third part concerns the characteristics of tortfeasor relevant for distribution.

3.2.1 Aims of Tort Law

To be able to understand the role of tort law concerning AI, it is important to understand the answers to these questions. More specifically, to understand our expectations of tort law in the regulation of AI, we need to elaborate on them in general. Behavior merits treatment under tort law if it detriments or destroys values attached to a person. Such treatment of the law sends two messages to the wrongdoer: (1) such behavior is undesirable; (2) it should not be repeated. This is a widely recognized goal of tort law often described as deterrence.

However, tort law does not sanction behavior *per se* but its consequences· That is what separates it from other fields of law. For instance, criminal law and misdemeanor law might deter one from behaving in a certain fashion without any reference to the consequence of their behavior. For instance, driving under the influence of alcohol is in many jurisdictions punishable regardless of whether real harm has been done. Another reason why behavior can be treated under tort law is to provide a mechanism of compensation to the victims of it which would be usually expressed through the imposition of an obligation to pay on the wrongdoer. Although it sanctions consequences, it creates expectations about the foreseeability of compensation to potential victims. If the occurrence happens, it provides a mechanism for monetary compensation. The broader implication of having injured parties satisfied is the preservation of social order. Namely, provided that it does not have foreseeable means to recover the loss, a victim may turn to private vengeance.[15] In the ideal scenario, the liability regime has two effects—*ex ante* and *ex post*. The *ex ante* effect is the induction of socially desirable behavior "in terms of reduction of a number of accidents and increase in safety investments",[16] and *ex post* to ensure compensation

[15] Shavell (2007), p. 35.
[16] Leenes et al. (2017), p. 11.

to the individual who suffered the harm by the wrongdoer.[17] The role of deterrence and compensation is seen differently depending on the jurisdiction. In general, common law jurisdictions treat the two goals as equal or even place deterrence overcompensation.[18] On the other hand, in the continental European legal tradition, the main role of tort law is to provide compensation, while "primary implementation of the deterrence notion is left to public law, above all criminal law; thus, compensation payments under the law of damages are limited to the full redress of the damage sustained".[19]

A creator of the LO draft, Mihailo Konstantinović, expressed a similar position, stressing that reparation of harm is the primary goal of liability rules in the law.[20] Consequently, the duty to compensate in B&H's law is placed as a duty independent of any prior relations between a tortfeasor and a victim. It is an obligation of its own. Article 16 of LO provides for a general duty to refrain from harming others. A primate of compensation over deterrence can be discerned from the wording of this provision. It does not prohibit conduct that leads to harm, but it only sanctions the harm itself. Legal theory has interpreted such wording as providing leeway for lawmakers to adopt various other rules to regulate behavior, whereas compensation remains the primary concern of tort law.[21] Such understanding is also clear from the norms of LO which guide the courts in the damages to be awarded. Article 190 of LO stipulates that the determination of damages to be awarded should be assessed with the goal of restoration of the material state of the person sustaining damage into the state it would have been without the damaging act or omission. This is the so-called principle of integral compensation.[22] Exceptionally, the courts are entitled to correct this amount in the following cases:[23]

1. if the liable person is in a poor material situation so that payment of full indemnity would bring it into poverty;[24]
2. in case of indemnity awarded according to the value the object had for the person sustaining damage if an object is lost or damaged by a criminal offence committed wilfully;[25]
3. If the tort-feasor has caused damage while doing something to the benefit of the person sustaining loss, the court may order a lower indemnity, while taking into account the degree of care the tort-feasor was otherwise applying in their own affairs;[26]

---

[17] Ibid.

[18] Oliphant (2015).

[19] Koziol (2012), p. 747.

[20] Konstantinović (1969a, b).

[21] Perović (1995), p. 52; Radišić (2004), p. 189; Karanikić Mirić (2009), p. 307.

[22] Ibid, 308.

[23] Karanikić Mirić (2009), p. 307.

[24] Article 191(1) of LO.

[25] Article 189(4) of LO.

[26] Article 191(2) of LO.

4. if an injured person contributed to the harm, and it is impossible to establish which part of the harm comes from it.[27]

Guido Calabresi's "The Cost of Accident" elaborates on the specific contents of the goals of liability law.[28] This classification provides an even more specific understanding of is ordered by the importance of goals and lists: (1) the reduction of the total accident costs, (2) the allocation of risk, and (3) the minimization of administrative costs of the system.[29] The reduction of accident costs can be further divided into primary accident costs, secondary accident costs, and tertiary or efficiency costs. Primary accident costs encompass all costs borne by the victim due to the harm suffered as well as the costs of taking precautionary measures by an injurer. Secondary accident costs include costs of risk-bearing due to a potential accident incurred with the purpose of risk spreading. Tertiary accident costs refer to the costs of administering a treatment of accidents. It is clear, however, that the aims of tort law have very specific instrumental purposes. Tort law rules ought to provide the greatest level of efficiency, and any departures must be justified by society's understanding of justice.

Beyond effects on private relationships, tort law fulfills broader societal goals. Observed through the lens of the law-in-action approach, it should signal whether a jurisdiction provides certainty to outside actors who might want to get involved. As the EU Parliament's Proposal from 2020 suggests in Recital (20), the aim is "not only to safeguard important legally protected rights of individuals, but also to determine whether businesses, especially SMEs and start-ups, can raise capital, innovate, research, and ultimately offer new products and services, as well as whether consumers trust such products and services and are willing to use them despite the potential risks and legal claims being brought in respect of such products or services".[30] The underlying public policy goals can be manyfold and tort law might act as a mechanism of social engineering with a potential to promote environmental, health, and safety goals.[31] However, such a broad understanding of tort law is specific to every society as well as to specific time where it is employed, provided, of course, that tort law is understood as something beyond a tool that allows individuals who suffered harm to receive compensation from the persons who caused it.

Apart from providing compensation, we expect the tort law to provide deterrence from the behavior deemed undesirable. What this means exactly in relation to AI is hard to define, except that it is clear that such behavior has to create harmful consequences treated by tort law. For a novel technology in which boundaries are still not clear, a treatment of consequences is an apt avenue, compared to ex ante

27 Article 192(2) of LO.

28 Calabresi (1970).

29 Ibid, pp. 26–29.

30 Resolution with recommendations to the Commission on a civil liability regime for artificial intelligence [2020/2014(INL)].

31 Kysar (2018), p. 56.

mechanisms such as licensing, safety standards, etc. Tort law is more subtle insofar as it does not curtail development by limiting behavior that has not generated any undesirable consequences. However, AI is peculiar because of its autonomy from humans. This is reflected in its independent decision-making not only from its owners and users but sometimes also from its creators. As such, it creates an interesting situation vis-à-vis potential parties that can be affected by moral hazards. Unlike in typical situations where humans behind any activity are in the focus, we can ask the question of who should be impacted by the regulators' rules—humans of AI itself.[32] Although this task is in reality often hard, humans can be incentivized. At least, we have prior experience with humans and their incentives as current approaches around the world concern the establishment of rules for humans, even if they act under the shield of various forms of legal persons. On the other hand, the incentives of AI as an autonomous entity are a new issue. Ai is an independent entity with the ability to improve itself based on prior experiences. With opacity as its characteristic, AI behaves unpredictably, and it is sometimes impossible to foresee its decisions. Unlike traditional software where all possible outcomes can be tested by the creators, AI does not offer that possibility. Liability rules can be approached from either a normative or economic perspective.[33] From a normative perspective, these rules are understood as prohibitions. The economic perspective treats liability rules as a cost of a certain decision. The latter approach suggests that liability rules can be breached if it is worthy to a wrongdoer, which often can be calculated ex ante. In case there is an unpredictable AI that does not have a straightforward prohibition embedded in its algorithm, it is likely to calculate whether the breach of liability rules is worthy.

Unless the legal prohibitions are easy to understand, how can developers integrate them into the algorithm? Thus, it is possible to have AI engage in risky activities without having humans to be even aware of it. One of the solutions is obviously to prohibit every questionable type of behavior, effectively preventing AI from exploring certain options in the process of machine learning. As a result, we might get a slower pace of AI improvement.

The result is unfavorable as well if we allow AI to interpret the meaning of legal rules. Not only they will inevitably tend to circumvent them, but there is also a fundamental problem of understanding the legal rules of non-human entities. This is especially emphasized if AI operates not only as a recommender but also if it executes actions in accordance with its interpretations of the law. An additional problem with AI lies in the fact that is it not human. It bears the supreme potential to make rational calculations, but the law is designed with more than reasonableness in mind. It bears an ethical component that cannot be reduced to mere mathematical calculation. Tort law for that reason operates with abundance of general standards instead of clear rules, as all potentially relevant situations cannot be predicted and we often have a holistic perspective of an accident only after it occurred. Reduction of

[32] Lemley and Casey (2019), p. 1368.

[33] Calabresi and Melamed (1972).

such complex calculations to rational variables for AI is not an easy task. The law is not able to do so even for humans.

Meeting the aims of tort law in the case of AI therefore requires rethinking traditional settings which now have to take into consideration specific characteristics of the object of regulation.

3.2.2 Distribution of Responsibility

If we agree that tort law aims at deterrence and compensation, the following question is who should be responsible to compensate? Is that the same person who can provide deterrence? As a truism, tort law attributes the duty to compensate to a person who caused the injury. Such a choice relies on the underlying principle of justice. In other words, the mere fact that one has suffered damage does not entitle them to a right to require compensation from a specific person. Our attribution of responsibility to a tortfeasor derives from a broader understanding that a person who caused the harm should have a duty to compensate. The two classic understandings of justice underlying such reasoning are corrective and distributive.

Corrective justice presupposes that the tortfeasor and injured parties have the same rights and duties and that one cannot be better off on the account of the other without justification.[34] Aristotle introduced the idea that a function of a system is to exercise corrective justice in Nicomachean Ethics.[35] If an accident occurs, a victim has a right to be restored to a position in prior to the accident. As a matter of principle, the compensation does not have to be in the money and ideally is not, as the best potential solution would be a restitution of the victim's position. There is a disagreement between the authors about whether might have a right to compensation without a corresponding duty of tortfeasor. One view is that a victim who suffered harm that cannot be attributed to any person who has to be compensated nonetheless deserves a right to be compensated.[36] Justification is that the victim is objectively worse off irrespective of whether there is a justification for wrongful conduct. There is also a view that considers that a victim's right to require compensation must correspond to a wrongdoer's duty to compensate and that one cannot exist without the other.[37] However, the mere causation between the tortfeasor action and suffered harm is not enough to entitle a victim to a right to compensation. It is necessary but not a sufficient condition, as it is accepted in a great number of legal systems. We will refer to that question in the following section.

Another question concerning corrective justice is whether one is entitled to commit a tort with beforehand consideration, realizing that justice would be served

[34] Honore (1995).

[35] Gordley (1997).

[36] Coleman (1992), p. 340.

[37] Weinrib (1980), p. 267.

if it compensated a victim. In his later work, Coleman stated: "Corrective justice is the normative principle that connects our first-order duties of care to others to a second-order duty of repair in the event we fail to discharge the first-order duties we have. At the bottom is the idea that our relations with one another are structured in part by the rights and duties we owe one another. We do not see each other merely as potential holding bins of some share of the world's welfare."[38] In the classic economic analysis of law understanding, the relevance between the first-order and second-order duties is not emphasized. While justice is one of the considerations along with the reduction of costs,[39] greater deference is given to the latter.

Distributive justice is a concept whereby goods and burdens should be distributed among members of a society in a just fashion. The idea stems from the philosophy of Aristotle and has been later a starting point for deliberation in tort law. If distributive justice concerns goods and burdens, it should place also "the burden of bearing the risk that his conduct may turn out to be harmful to others in return for the benefit to himself that will accrue should his conduct turn out as he plans".[40] What a person entitles to compensation for wrongdoing is not any specific interaction but the mere fact that it is a member of society. Aristotle explains that distributive justice means the power of deciding what is for the public interest and that corrective justice deals with private relationships. Corrective justice and distributive justice in tort law do not act separately. Some authors[41] have argued that they often have the same point to the extent that it is sometimes hard to distinguish between them, especially if the idea behind corrective justice is to protect a just distribution of resources.[42] In any case, both are grounded in the belief in the equality of people who interact. That idea was underlying Aristotle's Nicomachean Ethics as well as Immanuel Kant's understanding of morals:

> [M]an regarded as a person [rather than a mere animal], that is, as the subject of a morally practical reason, is exalted above any price; for as a person (homo noumenon) he is not to be valued merely as a means to the ends of others or even to his own ends, but as an end in himself, that is, he possesses a dignity (an absolute inner worth) by which he exacts respect for himself from all other rational beings in the world. He can measure himself with every other being of this kind and value himself on a footing of equality with them.[43]

Unlike distributive justice, corrective justice links specific harm suffered by a victim to a specific tortfeasor. While distributive justice would be concerned with a more general understanding of distribution within a community based solely on the well-being of its members, corrective justice grants a right against a specific person who is responsible for the harm. Apart from what is just, the distribution of responsibility

---

[38] Coleman (1992), p. 353.

[39] "'Moral' evaluations of the activities involved enter into the decision, and the aim of the ex post decision is to find not the cheapest but the best cost avoider." Calabresi (1970), p. 241.

[40] Honore (1995), p. 82.

[41] Benson (1992) and Weinrib (1992).

[42] Gordley (1997).

[43] Kant (1991), pp. 213–214.

also has to be in line with other aims of tort law. It has to provide deterrence as well as compensation.

A specific reference to AI would not be provided here as a separate chapter is devoted to the question of allocation of responsibility.

3.2.3 Considerations Relevant to the Duty to Compensate

Deterrence and compensation as the two main aims of tort law do not necessarily entail identical measures. The understanding of corrective justice allows for the separation of the two goals. Many factors attributed to a victim might lead to a conclusion that its duty to compensate an injured party would be unjust. At the same time, an injured party has suffered losses due to the conduct of a person violating its rights without consent. The modern tort law is familiar with this problem, and it deals with it in various ways. Without prejudice to the following chapters where these questions will be elaborated in detail, a brief categorization of considerations relevant to the duty to compensate is provided here. A default rule, stipulated in Article 154 of LO, is that whoever causes injury or loss to another shall be liable. To defend themselves, a tortfeasor must actively prove the presence or absence of certain circumstances, depending on the applicable basis of liability and the applicable law.

Situations, where tort law assigns a duty to compensate the one who caused harm without any possibility to be exonerated, are hard to find. A mere causal relationship between one's conduct and harm does not suffice to assign liability. This approach in its pure form perhaps exists in the realm of social or moral norms, but tort law considers it only as necessary but insufficient to assign one with a duty to compensate.[44]

A multitude of reasons why a tortfeasor might not be assigned a duty to compensate a victim exist.[45] First, a tortfeasor might exonerate one from the duty to compensate for harm if the duty of care has been met. For instance, a medical doctor might not be liable for a patient's deteriorated health if the treatment it provided has been appropriate and applied with sufficient care. Second, there are reasons related to a specific factual situation that rendered the harm unforeseeable. For instance, in a case where an individual is in the middle of a snowstorm on the mountain, they can break into a cabin by force in order to survive. An owner of a cabin has suffered harm, but the circumstances do not allow for attributing a duty to compensate to a person in danger. LO does not have a doctrine of necessity akin to, for instance, German Bürgerliches Gesetzbuch, but the courts can reach the same outcome by applying vis major in Article 177 with the same underlying reasoning. Furthermore, a duty to compensate can arise out of the application of negotiorum gestio doctrine

[44]Honore (1995), p. 81.

[45]Ibid, pp. 90 et al.

contained in LO, even if a tort law duty cannot be established. Third, the applicable law might not cover specific harm adequately. For example, pure economic loss is protected to a limited extent throughout Europe.[46] The limitation of duty to compensate a victim stems merely from the inability to interpret the applicable law to cover a specific type of harm. However, LO does not preclude recovery for pure economic loss as it sets out a very broad definition of damage.[47]

Fourth, considerations beyond specific cases might exclude the applicability of tort law. For, example the state might decide that some sorts of harm require compensation from publicly maintained funds. This approach relies heavily on distributive justice instead of corrective. When it exists, it is usually an exception from the rule that tort law governs matters of compensation. An example would be New Zealand where a publicly funded accident compensation scheme with the goals of minimizing the incidence and impact of injury was introduced in 1974.[48] The scheme assists with the cost of treatment and rehabilitation for all personal injuries, regardless of fault, and in exchange bans suing for compensatory damages.[49] In B&H, such an approach also exists to a certain extent. In case of a vehicle accident, if a victim cannot obtain compensation through the means of tort law, she is entitled to be compensated via the publicly held fund.[50] The fund is financed through the mandatory contribution of all vehicle owners. Unlike in the example of New Zealand where the tort law is not applicable, the B&H applies the fund as an additional level of protection for a victim in case (1) the harm has been done by an unknown vehicle only if it is non-pecuniary damage; (2) tortfeasor does not have a mandatory insurance contract that would entitle a victim to compensation; and in case of bankruptcy of an insurance company, if a victim cannot be compensated from the bankruptcy estate.[51] From the perspective of economic analysis of law, this might not be necessarily problematic, as the allocation of loss in this way can be efficient.[52] Moreover, a vague understanding of justice and fairness by Calabresi, additional keys in the allocation of loss along with the reduction of costs, does not bar such interpretation. However, a complete exclusion of tort law or supplementation of tort law with publicly funded schemes has the potential to undermine deterrence as a tortfeasor will not directly bear the costs of the harm it causes.

[46] Bussani and Palmer (2003), p. 120.

[47] Bukovac Puvača (2017), p. 399.

[48] Wallis (2017), pp. 38–39.

[49] Ibid.

[50] Law on Mandatory Traffic Insurance of the Federation of BiH (Official Gazette Federation B&H 57/20); Law on Mandatory Traffic Insurance of Republika Srpska (Official Gazette Republika Srpska 82/15).

[51] Article 66 of Law on Mandatory Traffic Insurance of the Federation of BiH; Article 51 of Law on Mandatory Traffic Insurance of Republika Srpska.

[52] Ibid.

A specific reference to AI would not be provided here as there are various potential reasons for not assigning a tortfeasor with a duty to compensate in the case of AI. They will be elaborated on throughout the work.

3.3 Law Between Innovation and Safety

Prevention of accidents and compensation are not the only goals of tort law. How else can we explain the rules whereby drivers are allowed to reach a speed of 130 km/h+ on highways, or how potentially lethal drugs are often sold without prescriptions? We do not want to equal the number of accidents to zero if a society receives benefits in exchange for their occurrence at an acceptable rate. The role of tort law is to ensure that the excessive exposure to the risk caused by the recklessness of the party who can manage the risk is reduced to a socially desirable level. This has traditionally been an endeavor of accident law—to achieve a balance between the risk and reward society has from one's behavior or invention.[53] If in the past we had been willing to sacrifice human lives for many purposes. For example, the construction of the Gotthard Base Tunnel through the Alps was highly beneficial as the duration of the trip was curtailed, although some of the consequences could have been predicted. During the execution of this project, nine workers lost their lives.[54] We are also willing to sacrifice the most important values such as human lives to a certain degree by allowing road traffic and not preventing vehicles from reaching high speed. Again, this can be understood as a conscious choice of modern societies given the available data on the number and cause of traffic accidents.

The mere operation of attaching a price tag to human lives seems inhumane. But, as economists would point out, there is an optimum level or a risk that is acceptable to society.[55] Calculation of the worth of invaluable values such as human lives is being done on many levels. For instance, in cases concerning robots that might cause physical harm to humans, the choice is in the hands of those who manufacture them. In a trolley problem, a textbook example of understanding morality and justice, humans are perplexed as they need to sacrifice invaluable values to protect other values of the same kind. They are put in a situation of determining which of the two merits more protection. If such decisions are adopted by opaque artificial agents, they would essentially deal with choices involving an understanding of morals. The idea itself sounds uncomfortable. Tradeoffs between innovation and protection of the most important values in a society are not therefore new. The question one might ask is what risk are we willing to take to have AI that is advanced and, perhaps even

---

[53] Calabresi (1970), p. 18.

[54] Memorial ceremony for deceased tunnel workers, available at: https://web.archive.org/web/20200427001530/https://www.alptransit.ch/en/media/press-releases/detail/news/memorial-ceremony-for-deceased-tunnel-workers-977/.

[55] Lemley and Casey (2019), p. 1368.

more important, better than in other parts of the world?[56] Additionally, who is the one who should make such decisions?

On the one side, the promises of AI are unprecedented. Provided they are delivered, the lives of people will be highly improved. Products and services touched upon by AI that possess sophisticated characteristics are inevitably going to improve the benefits for consumers. The comfort of being a passenger in a driverless car enables one to simultaneously stream a movie and enjoy the scenery while crossing the desired distance. The risks of wrong judgment a physician can make are going to be reduced if not eliminated with the introduction of AI tools that aid in establishing a diagnosis or performing treatments themselves. The benefits exceed the increase in the level of comfort. AI is a transformative technology with the potential to lift the ones who master it above those who do not. Market players who succeed have a chance to have a strong position beyond national borders. In the years of the emergence of the internet and so-called "big tech", a new set of companies emerged along and some of them have had an enormous impact. A similar scenario might happen with AI.

Liability rules are a part of the bigger picture. Strict tort law rules might provide a victim a secure and fast compensation, but at the same time, it might render a jurisdiction less attractive for investment and deployment of new technologies. On the other hand, tort law might be loosened in order to stimulate AI. This would effectively mean subsidizing innovation through tort law. The idea itself is not new as authors had proposed the use of liability to foster other social goals such fight against inequality and unemployment and achieving market competition.[57] The problem of having outside goals embedded in tort law lies in the potential of disturbing fundamental goals—deterrence and compensation. Loosening liability rules might remove an incentive for AI manufacturers to engage in overly risky activities, as compensation might be hard to obtain for a victim. It is possible to divorce deterrence from compensation and provide, for instance, victims with other means of recovery. But the problem of deterrence remains and the well-known way of tackling it is tort law. Provided we remove this incentive to deter from the realm of liability law, we will need to include other legal mechanisms that are, due to a lack of experience, less known and trustworthy.

A dichotomy between innovation and safety is not new and specific to AI. Societies have sacrificed safety to have higher quality of technology and such calculations are still made in contemporary times. The proper regulatory approach concerning AI has to have the same calculation in might—it needs to find a balance between acceptable risk considering potential benefits. And the benefits are very promising. They extend over the improved quality of everyday life as AI is a transformative technology that offers states the possibility to reposition on the global

[56] This question surpasses this work. Hence, it does not attempt to answer it. It is only worth noticing that innovation and protection of society have questionable validity if understood in terms of one being a negation of the other. It not clear whether there is a causational link between the two.

[57] Calabresi (1970), p. 32.

markets. Tort law is a tool used primarily for the compensation of victims and deterrence of tortfeasors. It can pursue other goals too. It can subsidize innovation a society deems appropriate. However, such goals mustn't annul the primary goals of compensation and deterrence.

B&H law does not recognize fostering innovation as a goal of liability law, at least directly. Historically, even before the adoption of LO, case law in Yugoslavia developed the concept of strict liability and applied it to modern technological developments considered as a source of increased danger. The applicable statutory law in Yugoslavia prior to World War II did not contain general rules on strict liability. However, under the influence of mainly Austrian and Soviet law,[58] courts in Yugoslavia adopted an understanding that the increased risk arising from an activity or a thing should correspond to a greater exposure to liability. Such development had also taken the attention of the drafters of LO. Mihailo Konstantinović had taken into account Yugoslavian history and developments in comparative law at the time, especially French law.[59] In the first, second, and final versions of the LO, the text included rules on strict liability. In general, Yugoslavian law had followed the European trends at the time. The arguments employed in discussions regarding strict liability in national legal systems around it had also been present in the case of LO.[60] The impact of the increased burden on innovation was one of them. However, in the case of Yugoslavia, this argument was not embraced very much. More precisely, the principle of *cuius commodum eius damnum* was understood differently by the drafters of LO. Mihailo Konstantinović considered that a person who benefits from a thing or an activity that is of increased dangerousness should compensate for harm. Individual benefits should be understood as related to specific things or activities and therefore liability should be specified too. Consequently, *cuius commodum eius damnum* does not entail the socialization of risks but an allocation according to a criterion of direct benefit from a thing or an activity.[61]

3.4 Law of the Horse

There is almost universal recognition of AI as a specific phenomenon. Lawmakers are increasingly deliberating on how to approach this issue. Many see its enormous potential for growth as well as a likelihood that it might transform labor, markets, or even warfare. However, the exceptionalism of AI does not necessarily mean it merits being treated as a different field of law. Regulation of new phenomena is not a new task in history, and the law has already many times managed to grasp innovation. With the emergence of the internet, similar questions have been raised. Prominent

[58] Bazala (1956) and Mihajlović (1975).

[59] Karanikić Mirić (2019a, b), p. 32.

[60] Cigoj (1983).

[61] Karanikić Mirić (2019a, b), p. 38.

scholars had championed two opposite positions. The advocate of the first view is Frank Easterbrook,[62] who criticized the endeavor to create cyberlaw as a distinct field of law. He argued that there is no coherent system of rules that would encompass all relevant legal questions and simultaneously have inner logic and structure.[63] This is exactly the reason why law and technology are approached through the compartmentalized (but often related) subject areas: "the traditional intellectual property topics (copyright, trademarks, and patents), biotechnology law, new media, telecommunications, and so on".[64] The proper approach to treat technology is, in his opinion, by general rules of law. They should be adapted to fit specific characteristics of a particular technology, but their underlying logic and structure can remain more-less untouched. The opposite approach had been advocated by Lawrence Lessig.[65] He recognized that technology can be understood as exceptional and therefore merits specific treatment. Studying cyberlaw, his opinion is useful as tensions in law present in the case of internet regulation can be understood properly only if the technology is treated as specific. Only then we can discern the proper way to treat these tensions. The discussion between the two opposite standpoints remains unsettled.[66]

Analogously, the following question can be raised: do we need specific rules for AI or general rules that can successfully deal with accidents caused by this technology? First, this work does not attempt to address characteristics of AI that render the entire legal treatment insufficient. It concerns only one question—tortious liability. Whether this technology merits a completely novel field of law is impossible to discern now as it is in its infancy and the progression is hard to predict. Therefore, premises for this discussion might potentially be ripe in the future, but not at the moment. We are aware, however, that AI has characteristics that undermine existing liability rules and fundamental principles of civil law, as the Report established.[67] Change of liability rules avoids being a subject of Eastbrook's observations as it compartmentally addresses AI. At the same time, to understand liability implications comprehensively, one cannot exclude the possibility of having to treat the technology comprehensively. Even compartmental treatment of an issue such as liability might be fueled by a holistic understanding of the legal implications of this technology.

Currently, we can discuss more specific questions such as whether we need new liability rules or whether the existing ones can properly address AI risks.

---

[62] Easterbrook (1996).

[63] He famously argued that studying technology in this fashion resembles studying questions related to horse, such as the question of their sale, breed, care etc. He stated that. "[a]ny effort to collect these strands into a course on 'The Law of the Horse' is doomed to be shallow and to miss unifying principles". Ibid.

[64] Cockfield (2004), p. 386.

[65] Lessig (1999).

[66] Calo (2015), p. 115; Cockfield and Pridmore (2007), p. 495.

[67] The Report, 5–9.

Preliminarily, it depends on the applicable law in a specific jurisdiction as well as the specific field of application of AI. The latter presupposes that there is a different exposure and tolerance to risk which are contingent on the field of application. Adaptations of liability rules have historically occurred as a response to new technological phenomena.[68] To adapt liability rules is not to leave the entire logic of liability law. The system remains coherent and interventions are conducted only in those parts where the entirety of the system no longer fulfills the aim of this field of law. Liability rules would therefore act as *lex specialis* concerning general rules of liability.

If there is a need to adapt specific rules of liability to particular applications of AI, the next question is who should do it. One option is to regulate it by statute and the other one is to leave it to the courts. Adaptation of general liability rules to new technologies is a delicate process. As Graham describes, it consists of several phases:

> First, the initial batch of cases presented to courts may be atypical of later lawsuits that implicate the innovation, yet relate rules with surprising persistence. Second, these cases may be resolved by reference to analogies that rely on similarities in form, and which do not wear well over time. Third, it may be difficult to isolate the unreasonable risks generated by an innovation from the benefits it is perceived to offer. Fourth, claims by early adopters of the technology may be more difficult to recover upon than those that arise later, once the technology develops a mainstream audience. Fifth, and finally, concerning any particular innovation, it may be impossible to predict whether, and for how long, the recurring themes within tort law and its application that tend to yield a "grace" period for an invention will prevail over those tendencies with the opposite effect. In short, it takes time for innovation, such as autonomous vehicles, to become fully assimilated within everyday tort law, and one rarely can anticipate the precise timetable for this process, or its final results.[69]

Unlike other branches of government, provided there are no procedural constraints, the court has to address the merits of the question presented before it. Furthermore, the parties in the case are in a position to scrutinize otherwise unreachable state actors. Kysar suggests that discovery rights in the hands of a plaintiff are powerful too "to uncover risk information, including information that may not have been disclosed to regulators".[70] An incentivized individual committed to the utilization of discovery rights could create an impact broader than in its case. The public might receive information that provides scrutiny over the work of wrongdoers, which might be particularly interesting if a defendant is a person who provides products or services on a large. If access to the court is provided to a broad group of plaintiffs, the level of scrutiny increases proportionally. This could be even more emphasized if attorneys are incentivized to foster the process via means such as contingency fees and collective redress. Until AI is fully developed and understood, the role of the courts might be even more important. Legislators cannot predict the risks of AI with certainty since the technology is still in an infantile stage. Although the lack of information can be mitigated by the sectoral and risk-oriented approach to a certain

---

[68] Zimmermann (1996), pp. 1130–1132.

[69] Graham (2012), p. 1242.

[70] Kysar (2018), p. 54.

extent, only ex-post measures such as court decisions allow for a complete assessment. The courts are, thereby, able to provide some time for legislators to deliberate on the appropriate approach in the form of legislation.

The role of the courts is limited. They do not possess knowledge relevant to making policy choices about highly sophisticated matters nor do they have democratic legitimacy. Also, other problems limit its regulatory function in practice. For instance, if the number of wrongdoers is high and their contribution to the harm cannot be calculated precisely, court rulings hardly impact the control of the risk of private individuals. In the environmental law, "any individual harm will be seen as the result of greenhouse gas emissions by literally billions of alleged wrongdoers, likely including the plaintiff herself. Such problems of defendant numerosity are at the very heart of the public policy challenges posed by climate change. Tort seems to offer only meager resources to overcome them".[71] AI can be developed by many actors who may contribute to various stages of the process. There could also be many deployers. The full potential of this technology can be achieved if it is part of a broader ecosystem where it interacts with other software. Since many actors have an impact on the output of the technology, it might be very hard to determine which of them should be liable. The situation could be even more complex since there could be many actors involved in the process of development and deployment of each part of a digital ecosystem. The number of potentially liable parties is high and there might not be an easy way to attribute liability. The court could also be limited by procedural constraints such as the statute of limitation or remuneration cap.

This question, of course, relies also on the tradition of a legal order. B&H belongs to the group of states where major doctrinal changes are instituted through a statute. However, the role of the courts in establishing a liability regime should not be neglected. First, as we mentioned in the previous section, the courts in Yugoslavia have a historical record of adapting liability rules in accordance with the current trends. They developed a concept of strict liability to meet the needs of technological innovation at the time. Second, the language used in LO is very broad. For instance, there is no definition of fault. Also, LO does not define a dangerous thing or a dangerous activity, or their correlation.[72] The vagueness of LO has been a point of discussion in countries that succeeded Yugoslavia and thereby still apply it or apply the law based on LO. For instance, there was an attempt in Serbia to provide a definition of dangerous things in 1993.[73] However, the initiative failed. Thus, the

[71] Ibid, p. 53.

[72] Mihailo Konstantinović stipulated that dangerous things are broader notion which include dangerous activities: "Ustvari, radi se uvek o odgovornosti za opasne stvari. Pojam opasne stvari je širi od pojma delatnosti koja predstavlja povećanu opasnost po okolinu i on ga potpuno obuhvata. Jer, praktično govoreći, pri svakoj delatnosti koja stvara povećanu opasnost za okolinu, mi se služimo stvarima, koje, ako već nisu opasne po svojoj prirodi, postaju opasne upotrebom." Konstantinović (1958), p. 300. However, this view is not universally accepted in the scholarship. See Popović (1986), pp. 505–511.

[73] Stanišić (2013), p. 95.

current law provides grounds for the courts to significantly expand existing rules and potentially cover AI.

3.5 The Proper Level of Liability Regulation

In general, the EU has an *ad hoc* approach when it comes to the regulation of private law. It sees "private law from a functional rather than a formal, and from a fragmented rather than a systematic, point of view, and only regulated areas which it deemed to be necessary in order to create the internal market".[74] In the past, several initiatives from scholars and various advocates in the EU had been made for the supranational organization to enter the field of private law, but most of them can be seen as more or less unsuccessful.[75] As some authors notice, the EU exercises jurisdiction in the domains where "the void" exists[76]—where the Member States have not already exercised their jurisdiction concerning the phenomena created by the application of (new) technology. The EU essentially fills the gap by adopting the rules that either set the scene from scratch or harmonize/unify divergent legal orders of MS which in the specific field have "such a short history that is not yet entwined into national legal orders creating insurmountable difficulties if replaced".[77]

While the points raised by the aforementioned authors might be grounded in the regulation of safety standards or other AI-related domains, they are not in the case of liability. First, the existence of legal gap does not exist in the case of AI liability. The MS legal orders have usually long-standing and comprehensive liability systems deeply rooted in tradition, which in some cases last for centuries. The new phenomena, whether it is AI or any new development and without prejudice to how unprecedented, is to be treated by the existing liability rules, regardless of the level of satisfaction with the outcome.

However, AI might bring a new perspective and open room for discussion. There are practical reasons for having rules on AI on level places beyond national legal systems. As a data-intensive technology, its unique characteristics entail the availability of large sets of data for processing to achieve fast and steady advancements in the technology. AI relies on borderless data flows and the lack of hurdles in obtaining and processing data that dictate the pace of improvement.[78] The magnitude of similarity of AI's environment is likely to faster improve its decision-making process. If AI takes into consideration liability rules as one of the parameters in the

---

[74] van Dam (2013), p. 156.

[75] See van den Berg (2007).

[76] Papakonstantinou and De Hert, EU lawmaking in the Artificial Intelligent Age: Act-ification, GDPR mimesis, and regulatory brutality, available at: https://europeanlawblog.eu/2021/07/08/eu-lawmaking-in-the-artificial-intelligent-age-act-ification-gdpr-mimesis-and-regulatory-brutality/.

[77] Ibid.

[78] Lohsse et al. (2019a, b), p. 15.

process of learning, the same or even similar rules increase it. Otherwise, rules in force in one jurisdiction do not have to be the same in others. EU generally harmonizes safety standards regarding a technology while liability rules are left to the Member States. However, it is unclear how AI is going to perceive them. As mentioned above, economic considerations of legal rules incentivize one to adjust behavior to reduce the costs of its actions. Whether AI itself make such calculations or will they be reserved exclusively for humans? How might AI do it in case the question to the previous question is affirmative? Answers to both questions are unclear. It is certain, however, that a familiar environment allows for a smaller number of trial-error rounds before a certain behavior can be deemed successful.

Also, the US and China are the world's frontrunners in AI development.[79] There is certainly more than one reason for it. The availability of data required for learning AI is reduced in the EU compared to its biggest global competitors due to the protective data privacy law.[80] A study by the European Investment Bank demonstrates the lower number of small and medium enterprises involved in AI and blockchain in the EU (1232), compared to China (1418) and the United States (2995).[81] The level of investment is lower in the EU as well. It also finds that "the United States and China together account for over 80% of the €25 billion of annual equity investments in AI and blockchain technologies, while the EU only accounts for 7% of this global amount, investing around €1.75 billion".[82] Irrespective of whether the current state of play in the field of harmonization of tort law impacts the position of the EU in the global race, it is possible that it might do so in the future when accidents start occurring on a higher scale. Therefore, the EU ought to avoid fragmentation of the legal system if possible and instead pursue a policy that provides fast and steady growth which entails a harmonized set of rules. Tort law should not be understood alone. Rather, one must take into account ancillary systems, such as private insurance and social security systems,[83] and even the harmonization of administrative and criminal law.[84]

Even in those industries where it had not been a frontrunner, the EU has often managed to be a very impactful player on the global level. Regulation of certain areas such as data protection and antitrust in the EU has changed global industries that modify their policies to comply with it. This has been recognized as the Brussels effect,[85] a manifestation of the EU's global regulatory influence. Even if the EU fails to become the world leader in AI development, the creation of a sound regulatory

[79] See Craglia (2018).

[80] For instance: Want Europe to have the best AI? Reform the GDPR, available at: https://iapp.org/news/a/want-europe-to-have-the-best-ai-reform-the-gdpr/.

[81] Artificial intelligence, blockchain and the future of Europe, available at: https://www.eib.org/en/products/advising/innovfin-advisory/ai-blockchain-and-future-of-europe-report.

[82] Ibid.

[83] Cristina Amato (2019), p. 161.

[84] Ibid.

[85] Bradford (2019).

framework, with a liability regime as an inevitable part of it, could be the way it might shape the technological landscape in the future.

The relevance of the EU's rulemaking for B&H is high. Although it is not a Member State, the EU is its number one trading partner. As they are not equal in size, B&H has to, voluntarily or not, adjust its law and practice to align with new trends set in the EU. Standard-setting on a supranational level does not necessarily have to be made in the EU though. Other international organizations have the potential to do the same and states such as B&H would be better off in such cases. Or, an international agreement would fit the same purpose. However, it is debatable whether any other international framework, apart from the EU, could be realistically expected. The Council of Europe, for instance, the other regional organization in Europe, is not primarily dealing with liability issues or technical standard-setting in the continent. Its current project, CAHAI,[86] is currently focused on whether an international legal instrument would be an apt solution for the protection of human rights from the risks generated by AI. Due to the complexity of the task and the diversity of participants, the consensus might not be reached any time soon. Therefore, it is even less likely to expect this organization to exit its traditional mandate and try to be a European legislator. The prospect of such developments occurring within the purview of organizations that are not focused solely on Europe is even less likely as the interests of the states involved are even more divergent thereby rendering the consensus hard to reach. B&H could benefit indirectly from the adoption of the legal framework on the EU level. First, as the accession of potential MS to the EU depends on the alignment of one's legal order with the *acquis,* B&H might be obliged to adopt the EU's standards and rules. Second, due to the proximity to the EU and dependence on its economy, B&H could adopt the rules as a matter of economic pragmatism to ease the exchange with the EU. Finally, if the Brussels effect occurs again in the case of the EU's AI regulation, B&H and other states might be impacted indirectly by the changed behavior of the manufacturers, deployers, and legislators outside the EU.

Lastly, the aforementioned discussion is relevant to the regulation of tort law in B&H. Currently, the entities and Brcko District claim jurisdiction to regulate the law of obligations. Due to the specific AI characteristics and analogously with the reasons listed in the case of the EU, having a single set of rules on the state level or highly harmonized rules on the level of its parts is favorable for AI development. This has already been done in B&H in the case of horizontal legislation which has great implications on technology, such as the Law on the protection of personal data, an entire set of intellectual protection laws, and the Law on the protection of consumers. Just as in the case of the EU, the decision regarding the appropriate level of regulation is a combination of expert and political considerations.

[86] Ad hoc Committee on Artificial Intelligence, available at: https://www.coe.int/en/web/artificial-intelligence/cahai.

3.6 Proper Time and Scope of Liability Regulation

In dealing with emerging digital technologies, a lawmaker faces the question of whether to regulate a phenomenon that it does not completely understand due to its novelty and sophistication. The situation is even more complex when the process of the development of technology is not completed at the time of the adoption of new rules because the direction in which the development might go cannot often be anticipated. The development of AI fits this description.

"At the early stages of a technology, it is particularly important to provide incentives to take care as manufacturers still have a lot to learn."[87] The new rules should not act as a slap on the wrist for carefree actors who can afford to compensate for the harm created without changing the wrongdoer's behavior. If manufacturers need to be provided with an incentive to care, they also need not be punished too severely if harm is done, especially if it did not involve excessive involvement in overly risky activities or lack of care. Finding a balance between these two opposite positions relies on the timeliness of the regulation, including liability rules.

Adoption of new liability rules can be understood as an expression of understanding of new phenomena that cannot be encompassed by the existing liability rules.[88] It can be claimed that, due to the ambiguous nature of AI in present days, lawmakers are not ready to assess whether the current liability rules are fit for the proper regulation of AI. The time lawmakers have to regulate depends on the current and imminent impact of new technologies on society. If the risk is not present or cannot be perceived in the foreseeable future, there is no need for any novelties. However, accidents involving AI are emerging around the world.[89] Assuming they will continue to appear, one might wonder whether it would be appropriate to adopt liability rules now, although we do not know all potential problems. An alternative would be to wait for understanding to be sufficiently comprehensive and act then. The problem with the first avenue is that we may miss some important points and then we will have a non-comprehensive regulation or an insufficiently good regulation. The problem with the second avenue is that we risk that the current law is not enough to cover everything, so the goals of cake law will not be met in the specific situations that AI produces. Both approaches should avoid overregulation. The timeliness of new rules should be constrained to only those modifications without which the outcome of the cases solved based on judicial interpretation of current rules would be unsatisfying. More precisely, statutory rules should be introduced only where courts are not able to adopt the current rules timely or at all.

[87] Wagner (2019), p. 52.

[88] Borghetti (2019), p. 72.

[89] Tesla in deadly California crash was on Autopilot: Authorities, available at: https://www.aljazeera.com/economy/2021/5/14/tesla-in-deadly-california-crash-was-on-autopilot-authorities; Tesla Model 3: Paris' largest taxi firm suspends cars after fatal crash, available at: https://www.bbc.com/news/world-europe-59647069; When a computer program keeps you in jail, available at: https://www.nytimes.com/2017/06/13/opinion/how-computers-are-harming-criminal-justice.html.

The proper time of regulation is related to the question of the scope of the new rules. The level of development and deployment of AI varies depending on the sector. Some industries such as finance, healthcare, and robotics, already regularly deploy AI or have a huge potential to do so in the near future. This is reflected in the investment they attract.[90] Due to the disparity among sectors, the question is whether new rules liability rules ought to be rules of general application or the rules applicable to particular sectors where AI is present, and which are in higher stages of development compared to other sectors. The main advantage of general rules of liability is the avoidance of a multitude of different rules that might be potentially applicable. Addressees of such rules might be puzzled by different regimes. Also, it would be necessary to deal with situations where harm arises from AI activity "at the boundary between industries or from a combination of activities by Al from multiple industries".[91]

The creation of a set of rules for specific industries or specific risks may be an easier task. It is easier to tailor rules for specific risks or other specific considerations such as the sensitivity of the sector than to provide general rules. Furthermore, the prevalence of risks in particular sectors where AI operates is easier to be identified. In other words, it is easier to assess specific risks of sectors where AI is already in use and to adopt specific rules pertaining to them than to endeavor to discern rules of general application related to AI. Another advantage of sector-specific liability regulation is the possibility of limiting it in those areas where a lawmaker might seem desirable.[92] We previously discussed that tort law might be used for achieving various societal goals. One of them is to subsidize innovation through loosening liability rules for those involved in the development and deployment of technology. Subsidizing innovation through liability rules is a very complex operation that might have undesired effects. For example, they might incentivize the AI industry to engage in moral hazard—to provide a suboptimum level of care since the rules in force might allow so, by providing remuneration caps, regulatory safe harbors etc.

While using tort law for such purposes is inherently vague, the impact of undesired side effects might be curbed as the scope of the rules is limited to a particular sector. In other words, the spill-over effects of such risky regulatory measures will be limited if they apply only to specific sectors. Furthermore, perhaps the market will operate differently in various sectors and there might not be the need for adaptation of rules if the market itself addresses some of the risks,[93] such as lack of deterrence.

---

[90] Global Artificial Intelligence Industry Whitepaper, available at: https://www2.deloitte.com/cn/en/pages/technology-media-and-telecommunications/articles/global-ai-development-white-paper.html.

[91] Yoshikawa (2020), p. 1174.

[92] Ibid.

[93] Veljanovski (2010), pp. 21 et seq.

The decision between the adoption of general or sector-specific liability rules does not necessarily mean that one avenue excludes the other. Rather, the search for the general rules of liability for AI can be deemed as a multi-step process:

> As a first step…, therefore, there is a need to produce sectoral, risk-based liability rules for specific autonomous systems of particular practical importance (e.g. motor vehicles and medical robots). A second step would see these sectoral rules expanded into a general liability rule based on risk, which would, as far as possible, exclude gaps in protection and value contradictions.[94]

The appropriate time to adopt new liability rules and the question of their scope are related to the same questions concerning safety standards. Liability rules regulate ex post facto effects of certain activities involving this technology, while safety standards would provide ex ante rules. Some standards concerning particular industries where AI is present have been established, such as the case with the aforementioned statutes adopted in France, Germany, and the UK. However, general standards concerning AI are still not in force. AI Act proposal is the first piece of legislation to my knowledge that has general product security and technical standards as its subject matter. Without prejudice to the following sections which will discuss the relationship of safety standards with liability rules, it can be noted at this point that the coexistence of both types of rules is desirable for the appropriate regulation of technology. Also, just like in the case of liability rules, safety, and standards are easier to be identified on the level of particular sectors than in general as they can reflect more familiar and specific problems.

B&H's LO recognizes specific liability regimes for various types of activities and sources. Apart from the general clause on strict liability, it provides specific rules of strict liability for accidents caused by a motor vehicle in motion,[95] product liability,[96] liability of state for terrorist Acts, street demonstrations or public events,[97] liability of organizer of performances,[98] liability due to refusal to render necessary aid,[99] liability relating to a duty to conclude a contract,[100] and liability relating to conducting affairs of general interest.[101] Apart from that, courts have established specific regimes for certain activities through the interpretation of general clauses of LO. Examples are the liability of medical institutions for harm caused to patients[102] and towing vehicles.[103] Also, as we mentioned, even before the adoption of LO, the courts have developed concepts in order to tackle technological changes throughout

---

[94] Revolidis and Dahi (2018), p. 123.

[95] Article 178 LO.

[96] Article 179 LO.

[97] Article 180 LO.

[98] Article 181 LO.

[99] Article 182 LO.

[100] Article 183 LO.

[101] Article 184 LO.

[102] Supreme Court of Federation B&H, case number P 091661 11 Rev, 21.05.2012.

[103] Supreme Court of Federation B&H, case number 070-0-Rev-06-000939 od 23.08.2007.

Yugoslavia. Thus, sector-specific regimes introduced by legislators or the courts would not be a novelty for B&H law.

3.7 Design of Liability Rules

Although AI generates specific risks it does also have many characteristics that mirror or highly resemble traditional sources of harm. Recognition of similarities could be useful as current liability regimes have been designed to address them. Provided that traditional risks can be to a certain degree isolated from other, disruptive characteristics of AI, the current concepts can be applied. They should be applied since the liability regimes that are in force are well-oiled systems that have passed the test of time.

Understanding different risks and the ability to isolate them would foster proper regulatory response. The European Law Institute's "Response to the Public Consultation on the White Paper: On Artificial Intelligence"[104] advocates a targeted approach, whereby traditional physical risks would be tackled with current liability regimes, while social risks require the use of more sophisticated regulatory techniques or rather a combination of existing techniques that target specific risks and sectors where they appear.[105] This proposal isolates risks that cannot be dealt with by present liability rules. Thereafter, it further curtails the target by isolating sectors where the risk is material. Such an approach aims at shrinking the application of new and unreliable liability rules to situations where it is necessary only. A further elaboration of the risk-based approach to liability regulation has been made by Christiane Wendehorst. In order to determine a proper regulatory response, this author created a taxonomy of risks generated by AI. It consists of several classifications of risks that aid in determining a proper basis of liability and addressees of liability. She stresses the importance of differentiation between risks based on the type of harm,[106] whether they are generated freely or under the influence of technology,[107] whether they can harm an individual or entire system,[108] and whether a risk is a characteristic of the specific intended function.[109]

Focusing on sectors where the AI risks are high provides an additional tool to achieve precision in what new liability rules should target. For instance, certain risks

---

[104] European Law Institute, Response to the public consultation on the White Paper: On Artificial Intelligence—A European approach to excellence and trust, COM(2020) 65 final, available at: https://www.europeanlawinstitute.eu/fileadmin/user_upload/p_eli/News_page/2020/ELI_Response_AI_White_Paper.pdf.

[105] The advocated approach includes a combination of a set of fully horizontal principles, a list of blacklisted AI practices, and a creation of a regulatory framework for defined high-risk applications.

[106] Those are physical risk, pure economic risk, and social risk.

[107] Those are direct risk and intermediated risk.

[108] Those are individual risk and systemic risk.

[109] Those are typical risk, atypical risk, and general risk.

related to the application of AI can be limited in some sectors and simultaneously troubling in others. Also, it is possible that certain risks are only sector-specific and do not appear in the case of the application of AI in other spheres. The advantages of risk-based regulation of liability are manyfold. Current liability regimes for non-peculiar risks would remain the same, providing certainty to the current expectations of all actors involved. There would be no need to disrupt current business practices or the behavior of consumers. Novelties would be limited only to specific risks that cannot be dealt with by current practices. The predictability of the regulatory environment is a sign of a favorable environment for innovations, provided that the rules do not create red tape. Adaptations of product liability and extension of fault liability are certainly steps in that direction, along with the imposition of strict liability only to those sectors and practices where AI generates high risks.

Understanding AI risks allows for the application of familiar liability concepts, provided they can be treated in isolation. Furthermore, the determination of sectors where the risks are increased or specific allows for regulation that would be designed to meet exactly those risks, while the general liability regime would remain untouched. Therefore, at the outset of technology, the risk-based approach is an apt avenue as it would allow the preservation of successful components but at the same time adjust to a novel phenomenon.

Unfortunately, lawmakers in B&H have not announced a strategy to adopt a risk-based approach or any of the concepts of better regulation or smart regulation. As scholarship stipulates, although B&H has characteristics of economic federalism, none of the lawmakers significantly utilizes means of such an approach.[110] Seminal examples would be rules on the regulatory impact assessment in force at the state level and the level of entities.[111] However, these instruments are inconsistently applied in FB&H, although they bear the potential to have a comparative overview throughout B&H, often a complex task due to its complex and asymmetric structure.[112] There is a lack of evidence regarding this approach concerning the regulation of new technologies such as AI.

3.7.1 AI-Specific or Technology-Neutral Approach

Regulation of liability is concerned with the detrimental consequences of a certain activity or phenomenon. We previously expounded on why AI deserves to be singled out for various reasons from a general liability regime. If that stipulation is accepted, the question is how can we determine specific consequences of AI

[110] Imamović Čizmić (2018), p. 810.

[111] Ramić, Procjena učinaka propisa u Bosni i Hercegovini – stvarnost ili mit?, available at: https://eu-monitoring.ba/procjena-ucinaka-propisa-u-bosni-i-hercegovini-stvarnost-ili-mit/.

[112] Imamović Čizmić (2018), p. 811.

resulting in damage? As an emerging digital technology, it is highly sophisticated and opaque. In some situations, we might not be able to fathom whether it caused harm or not. This question is not novel, however. Highly sophisticated human inventions had previously caused harm and tort law had dealt with it through adaptation or adoption of various doctrines, such as strict liability, the lowered burden of proof etc. A more complex question concerns the interaction of AI with other emerging technologies and their joint impact.

Emerging digital technologies are increasingly interconnected. Harm might occur when they act in concert. If we establish that AI deserves specific liability rules, one might wonder whether the same approach should be applied to all emerging digital technologies. This question is closely related to the one mentioned in Chap. 2 when we discussed briefly how to define AI for civil liability. The task of defining AI in a legal document is hard due to the lack of overall consensus on the meaning of this term as well as its changing (evolving) nature. From the perspective of civil liability, defining the harmful consequences of this technology is hard as well as there might not be differences and other sources of harm. Similarly, even if we manage to overcome this impediment, it would be very hard to differentiate between AI and other emerging digital technologies it acts in concert with. If, for example, the harm is caused by joint action of various components of a digital ecosystem, of which AI is only a part, it might be very hard to attribute liability to only one of them. A struggle might be even harder if different liability regimes would apply to different components of a digital ecosystem.

This dilemma is broader than a simple binary choice between technology-neutral and technology-specific approaches to liability. The former approach would treat harm by liability rules irrespective of its source. It would be blind to specific characteristics of AI or its role in society. On the other hand, a technology-specific approach would entail specific liability rules that would be applied strictly to AI. But, although a preferable avenue at first glance, there are problems caused by this approach too, as we have seen. A third approach would be to treat AI as well as all other connected emerging technologies under the same liability rules, as well as all activities surrounding a single AI. In the words of the German Data Ethics Commission: "the sociotechnical system as a whole must be considered, or in other words all the components of an algorithmic application, including all the people involved, from the development phase – for example, the training data used – right through to its implementation in an application environment and any evaluation and adjustment measures".[113] Notably, Dataethikommision uses the term algorithm instead of AI, but it does so arguably as the focus of its work is on the algorithmic impact on data in general, and not only on the impact of AI.

In the Report, the Expert group uses the umbrella term "emerging digital technologies" to assess challenges to current rules of liability. This can be understood as a materialization of the third approach. However, the Report also recognizes: "It is,

[113] Opinion of the Dataethikommision, 20, available at: https://www.bmj.de/DE/Themen/FokusThemen/Datenethikkommission/Datenethikkommission_EN_node.html.

therefore, necessary to consider adaptations and amendments to existing liability regimes, bearing in mind that, given the diversity of emerging digital technologies and the correspondingly diverse range of risks these may pose, it is impossible to come up with a single solution suitable for the entire spectrum of risks."[114] Therefore, while there might be concerns about liability law caused by the joint impact of AI and other related technologies, a single set of rules that would govern them all might not be possible to achieve. In such a setting, a definition of emerging digital technologies is less relevant at this point as it can be made specifically with respect to specific technologies that fall within the purview of this term. Specific definitions can be provided for all technologies recognized as emerging and digital and which merit being defined in the first place.

Diversity of sets of rules allows for the avoidance of a trap one might fall into with the term it—liability rules for emerging digital technologies should not be technology-neutral, but they allow for flexibility to lawmakers as new rules can be attributed to specific technologies incrementally. At the same time, the addressees of the new rules might not be perplexed by the uncertainty of terminology used as specific rules are to be used for specific technologies, provided there is coherence between them. A technology-specific approach to the regulation of liability for AI is desirable. It should take into account the specific risks of this technology as well as its joint impact with other emerging digital technologies.

3.7.2 *Regulatory Technique*

Since the introduction of the Digital Single Market Strategy,[115] the EU has started to adopt an approach to technology that does not rely on a specific set of rules and corresponding obligations as much as on the identification of specific situations with increased risks emerging. When they are identified, specific measures aiming at increasing accountability of public and private sectors are adopted.[116] The new rules thereby are sensitive to specific risks envisioned by lawmakers. "Risk-based regulation is commonly taken to mean that regulators operate decision-making frameworks and procedures to prioritize regulatory activities and the deployment of resources according to an assessment of the risks that regulated firms pose to the regulator's objectives."[117] The application of risk-based regulation entails

[114] Report, 5.

[115] Communication from the Commission to the European Parliament, the Council, the European Economic and Social Committee and the Committee of the Regions: A Digital Single Market Strategy for Europe (COM/2015/192 final).

[116] Giovanni De Gregorio and Pietro Dunn, Profiling under Risk-based Regulation: Bringing together the GDPR and the DSA, 3, available at: https://assets.ctfassets.net/iapmw8ie3ije/5EuxLPaUIsgGt7R6PgeuFK/c9269e55e10bb2a7a0b392624c08f4d0/De_Gregorio_Dunn_My_Data_is_Mine__1_.pdf.

[117] Baldwin and Black (2016), p. 567.

assessment of the risk, a process which involves various methodologies and processes.[118] The underlying principle of this approach is: "the greater the potential for harm, the more stringent the requirements and the more far-reaching the intervention by means of regulatory instruments".[119] However, even within the EU, the risk-based approach does not materialize in the same way. Rather, it depends on the field of application and desired goals set by the lawmaker. For, instance, the GDPR and Digital Services Act.[120] This regulatory technique is an expression technocratic approach to governance that aims at avoiding "over-regulation, legalistic and prescriptive rules, and the high costs of regulation".[121] Although the EU has been a champion of this approach recently, the risk-based approach has not been a hallmark of its regulation. Rather, national lawmakers have also employed it in the regulation of technology.[122]

Regulation of risk, however, has to impose a specific set of duties on a person to be effective. At a certain point, an understanding of risk has to be materialized into traditional legal proceedings.

When regulators seek to take formal enforcement action such as imposing fines or instituting prosecutions, they will then have to reconfigure the risk according to a legal framework. As Hawkins's research illustrates, what field officers may see as the relevant set of risks, and the correct data to support their claim, may not be the same as is recognized in law: events have to be reconstructed from the language of risk into one of duties and liabilities.[123]

Risk-based regulation of AI does not mean that all legal instruments regulating AI are supposed to recognize and treat the same risks. By analogy, legal instruments adopted by the EU in the area of data privacy do not recognize and regulate the same risks in a uniform fashion. De Gregorio and Dunn noted that different legal instruments might tackle different risks stemming even from the same technologies.[124] Similarly, a risk-based approach to AI does not mean that the same risks of AI will be regulated by different legal instruments. The risks might be different. Also, they might be the same but approached by different perspectives. However, legal instruments must not contradict each other and thereby impose either too heavy a regulatory burden or vague and confusing duties. The following sections will

---

[118] Hutter (2006); Alemanno (2013).

[119] Opinion of the Dataethikommision, 20, available at: https://www.bmj.de/DE/Themen/FokusThemen/Datenethikkommission/Datenethikkommission_EN_node.html.

[120] Proposal for a Regulation of the European Parliament and of the Council on a Single Market for Digital Services (Digital Services Act) and amending Directive 2000/31/EC (COM/2020/825 final).

[121] Macenaite (2017), p. 509.

[122] Black (2005), p. 510.

[123] Baldwin and Black (2016), p. 588.

[124] Giovanni De Gregorio and Pietro Dunn, Profiling under Risk-based Regulation: Bringing together the GDPR and the DSA, 11, available at: https://assets.ctfassets.net/iapmw8ie3ije/5EuxLPaUIsgGt7R6PgeuFK/c9269e55e10bb2a7a0b392624c08f4d0/De_Gregorio_Dunn_My_Data_is_Mine__1_.pdf.

address more extensively the role of ex ante regulation of AI and its relation to the question of tortious liability.

The risk-based regulation of liability reflects this approach as well. In the Parliament Resolution from 2020, there is a different treatment of AI depending on two criteria. First, the sector in which the system is employed (healthcare, transport, energy, and parts of the public sector) and the risk of significant and unavoidable harm to the affected persons (uses with a significant impact on the affected persons). If a particular AI system meets the requirements, strict liability will be applicable. Such a system would be considered high-risk and merit different treatment: "(…) an AI-system that entails an inherent high risk and acts autonomously potentially endangers the general public to a much higher degree; (…) based on the legal challenges that AI-systems pose to the existing civil liability regimes, it seems reasonable to set up a common strict liability regime for those high-risk autonomous AI-systems"[125] Conversely, fault-based liability remains the default basis of liability. The Resolution has been the subject of numerous criticisms.[126] However, it was only an invitation to the Commission to propose a text of a legally binding instrument and does represent a final position of the EU Parliament. Specific categorization of risk and its treatment with different rules of liability could be modified. If nothing else, the Resolution was a signal of the acceptable approach to the final decision-maker in the legislative process in the EU and depicts what might be expected to become binding law. However, as previously mentioned, the rather mild adaptations of the EU law had been adopted as a new approach instead. They envisage updates to the PLD and a new instrument, the AI Liability Directive.

That being said, it is important to discuss how this is relevant for B&H. First, the aforementioned arguments apply. B&H heavily relies on the commercial and political relationship with the EU. It aims at becoming a Member State and therefore incrementally aligns its legal order with the EU. In the domain of technology, B&H still does not have a digital strategy on the state level, due to mainly political reasons. It does not have a developed policy it pursues and its laws are a patchwork of legal instruments adopted on the state and lower levels. However, when it does act in the field of technology, it usually looks upon the EU. For example, data privacy legislation had been adopted in line with the Data Protection Directive 95/46/EC.[127] Now, after the adoption of the GDPR, the B&H Data Protection Agency has prepared a new text of the law that is in line with it. Furthermore, as the tort law is regulated by the Member States in the EU, B&H might simply replicate the actions

[125] Recital 3 of the Proposal.

[126] Henrique Sousa Antunes, Civil liability applicable to artificial intelligence: a preliminary critique of the European Parliament Resolution of 2020, available at: https://papers.ssrn.com/sol3/papers.cfm?abstract_id=3743242; European Law Institute, Response to the public consultation on the White Paper: On Artificial Intelligence—A European approach to excellence and trust, COM(2020) 65 final.

[127] Directive 95/46/EC of the European Parliament and of the Council of 24 October 1995 on the protection of individuals with regard to the processing of personal data and on the free movement of such data COM(1990)314.

of the EU's Member States. As it might adopt the same ex ante requirements, it might adopt the analogous adaptations of its civil law. Moreover, as EU AI's legislation potentially has extraterritorial reach, B&H just like any other non-EU state might not have a choice except to opt to comply with it in order to continue interacting with the biggest economic block in the world.

3.8 Classification of Risks

If the regulatory technique has to demonstrate sensibility towards risks and allocate appropriate burden accordingly, the following question is how to determine risks. This is not the only pending question though. After the criteria for liability risk assessment have been established, the law has to determine what it means to treat risks differently. As we could briefly see in the previous section, the main sanction envisaged by the EU Parliament is the attribution of strict liability to high-risk AI and fault-based liability where the risk is not high. However, as national law governs tort law in the EU, national lawmakers can adopt many other devices in order to balance the positions of involved persons. Classification of risks might act as a starting point in applying specific liability rules as well as understanding the implications of their application. For instance, in case of attribution of liability, the reasons for harm might be attributed either to: manufacturers (for example, product defect), users (for example, misuse or failure to update), AI itself (black-box), or a victim (for example jaywalking in traffic). Such classification is useful in understanding the implications of applying the current rules of allocation and it might provide an insight into what could be done if a problem is detected.

Let's turn back to the question of establishing criteria that should be employed to determine whether AI is high-risk. Article 3 of the Resolution stipulates that high risk "means a significant potential in an autonomously operating AI-system to cause harm or damage to one or more persons in a manner that is random and goes beyond what can reasonably be expected; the significance of the potential depends on the interplay between the severity of possible harm or damage, the degree of autonomy of decision-making, the likelihood that the risk materializes and the manner and the context in which the AI-system is being used".[128] Clearly, whether an AI poses a high risk depends on many factors. Wagner considers that only two of these factors impact risk relevant for liability—the probability of the occurrence of damage and the severity of the threatened damage.[129] In this author's opinion, other factors taken into account by the EU Parliament's definition might be relevant for other fields of law, but they are not for civil liability.

The additional way to achieve precision in what new liability rules should target is to focus on the sectors where the AI risks are inherently high. For instance, certain

[128] Article 3 of the Resolution 2020.

[129] Wagner (2021), p. 10.

risks related to the application of AI can be limited in some sectors and simultaneously troubling in others. Also, it is possible that certain risks are only sector-specific and do not appear in the case of the application of AI in other spheres. This is not universally accepted as some authors consider that limiting liability rules to sectors should be not pursued and that the nature of AI application and its inherent risks are preferable criteria.[130] German Datenethikkommission points out that various other criteria should be taken into account for the assessment of risk related to the application of AI. It argues that classification of risks should take into account the value of the legal interests and interests concerned, the magnitude of potential harm, the particular sensitivity of the data used, the amount of possible damage for individuals or groups (including non-material damage or loss of benefit that is difficult to quantify in monetary terms), the number of people affected, the sum of the potential damage and to take into account the damage to society as a whole, which can go far beyond the mere summation of individual damage.

The effects of the use of AI also depend on the area of application, should be considered in terms of their ecological, social, psychological, cultural, economic, and legal dimensions.[131] ELI claims that classifying certain AI applications should be based on the sector but rather "on the basis of the nature of the application and its inherent risks".[132]

Apart from the Resolution, to my knowledge, the scholarship has so far provided classifications of AI risks based on various criteria. Wenderhost recognizes two types of risks that entitle a person to compensation. The first is functionality risks, and the second is safety risks. Functionality risks "comprise risks of the software or other product not performing properly, ie the user not getting 'good value for money'".[133] An example would be a handwatch with non-functioning arrows. Safety risks encompass "all risks of harm that may be caused to people or to assets and values different from the relevant product itself."[134] An example would be a washing machine that tears clothes. While the first category of risks is regulated by contract law, the second one is subject to tort law and therefore a focus of this work. This author further classifies safety risks into several criteria: (1) the type of harm caused; (2) whether the risks are caused by the free decision of a third party which was in some way instigated or facilitated by the technology or not; (3) whether the harm affects only individuals or has a broader effect on society or economy as a whole; (4) typicality of risk that a person can expect. This author creates a matrix whereby an application of AI is seen through the lenses of all criteria. Depending on the result, the appropriate basis of liability and appropriate defenses are afforded in each

[130] European Law Institute, Response to the public consultation on the White Paper: On Artificial Intelligence—A European approach to excellence and trust, COM(2020) 65 final, 10.

[131] German Data Ethics Commission, Report on Data and Algorithmic Systems, 2019, 173.

[132] European Law Institute, Response to the public consultation on the White Paper: On Artificial Intelligence—A European approach to excellence and trust, COM (2020) 65 final, 10.

[133] Wendehorst (2020), p. 161.

[134] Ibid.

situation. Such classification of AI risks is relevant, as we can see, to a limited set of questions concerning civil liability. It does not, for instance, (directly) touch upon the questions such as the allocation of liability or burden of proof. The output of this author's work is a matrix of risks classified by the aforementioned criteria. It can be used for determining the basis of liability and available defenses.[135]

As the above discussion demonstrates, many criteria can be used to establish whether AI can be considered high-risk and therefore attributed with strict liability. However, this is not their only potential use. Depending on specific characteristics of risks, lawmakers can decide whether to adopt a different regulatory technique that would more suitable. For instance, ELI suggests that while mild adaptations of the current liability framework would be sufficient to tackle physical risks, social risks would require a more subtle approach, including a combination of regulation, co-regulation, self-regulation, and blacklisting in lieu of mandatory requirements.[136]

As the afore discussion demonstrates, the classification of risks can be done on various criteria. Currently, B&H's law does allow the courts to impose strict liability by selecting any of those they consider generating dangerousness. However, other important considerations, such as the allocation of liability and the position of all parties involved cannot be solved by the courts. Changes would require statutory intervention. Moreover, the judges should not be the only ones involved in the discussion about AI risks. There is no consensus reached internationally and even less in B&H where the discussion is very scarce in the first place. A broader debate is therefore necessary in order to assess the problems comprehensively.

3.8.1 The Problem of Intermediated Risks

A special set of problems arises when a human makes a decision that causes harm, but the decision has been influenced by AI. AI does not act as a tortfeasor or a source of harm, strictly speaking, but its contribution nonetheless cannot be neglected. Imagine if an AI-driven medical device suggests that a doctor should apply specific treatment to a specific patient. The doctor is the one who ultimately decides to do it. If the treatment turns out to be detrimental to the patient's health due to a wrongly assessed diagnosis, should the doctor be liable? Or, should manufacturers of AI be liable? As Wendehorst puts it, "intermediated risks are risks that materialize only in combination with the free decision of a third party, which was, however, instigated or facilitated in some way".[137]

Admittedly, this problem is older than AI. In the famous United States case of poisonous mushrooms, plaintiffs were mushroom enthusiasts who became severely

---

[135] Wendehorst (2020), p. 170.

[136] European Legal Institute, Response to the public consultation on the White Paper: On Artificial Intelligence—A European approach to excellence and trust, COM(2020) 65 final, 8.

[137] Wendehorst (2020), p. 35.

ill from picking and eating mushrooms after relying on information in The Encyclopedia of Mushrooms.[138] The question was whether a publisher of the said book had a duty to the accuracy of the contents of the books it publishes. The United States Court of Appeals, Ninth Circuit stated that the answer was negative and that "there is nothing inherent in the role of publisher or the surrounding legal doctrines to suggest that such a duty should be imposed on publishers". This court differentiated between a physical product and a set of ideas. It suggested that while a physical product may be defective, a producer will not be held liable in case the disseminated ideas are inaccurate.

Relevance for AI accidents exists when AI acts as a generator of an idea of human behavior. If a human agrees to AI's suggestions, the question is whether responsibility for such actions should be attributed to humans exclusively. If the analogy with the poisonous mushroom case is applied, it can be argued that potentially false information AI provides does not constitute sufficient grounds for the persons behind it to be held liable. After all, humans are the ones who ultimately make a decision and cause harm. Likewise, they can decide not to follow the suggestions and act otherwise. In an interesting recent case of VI v KRONE-Verlag Gesellschaft mbH and Co KG,[139] the European Court of Justice had to decide whether a piece of false information on herbal medicinal advice for treating rheumatic pain provided in an Austrian medical journal could be the basis for a product liability claim. The court held that some advice in a newspaper cannot be considered defective under PLD.

However, it seems that this was not the principal reason for this court's refusal to make a different decision. Paragraph 32 it raises the following question: "whether health advice which, by its nature, constitutes a service, can […] result […] in the newspaper itself being defective in nature". In the analysis, it concludes that it does constitute service and paragraph 39 concludes that "inaccurate health advice which is published in a printed newspaper and concerns the use of another physical item falls outside the scope of Directive 85/374 and is not such as to render that newspaper defective and the 'producer' strictly liable pursuant to that directive, whether they are the publisher or the printer of that newspaper or even the author of the article". One of the commentators noted that the problem with this decision is a lack of conclusiveness.[140] The Court of Justice fails to determine whether all information can be considered a service. If only repeatedly stipulates in the decision that advice constitutes a service. Therefore, we cannot be sure what are the boundaries of this reasoning. For instance, what is the rule that governs information which is not per se advice? We can make a conclusion based on analogy, but the Court of Justice's interpretation leaves an open door for different conclusions. In their

[138] Wilhelm Winter, Cynthia Zheng, Plaintiffs-Appellants, v. G.P. PUTNAM'S SONS, Defendant-Appellee, available at: https://h2o.law.harvard.edu/cases/5449.

[139] (Case C-65/20) ECLI:EU:C:2021:471.

[140] Elias van Gool, Case C-65/20 Krone: Offering (some) clarity relating to product liability, information and software, available at: https://europeanlawblog.eu/2022/01/19/case-c-65-20-krone-offering-some-clarity-relating-to-product-liability-information-and-software/.

opinion, Advocate General Hogan followed the line of reasoning outlined in the poisonous mushroom case. It separates the physical properties of products from the information contained therein and suggests that PLD should apply only to the former. This criterion, however, had not been used by the Court of Justice as it deflected to address this question conclusively by invoking the limitation of PLD to products.

Differentiation between the physical features of the product and the information it provides to users is not the only potential criterion to be applied. Wendehorst suggests that one can differentiate between functionality and mere content:

> Where a medical recommender system suggests a particular diagnosis and treatment this suggestion is generated by the system and its specific functionality. This can be compared to the functionality of a traditional medical device, such as a thermometer—if a thermometer falsely indicates that the patient's body temperature is normal, while really the body temperature is 41 degrees Celsius, there would be not the glimpse of a doubt that this falls potentially under the PLD, and the same should hold true for strict liability. Where, however, a medical journal publishes scientific articles online, and one of the articles includes wrong information, the functional equivalent would be a printed book and this would be merely a question of content displayed.[141]

When it comes to AI, it should be noted the problem of intermediated risks should take into consideration other factors too. As, with other digital products, does not merely convey information. Rather, "it constitutes an operational entity that can be used directly like a traditional consumer good for the specific purpose for which it has been designed".[142] Arguably, this problem would not exist in the case of LO. There is no definition of product or defect. The court has room for interpreting wrongful information in the case of AI as a defect. When it comes to functionality, as Wendehorst mentioned, it might be hard to assess whether a piece of defective information constitutes a functional deficiency or merely a content deficiency. In theory, the former would be relevant for establishing duties to compensate for harm as they would meet PLD requirements while the latter would not be treated as such.

Perhaps functionality can be further elaborated based on the level of specificity of instruction provided by AI. If AI provides advice for a specific situation and invites a person to take a specific action accordingly, this is different from advice in a newspaper. For instance, a device suggests that a doctor should provide a specific treatment in the case of a specific patient. This is way more specific than some advice in a newspaper. Provided that humans provided the required data, AI assessed the specific situation of a very concrete patient and offered a bit of tailored advice. In this example, it can be seen why an AI recommender can be understood as an operational entity compared to a newspaper.

Furthermore, digital products do not fit the difference between products and services, a line of reasoning championed by PLD and the Court of Justice.

---

[141] Wendehorst (2020), p. 32.

[142] Elias van Gool, Case C-65/20 Krone: Offering (some) clarity relating to product liability, information and software, available at: https://europeanlawblog.eu/2022/01/19/case-c-65-20-krone-offering-some-clarity-relating-to-product-liability-information-and-software/.

Information used in digital products has a different meaning and should be treated separately from traditional products. B&H product liability should be amended in this respect. As it has been mentioned in Chap. 4, there is a lack of harmonization in entity product liability regulation.

Proper treatment of intermediated risks in relation to AI and digital products, in general, is beyond the scope of this work. It requires further research and the work of the EU Commission that is going to revise the PLD will be very telling in this respect.

3.9 Safety Standards and Insurance and Compensation Funds

Regulation of liability for AI should be understood only as a piece of a greater regulatory puzzle. The entire regulation of risk is rather a mosaic of mechanisms that jointly seek to provide a balance between the risks and benefits of this technology. Some mechanisms of risk regulation are designed to operate ax ante, while others operate ex post. The liability regime is only a part of the legal framework. Its main goal is to provide compensation to the injured party that is affordable and timely. However, liability and tort adjudication have a broader policy impact and should not be treated merely as dispute resolution mechanisms that settle the interests of the involved individuals.

Understanding AI risks and their proper classification, a topic of our discussion in previous sections, allow for regulation that would be designed to meet exactly those risks. However, regulation of liability does not depend only on the proper understanding of AI risks. Rather it also has to take into account whether other regulatory tools are at the disposal. If they are used to prevent or curb a certain risk, then the liability rules can also be modified accordingly. A selection of specific ex ante measures by lawmakers is not an easy task. Regulation of liability and specific liability regimes depend on other rules in place. In the words of Rawls: "those institutions and actions are right which of the available alternatives produce the most good, or at least as much good as any of the other institutions and acts open as real possibilities".[143] Some authors consider that consider both options as mutual substitutes which ought to correct externalities.[144] However, such a view has in mind deterrence as the main goal of liability law, which is now a view shared in continental Europe, including B&H, as we established before. With some exceptions, ex ante measures do not offset harm suffered by an injured party. Rather, they either prevent harm from occurring or foster the enforcement of liability rules.

A complex relationship between ex ante regulatory measures and liability as an ex post mechanism is also evident when it comes to the order in which they should be

[143] Rawls (1973), pp. 24–25.

[144] Kovac (2020), p. 128.

applied. Especially when it comes to new technologies such as AI, it is important to have some standards set as a reference point for the assessment behavior of both tortfeasor and victim. In theory, ex ante rules go hand-in-hand with liability rules and should therefore coexist.[145] Ex ante rules remove problems of applying abstract standards in liability law, such as foreseeability or duty to care, providing a context for the appropriate application in specific situations. At the same time, liability limits the costs of regulation.[146] It provides optimization of risk via an ex post mechanism. Thus, overly burdensome red tape is avoided.

Some combinations of various ex-ante devices and their interplay with liability rules are very hard to assess from the perspective of an effect they might yield. What works in the case of certain domains might not work in the case of others. The problem with designing a regulatory framework is exacerbated due to the specific characteristics of AI and its relationship with other emerging digital technologies. A tool at the disposal of lawmakers is the so-called regulatory sandbox. It is a process conducted in cooperation with lawmakers and participating business entities where the effects of a certain regulatory framework are tested.[147] Before putting regulation in force, it would allow businesses and regulators to see how the law would appear in practice. For businesses, a regulatory sandbox also provides a test for their products and services in conditions akin to the real world, which cannot be always replicated in projections and simulations.[148] The United Kingdom Financial Conduct Authority defines it as "a 'safe space' in which businesses can test innovative products, services, business models and delivery mechanisms without immediately incurring all the normal regulatory consequences of engaging in the activity in question".[149] Regulatory sandboxes, however, are not universally acclaimed. Some authors argue that their application actually slows down innovation.[150] For instance, consumers might think that products or services tested in such an environment might be endorsed by regulators and thus be perceived as safe.

The concept has been endorsed so far by the EU institutions. The EU Council issued the Conclusion of 16 November 2020 on regulatory sandboxes and experimentation clauses as tools for an innovation-friendly, future-proof, and resilient regulatory framework that masters disruptive challenges in the digital age.[151] It recognized the importance of regulatory sandboxes and called for the exchange of

---

[145] Schmitz (2000).

[146] Rose-Ackerman (1991).

[147] Allen (2019).

[148] Katerina Yordanova, The Shifting Sands of Regulatory Sandboxes for AI. KU Leuven Research Paper, 2019.

[149] Financial Conduct Authority, Regulatory sandbox, available at: https://www.fca.org.uk/publication/research/regulatory-sandbox.pdf.

[150] Dan Quan, A few thoughts on regulatory sandboxes, Stanford University, Stanford PACS, 2019, available at: https://pacscenter.stanford.edu/a-few-thoughts-on-regulatory-sandboxes/.

[151] Council Conclusions of 16 November 2020 on regulatory sandboxes and experimentation clauses as tools for an innovation-friendly, future-proof and resilient regulatory framework that masters disruptive challenges in the digital age 12683/1/20 REV 1 (2020) 13026/20.

"information and good practices".[152] The AI Act followed the lead and, along with setting "a basic framework in terms of governance, supervision, and liability",[153] included regulatory sandboxes as a mechanism in support of innovation. Employing this regulatory tool is not really entirely the EU's idea, as the United Kingdom and Norway had previously developed their national AI sandboxes.[154]

Although it is important in fostering the adoption of appropriate regulation, regulatory sandboxes themselves do not create a substantive set of rules.[155] Auxiliary tools do so are myriad. A list, as well as their characteristics, vary among authors. Due to their recognition in literature and by lawmakers, some of them will be expounded below.

3.9.1 Safety Standards

Safety standards can be described as a set of rules which producers have to satisfy in order to have their products released on the market. But it is more than that. It also includes a system of surveillance of whether the standards have been met as well as a power to impose measures to secure compliance.[156]

Safety standards and rules of liability are complimentary.[157] "The former defines under which conditions a product may be deemed safe and released onto the market. The latter identifies who shall bear the consequences of damage caused by a product, balancing the need of ensuring users' protection and that of allowing products to be distributed for profit".[158] This is the reason why they need to be adopted concerning one another. Along with determining who should bear the consequences of harmful events, safety rules also aid in applying a proper basis of liability. Moreover, in some jurisdictions, other questions such as the burden of proof as well as the standard of proof and standard of proof an injured party have to be met.[159] In the case of AI, the Report suggests that a lack of conformity with the safety rules of AI should lead to a

---

[152] Ibid.

[153] AI Act Explanatory memorandum, 15, available at: https://eur-lex.europa.eu/legal-content/EN/TXT/?uri=CELEX%3A52021PC0206.

[154] Truby et al. (2021), pp. 1–29 at 18.

[155] In context of liability, this is especially clear in Article 5(4) of AI Act: "Participants in the AI regulatory sandbox shall remain liable under applicable Union and Member States liability legislation for any harm inflicted on third parties as a result from the experimentation taking place in the sandbox."

[156] Bertolini (2020), p. 48.

[157] European Commission (2020). Report from the Commission to the European Parliament, the Council and the European Economic and Social Committee. Report on the safety and liability implications of Artificial Intelligence, the Internet of Things and robotics, European Commission, 12.

[158] Bertolini (2020), p. 51.

[159] Amato (2019), pp. 79 et al.

reversal of the burden of proof.[160] Such suggestion is premised on the opaque nature of emerging new technologies and the increased risk they generate, "in particular the pace at which these technologies are evolving, and the necessity of imposing a duty on providers to monitor the market and react more quickly to new threats than any rulemaker could".[161]

General safety rules for AI currently do not exist. There is an attempt to regulate some sectors where AI's presence is significant. This is the case with autonomous vehicles, where, as we mentioned before, some states have already passed legislation. When it comes to establishing general AI rules, the EU is a global leader. At the outset of her term as the head of the EU Commission, Ursula von der Leyen introduced a plan to regulate AI.[162] It presented the AI Act, an attempt to provide the first horizontal regulation of AI. As Veale and Zuiderveen Borgesius point out, the AI Act is only one of the instruments the EU Commission has in mind when it comes to creating a legislative framework for AI.[163] This proposal was risk-based, and it assigns a specific framework depending on the classification of an AI. It differentiates between four levels of risks: (1) unacceptable risks (Title II); (2) high risks (Title III); (3) limited risks (Title IV); and (4) minimal risks (Title IX). After negotiations, it was adopted and, on 13 June 2024, the President of the Council of the EU and President of the European Parliament officially signed the AI Act.

Unacceptable risks are the practices deemed prohibited. The list includes manipulation, social scoring, and "real-time" and "remote" biometric identification except for purposes of law enforcement under certain conditions. Just like unacceptable risks, minimal risks also create certain obligations. There are no binding safety standards imposed for this category. AI Act only encourages the Member States and the EU to adopt voluntary codes of conduct.[164] When it comes to binding requirements, it provides specific lists based on risks. Two categories of risk are recognized: high-risk and limited-risk.

High-risk requirements mostly create duties for the provider, a "person or body that develops an AI system or that has an AI system developed with a view to placing it on the market or putting it into service under its own name or trademark". Standards to be met range from the pre-marketing phase as well as after the AI has

---

[160] Report, 49.

[161] Ibid.

[162] Ursula von der Leyen, A Union that Strives for More: My Agenda for Europe, Political Guidelines for the Next European Commission 2019–2024, 2019.

[163] Veale and Zuiderveen Bergesius, Demystifying the Draft EU Artificial Intelligence Act, available at: https://osf.io/preprints/socarxiv/38p5f, 2. The authors mention the following legislative proposals: he draft Digital Services Act (with provisions on recommenders and research data access); the draft Digital Markets Act (with provisions on AI-relevant hardware, operating systems and software distribution); the draft Machinery Regulation (revising the Machinery Directive in relation to AI, health and safety, and machinery); announced product liability revision relating to AI; the draft Data Governance Act (concerning data sharing frameworks).

[164] AI Act, Article 39.

obtained approval to enter the market.[165] The list of duties is extensive, and I will only briefly refer to them. A provider must create a quality management system that ought to be updated throughout the lifetime of an AI. Furthermore, datasets used to train AI have to be of a specific quality, and the AI has to meet requirements of accuracy, robustness, and cybersecurity. A provider also needs to provide standardized technical documentation and information for purposes of transparency and registry in the public database. Moreover, human oversight of AI has to be ensured.[166] Limited-risk requirements concern transparency requirements for AI users and providers. Providers need to disclose when natural persons interact with an AI bot by providing appropriate design and development to an AI. Users of AI provide information in case of employment of an emotion recognition system, a biometric categorization, or deepfake technology.[167]

Once established, safety standards will provide for a better understanding of the terminology in liability law. However, although they act in synergy, safety standards, and liability rules operate on different levels.[168] Product liability operates with the notion of defect, which itself relies on the notion of safety.[169] In order to defend itself successfully, a producer has to demonstrate that the product was not defective. It is possible that a product has satisfied all safety standards but has nonetheless caused damage due to a defect. Likewise, in case a producer fails to satisfy all standard requirements, it does not automatically mean that its product is defective. Defendants may resort to alternative methods to show that the product meets the fundamental safety requirements.

3.9.2 Insurance and Compensation Funds

A combination of liability rules with schemes such as insurance and more rarely compensation funds is not a new idea. As Borgers notes, this is exactly the way societies tackle damages caused by the application of sophisticated technological inventions.[170] The main purpose behind having a financial scheme along with liability rules is to increase the position of an injured party. Essentially, it is projected that emerging digital technologies have the potential to detrimentally affect the position of an injured party, especially in the case of consumers. By introducing an insurance or a compensation fund, along with a favorable legal framework, such a

165 Kop (2021).

166 Ibid.

167 Article 52 describes it as an AI that "generates or manipulates image, audio or video content that appreciably resembles existing persons, objects, places or other entities or events and would falsely appear to a person to be authentic or truthful".

168 Bertolini (2020), p. 51.

169 See Chap. 4.

170 Borges (2019), p. 148.

position might be enhanced. Kovac argues that the minimum asset requirement of a person engaging in activity concerning AI would be necessary for achieving the same purpose.[171] However, it is unclear whether such a requirement would prevent small and medium enterprises from entering the market or make it more difficult. The position of an injured party is the subject of a separate part of this work— Chap. 6. Thus, at this point, the interplay between the insurance and compensation funds with liability rules will be in focus.

The idea has been endorsed by the EU Parliament's Resolution of 2017 which stipulates "a compulsory insurance scheme [...] whereby [...], producers or owners of robots would be required to take out insurance cover for the damage potentially caused by their robot". Unlike some ideas of this document, mandatory insurance survived the criticism and found its place in the Resolution of 2020 too. This document envisages mandatory insurance for AI classified as high-risk. In fact, this solution replicates a well-oiled system that has existed for decades around Europe. In the case of motor vehicles, the law in B&H envisages a combination of strict liability of a driver with mandatory insurance. The same scheme exists in the EU, as it has been harmonized by the Motor Insurance Directive.[172] High-risk AI is treated by strict liability, which is also the case with motor vehicle accidents where harm is caused to third parties. Obviously, the resemblance between motor vehicles and high-risk AI is not absolute, but at least the effects of a combination of liability rules and mandatory insurance have been tested in practice. Even in the case of fault-based liability, B&H law has experience with mandatory insurance. This is the case of an accident caused by a motor vehicle in motion where a tortfeasor and a victim operated motor vehicles.[173] An example is the profession of lawyers[174] and the notary public.[175]

Provided that mandatory insurance for AI is established, two potential parties might be obliged to possess it—manufacturers and operators. The question of a choice between them is related to the allocation of liability. Currently, under the law of B&H, a manufacturer is generally not held responsible for accidents caused by a third party. Thus, it would not make sense to impose an obligation to have insurance if liability rules do not change accordingly. Another argument is posited by Borges in favor of mandatory manufacturer insurance. Competition between manufacturers and importers of AI as well as between domestic and foreign manufacturers requires that manufacturers have mandatory insurance.[176] Mandatory insurance for operators

[171] Kovac (2020), p. 121.

[172] Directive 2009/103/EC of the European Parliament and of the Council of 16 September 2009 relating to insurance against civil liability in respect of the use of motor vehicles, and the enforcement of the obligation to insure against such liability.

[173] Article 178 LO.

[174] Law on attorney profession (The Official Gazette FB&H 27/03 21/09), Law on attorney profession RS (The Official Gazette Republika Srpska 80/2015).

[175] Law on notary public FB&H (The Official Gazette FB&H 45/02), Law on notary public RS (Official Gazette Republika Srpska 86/03, 2/04, 74/05).

[176] Magnus (1998).

is more akin to present mandatory insurance schemes in B&H than mandatory insurance for manufacturers. A risk of solvency is presumably higher if a liable party is an operator than a manufacturer. Thus, an introduction of mandatory insurance for operators would not disturb the entire system significantly as in the case of manufacturers. However, insurance is a mechanism based on the market. There must be an interest of insurers to provide services. In the case of general AI insurance, its existence might be dubious due to potentially incalculable and unforeseeable risks.

Thus, unlike the solution envisaged in the EU Parliament Resolution of 2020, it seems more realistic to introduce mandatory insurance based on sectors where the risk of liability can generate an insurance market. Finally, such a solution would replicate sector-based regulation of insurance which is already in place.

The Resolution of 2017 also advocates for the introduction of compensation funds as a coexisting mechanism for mandatory insurance.[177] Compensation funds are not a novelty in the law of B&H. Along with the EU Parliament's suggestion, it coexists with mandatory insurance in B&H. This is the case with the motor vehicle sector, where mandatory insurance is envisaged in the entities' legislation on mandatory vehicle insurance. In Federation BiH and Republika Srpska, respective statutes introduce the "Protective Fund", entity-operated bodies which provide compensation to persons who suffered harm in traffic accidents. The funds are designed to operate as a safety net for losses that cannot be covered by a mandatory insurance scheme. The coverage of losses in BiH by mandatory insurance and compensation funds is only sector-specific and therefore there is a lack of experience with this regime in other fields. Also, there is a lack of experience with having compensation funds as an alternative to mandatory insurance. They operate as supplementation to mandatory insurance, and not as a substitute for it. This is contrary to what the Resolution of 2017 suggests when it invites the Commission to decide whether to create a "general fund for all smart autonomous robots or to create an individual fund for each and every robot category and whether a contribution should be paid as a one-off fee when placing the robot on the market or whether periodic contributions should be paid during the lifetime of the robot",[178] and to ensure "that a compensation fund would not only serve the purpose of guaranteeing compensation if the damage caused by a robot was not covered by insurance".[179]

The problem with having such a comprehensive compensatory scheme in B&H is not only a lack of experience. The introduction of a compensation fund would necessarily require naming the parties who would contribute to the fund. Those

[177] European Parliament, Resolution of 16 February 2017 with recommendations to the Commission on Civil Law Rules on Robotics, P8_TA-PROV(2017)0051, Recital 58.

[178] European Parliament, Resolution of 16 February 2017 with recommendations to the Commission on Civil Law Rules on Robotics, P8_TA-PROV(2017)0051, Recital 59 (d).

[179] European Parliament, Resolution of 16 February 2017 with recommendations to the Commission on Civil Law Rules on Robotics, P8_TA-PROV(2017)0051, Recital 59 (c).

could be taxpayers or manufacturers and users of AI. To place the burden on the general population is a broader policy whereby the costs of digital transformation should be borne by the population and not only the ones who are directly involved in an accident. Consequently, manufacturers and users would not be incentivized to optimize the risk of AI as they would not be the cost bearers of losses. The effect of deterrence liability rules would hence be lost. To determine that manufacturers and users of AI should be compensated the fund has also problems. The very notion of AI seems vague, so the mere determination of who manufacturers and users are is difficult. Also, the costs of administration of compensation funds might be high, depending on the scope of covered risks and organizational complexity. Moreover, B&H is a small market, compared to the neighboring EU and other global players. One can argue that it is too small and not developed enough to be able to insist on such innovative rules which do not necessarily favor innovation. As such, it might be avoided by innovators who might determine that the costs of facing such regulatory novelty would not match the benefits of being present in the B&H market.

Mandatory insurance and compensation funds might be a part of a broader liability framework but to a limited extent. As is the case with motor insurance and compensation funds in B&H, they can be employed to a clearly defined set of risks, but not to cover all AI risks.

References

Books

Alemanno A (2013) Regulating the European risk society. In: Alemanno A et al (eds) Better business regulation in a risk society. Springer

Benson P (1992) The basis of corrective justice and its relation to distributive justice. Iowa Law Rev 77:515, 530

Bertolini A (2020) Artificial intelligence and civil liability. Policy Department for Citizens' Rights and Constitutional Affairs

Black J (2005) The emergence of risk-based regulation and the new public risk management in the United Kingdom. Public Law

Borges G (2019) New liability concepts: the potential of insurance and compensation funds. In: Lohsee S, Schulze R, Staudenmayer D (eds) Liability for artificial intelligence and the internet of things: Münster Colloquia on EU law and the digital economy IV. Nomos, p 148

Borghetti J-S (2019) How can artificial intelligence be defective? In: Lohsee S, Schulze R, Staudenmayer D (eds) Liability for artificial intelligence and the internet of things: Münster Colloquia on EU law and the digital economy IV. Nomos

Bradford A (2019) The Brussels Effect: how the European Union rules the world. Oxford University Press

Bussani M, Palmer V (2003) The liability regimes of Europe – their façades and interiors. In: Bussani M, Palmer V (eds) Pure economic loss in Europe. Cambridge University Press

Calabresi G (1970) The costs of accidents: a legal and economic analysis. Yale University Press

Cigoj S (1983) Član 173. Pretpostavka uzročnosti. In: Komentar Zakona o obligacionim odnosima, Savremena administracija, Beograd

Cotterrell R (2008) The struggle for law: some dilemmas of cultural legality. Int J Law Context 4(4): 373–384. https://doi.org/10.1017/S1744552309004042
Craglia M (ed) (2018) Artificial intelligence: a European perspective. Publications Office of the European Union
Gordley J (1997) Tort law in Aristotelian tradition. In: Owen GD (ed) The philosophical foundations of tort law. Oxford University Press
Hart HLA (1968) Punishment and responsibility: essays in the philosophy of law
Honore T (1995) The morality of tort law. In: Owen GD (ed) Philosophical foundations of tort law. Oxford University Press
Hutter MB (2006) Risk, regulation, and management. In: Taylor-Gooby P, Zinn J (eds) Risk in social science. Oxford University Press
Kant I (1991) The metaphysics of morals (trans: Gregor M)
Karanikić Mirić M (2009) Krivica kao osnov deliktne odgovornosti u građanskom pravu. Beograd
Karanikić Mirić M (2019a) Objektivna odgovornost za štetu. Službeni glasnik
Karanikić Mirić M (2019b) Postjugoslovenski "život" pravila o vanugovornoj odgovornosti u Srbiji. In: Možina D (ed) Razvojne tendence v obligacijskem pravu: Ob 40-letnici Zakona o obligacijskih razmerjih, p 274
Konstantinović M (1958) Osnov odgovornosti za prouzrokovanu štetu. Arhiv za pravne I društvene nauke, Belgrade
Konstantinović M (1969a) Obligacije i ugovori: skica za zakonik o obligacijama i ugovorima. Pravni fakultet u Beogradu
Konstantinović M (1969b) Obligaciono pravo. Beleške sa predavanja
Kovac M (2020) Judgement-proof robots and artificial intelligence a comparative law and economics approach. Palgrave Macmillan
Koziol H (2012) Basic questions of tort law from a Germanic perspective
Kysar D (2018) The public life of private law: tort law as a risk regulation mechanism. Eur J Risk Regul 9(1)
Lohsse S, Schulze R, Staudenmayer D (2019a) Liability for artificial intelligence. In: Lohsee S, Schulze R, Staudenmayer D (eds) Liability for artificial intelligence and the internet of things: Münster Colloquia on EU law and the digital economy IV. Nomos
Lohsse S, Schulze R, Staudenmayer D (2019b) Liability for artificial intelligence and the internet of things. Nomos
Magnus U (1998) Elemente eines europäischen Deliktsrechts. ZeuP 606
Oliphant K (2015) England and the Commonwealth n. 5/57. In: Koziol H (ed) Comparative stimulations for developing tort law. Jan Sramek Verlag
Perović S (1995) Predgovor, Zakon o obligacionim odnosima, Službeni list, Beograd
Radišić J (2004) Obligaciono pravo, Opšti deo, sedmo izdanje. Nomos, Belgrade
Rawls J (1973) A theory of justice. Oxford University Press
Revolidis I, Dahi A (2018) The peculiar case of the mushroom picking robot. In: Corrales M, Fenwick M, Forgó N (eds) Robotics, AI and the future of law. Springer, p 69
Rose-Ackerman S (1991) Tort law as a regulatory system. AEA Pap Proc 81(2)
Shavell S (2007) Economic analysis of accident law. Harvard University Press, p 35
Van Dam C (2013) European tort law, 2nd edn. Oxford University Press
van den Berg AJP (2007) The politics of European codification: a history of the unification of law in France, Prussia, the Austrian Monarchy and the Netherlands. Europa Law Publishing
Veljanovski C (2010) Economic approaches to regulation. In: Baldwin, Cave, Lodge (eds) The Oxford handbook of regulation
Wagner G (2019) Robot liability. In: Lohsee S et al (eds) Liability for artificial intelligence and the internet of things: Münster Colloquia on EU law and the digital economy IV. Nomos
Wagner G (2021) Haftung für Künstliche Intelligenz – Eine Gesetzesinitiative des Europäischen Parlaments. ZEuP 545, 556, available at: https://beck-online.beck.de/Dokument?vpath=bibdata%2Fzeits%2Fzeup%2F2021%2Fcont%2Fzeup.2021.545.1.htm&anchor=Y-300-Z-ZEUP-B-2021-S-550#FNA32

Weber M (1948) Essays in sociology (trans: Gerth HH, Mills CW). Routledge & Kegan Paul, London
Weinrib E (1992) Corrective justice. Iowa Law Rev 77:403
Zimmermann R (1996) The law of obligations: Roman foundations of the Civilian tradition. Oxford University Press

Articles

Allen JH (2019) Tort law as a regulatory system. AEA Pap Proc 81(2):54–58
Amato C (2019) Product liability and product security: present and future. In: Lohsse S, Schulze R, Staudenmayer D (eds) Liability for artificial intelligence and the internet of things. Nomos, p 161
Baldwin R, Black J (2016) Driving priorities in risk-based regulation: what's the problem? J Law Soc 43:4
Bazala B (1956) Odgovornost za štetu prouzročenu pogonom cestovnih motornih vozila, Naša zakonitost. God. 10, 3, 4 and 5
Bukovac Puvača M (2017) Ekonomski gubitci kao šteta u hrvatskom odštetnom pravu... Zb. Prav. fak. Sveuč. Rij. (1991) 38(1):397–418
Calabresi G, Melamed AD (1972) Property rules, liability rules, and inalienability: one view of the Cathedral. Harv Law Rev 85:1089
Calo R (2015) Robotics and the lessons of cyberlaw. Cal Law Rev 103:513
Cockfield JA (2004) Towards a law and technology theory. Manit Law J 30:383
Cockfield JA, Pridmore J (2007) A synthetic theory of law and technology. Minn J Law Sci Technol
Coleman J (1992) The mixed conception of corrective justice. Iowa Law Rev 77
Easterbrook HF (1996) Cyberspace and the law of the horse. University of Chicago Legal Forum
Graham K (2012) Of frightened horses and autonomous vehicles: tort law and its assimilation of innovations. Santa Clara Law Rev 52
Imamović Čizmić K (2018) Aplikacija koncepta bolje regulacije u Bosni i Hercegovini – ograničenja i solucije. In: Conference Proceedings: 2nd International Scientific Conference on Economics and Management - EMAN
Kop M (2021) EU Artificial Intelligence Act: The European Approach to AI, Transatlantic Antitrust and IPR Developments 2021, available at: https://law.stanford.edu/publications/eu-artificial-intelligence-act-the-european-approach-to-ai/
Leenes R et al (2017) Regulatory challenges of robotics: some guidelines for addressing legal and ethical issues. Law Innov Technol 9:1–44. https://doi.org/10.1080/17579961.2017.1304921
Lemley AM, Casey B (2019) The University of Chicago Law Review, Remedies for Robots
Lessig L (1999) The law of the horse: what cyberlaw might teach. Harv Law Rev 113
Macenaite M (2017) The "Riskification" of European data protection law through a two-fold shift. Eur J Risk Regul 8
Mihajlović S (1975) Odgovornost za štetu pričinjenu izvorom povećane opasnosti, Glasnik Advokatske komore Vojvodine, br.4/75, Novi Sad
Popović D (1986) Odgovornost za opasnu delatnost u jugoslovenskom pravu. Anali Pravnog fakulteta u Beogradu, br.5/86
Rudolf von Jhering (2008) The Struggle for Law, trans Lalor, J. J. Union, NJ: Lawbook Exchange reprint
Schmitz P (2000) On the joint use of liability and safety regulation. Int Rev Law Econ 20(1)
Stanišić S (2013) Prilog raspravi o opasnim stvarima i opasnim djelatnostima. Godišnjak Fakulteta pravnih nauka 3:3
Truby J et al (2021) A sandbox approach to regulating high-risk artificial intelligence applications. Eur J Risk Regul

Wallis AK (2017) No-fault, no difference: no-fault compensation for medical injury and healthcare ethics and practice. Br J Gen Pract 67(654):38–39, available at: https://www.ncbi.nlm.nih.gov/pmc/articles/PMC5198606/
Weinrib E (1980) The case for a duty to rescue. Yale Law J 90:2
Wendehorst C (2020) Strict liability for AI and other emerging technologies. J Eur Tort Law 11(2)
Yoshikawa J (2020) Sharing the costs of artificial intelligence: universal no-fault social insurance for personal injuries. Vanderbilt J Entertain Technol Law 21:1155

Chapter 4
Bases of Liability

4.1 Introduction

Just like the French Code Civil, LO contains general and often very broadly formulated rules that are prone to different interpretations. The rules of liability in LO have not been amended substantially ever since its adoption in 1978. B&H is an exception in this respect. Other Yugoslavian successor states have modified their LO's in order to modernize and/or adjust to the European trends and obligations.[1] However, the broad wording and changes in context and operation indicate that development has occurred.

There is leeway for the application of both fault liability and strict liability in the case of AI. A solution that envisages the either-or approach does not take into account the diversity between AI as well as between risks they generate. Moreover, they do not take into account that more than one person can be held accountable for an AI accident. As will be elaborated in the following chapter, manufacturers and holders/operators can be a part of the equation, which is especially favorable from the perspective of a victim. However, due to the specificities of their position vis-à-vis an accident, the basis of liability applicable to a person might differ.

Traditional bases of liability that exist throughout Europe are strict and fault liability. B&H law prescribes general rules on fault-based liability and strict liability too. Strict liability is set as a general clause with specific provisions on certain applications of activities. Furthermore, LO prescribes product liability and vicarious liability. This chapter will first discuss strict and fault-based liability and the challenges created by AI. These are manyfold. It requires rethinking of the fault-based liability standards of a reasonable person and reasonable expert. It should be noted that although our law does not and, in my opinion, should not aim at policing AI but humans around it, AI's autonomy and opacity generate very peculiar risks that

[1] Bevanda (2007), p. 16.

N. Muftić, *Artificial Intelligence and Tortious Liability*, European Union and its Neighbours in a Globalized World 21, https://doi.org/10.1007/978-3-031-86453-7_4

render the assessment of human behavior difficult. Unlike strict-based liability, fault requires a clear set of duties of a human. If they are hard to discern or if a human cannot control AI by performing them, the case for fault-based liability is difficult to establish. Fault-based liability should be applied in every case where the duties of responsible persons can be clearly defined, provided that there is no increased dangerousness of AI. If AI is of increased dangerousness, strict liability should be applied, as LO suggests. The borderline cases would be those where a duty of care cannot be easily formulated and there is no increased dangerousness. LO assists in such cases as it provides a presumed fault, meaning that the responsible person has to prove a lack of fault. In AI accidents, such settings are favorable as persons who operate AI are in a favorable position to provide evidence of their innocence. They naturally have more knowledge of a particular AI than the victim. In the long term, the duties of operators should be clearly established, either via a statute or judicial development. At the moment, they are very hard to formulate, so the focus can be on those that appear in specific sectors, such as self-driving vehicles.

Strict liability seems like a solution in these situations. However, although the current regulation of fault-based liability and strict liability in LO provides significant leeway for adaptation to AI by court intervention, some fundamental issues need to be resolved. One of them is, for example, whether autonomy and opacity themselves constitute increased dangerousness and consequently require the application of strict liability. Dangerousness should be assessed with a traditional understanding of this notion in mind. It should also take into account the peculiar characteristics of AI. Autonomy, opacity, and other characteristics alone should not constitute dangerousness. Exceptionally, when they operate in specific areas, such as biometric identification, AI should be deemed increasingly dangerous in every situation. Of course, increased dangerousness requires ex-ante regulatory responses that are beyond liability law. Such safety measures should assist courts in adjudicating cases and victims in obtaining compensation. Strict liability can be curtailed also based on the type of harm. It should apply only to physical risks, as pure economic risks and social risks generate other types of problems in relation to this basis of liability.

After setting the scene, it is necessary to discuss product liability, vicarious liability, and non-compliance liability. Product liability is regulated vaguely in LO and the courts have a significant role in interpretation and application. There is no definition of product, producer, or defect. Since the amendments to PLD have been adopted recently, LO will be interpreted considering the most significant findings. Product liability, as envisaged in LO, provides solid ground for dealing with AI. Although it is relatively old, it is broad enough to cover potential problems that are characteristic of this technology. Interestingly, it sometimes provides the injured party with a higher degree of protection than PLD. An example is presumed causation which is foreseen for product liability in PLD due to the application of general rules on strict liability. The main objection to LO is the lack of definitions of the most relevant terms in product liability, such as producer, product, defect, etc.

Although courts have leeway to interpret them in order to cover AI, there is an inherent problem of lack of predictability. Lawmakers should also take into account that there is currently a lack of harmonization in entities and on the state level when it comes to consumer protection legislation. Due to the potential of different interpretations, there is a problem of uncertainty related to relevant terminology which potentially affects the scope of application of product liability. Unfortunately, there is no official interpretation to my knowledge rendered by the courts, that would successfully deal with this conundrum. Although general formulations used by legislators in product liability provide leeway to the courts to adapt them to the changing landscape, some specific provisions should be construed by legislators. Those are defenses related to externally supplied data and defense of a producer of components, especially digital ones. In theory, these defenses can already be construed by the courts too due to the broad terminology of the applicable defenses in LO. However, there is an inherent lack of knowledge of technology on the side of courts and a corresponding lack of certainty on the side of manufacturers.

Vicarious liability will be addressed too. Although it does not apply to AI, it is an important question as it presupposes the liability of humans and legal persons for their auxiliaries. Nonetheless, a relationship between persons and animals in their control can act as a model for the application of LO to the harm caused by AI. Not much attention has been devoted in this work to non-compliance liability as it presupposes the existence of clear standards and duties concerning AI. Although it will operate as an important piece of the puzzle in the future, it can be established only after our understanding of AI is thorough and main policy issues have been settled.

Non-compliance liability might be important when we have clear standards and well-grounded industrial practices. It relies on a deep understanding of technology since it prescribes that a person shall be liable if she fails to comply with duties prescribed by the law. Currently, we do not have such duties crafted specifically for AI. They will certainly be developed over time, likely on a sectoral basis. Until that happens, non-compliance liability will remain inoperable.

Lastly, there is a question of contractual and tortious liability which may be applicable. These differences significantly affect the injured person's right to obtain compensation as well as the amount of compensation. The law is silent on whether contractual and tortious liability can be cumulated. Scholarship and courts have often divergent and indefinite positions. This is an issue that requires legislative action in order to equalize the positions of victims. On a level of principle, it may be necessary to allow victims to avail of tortious liability as it provides a greater scope of rights. This is especially so since borderline cases can be even more complex due to the peculiar characteristics of AI.

4.2 Historical Perspective of the Development of the Bases of Liability

Legal norms are not a static category. Tort law in Europe is prone to changes over time. This process, or rather, a development[2] is characterized by great diversity. The agents of changes, background motivation, and how they occur vary. As Ibbetson and Bell noted, the meaning of rules might change by formulation, interpretation, context and relevance, and operation of law.[3] The formulation refers to the wording of a rule, while interpretation refers to its understanding. A rule might be different although the wording does not change. However, if a formulation changes, this might be a clear indication of a change of the rule. Context and relevance provide inputs for a different interpretation of the rules. For example, after the adoption of the Law on general product safety standards,[4] a term defect of a product contained in Article 179 LO is supposed to be interpreted in light of it. Lastly, the liability rules change their meaning also in relation to how are they being enforced. For example, although they are available without specific de minimis limitations, medical liability claims are the most prevalent in cases of serious injuries.[5] This might suggest that there are other devices used for less serious injuries[6] (or perhaps none) and that the courts might interpret general liability rules only with serious injuries in mind.

Development of the basis of liability which would be of the most interest to us is the one related to technology and specific activities that generate increased risk. As AI bears disruptive potential for the current liability system, it would be useful to establish how other technologies in the past have impacted the development of law. The development of technology is a historical constant as well as the injuries it creates. In the words of Jonathan Morgan, it often merely brings new ways to inflict old harm.[7] However, not all developments are linear. Certain developments inflict harm that is of different quality. For example, environmental pollution caused by artisans in earlier agricultural societies had been localized. Technology at the time was not advanced enough to allow a potter to generate fumes which could create serious harm. Things were different after 1850 in Europe. As Bell and Ibbetson note, harms caused by new technologies were much different in terms of "scale, intensity and the potential persistence of noxious industries of an industrial era".[8] Rapid urbanization was marked by an increased number of traffic accidents. The mere increase in the number of vehicles and private car ownership caused this problem.

---

[2]The term development is used as to reflect any changes in which the law is understood by the legal community as a standard of conduct or in the way it is applied in practice. See Ibbetson and Bell (2010).

[3]Ibbetson and Bell (2010), p. 128.

[4]Official Gazette BiH 45/04, 102/09.

[5]Hondius (2010), p. 9.

[6]Ibid.

[7]Morgan (2017), p. 524.

[8]Ibbetson and Bell (2010), p. 138.

This novelty was followed by another one—due to the development of medicine, victims had a greater chance to survive than before.[9] The problem was not only in the number of vehicle accidents. Many specific legal problems occurred.[10] Along with the increased number of traffic accidents, vehicle insurance became prevalent: "In France, as in all other industrialized countries, tort liability in the automobile accident field has become a mere infrastructure. In practice, insurers compensate for damages."[11] The legal systems around Europe responded differently, probably due to a specific local context. However, the responses converged at some point. That can be noticed in the application of strict liability,[12] and later the establishment of mandatory vehicles.[13]

Two outputs of increased industrialization were also influential in shaping the bases of liability and tort law in general. The first output was emissions caused by industrial activities. Due to an increased number of factories and high-scale production workshops, neighbors of such facilities had been forced to tolerate a higher degree of emissions. Smells, noise, and various other kinds of emissions had not been a novelty, but a traditional artisan neighbor could not produce any of those to a such high scale. Moreover, rapid urbanization throughout Europe has brought people closer to one another more than before, which increased the potential impact of emissions. Again, the responses of European states varied. They typically included proprietary and tortious concerns and the adoption of status as a form of regulatory intervention. When it comes to the basis of liability "there was a clear tendency for tortious remedies to fall into line with the orthodox undercurrent of fault liability, while proprietary remedies would be granted independently of any

[9]Ibid, 34.

[10]Ibid, 114:

1. The scale of the accidents—more people might be injured, especially in a railway accident.
2. The speed of the events might make it dii cult for witnesses to see reliably what had happened and to provide sufficient evidence.
3. Many of the causes of accidents, particularly those involving cars, would not be just the vehicle, but the environment within which it was travelling: the road surface, the lighting and the weather.
4. The complexity of the mechanisms would make it harder for the conscientious railway company or car owner to ensure that the vehicle was safe before it was used. Was that person really to blame if an injury occurred? Given the novelty of the technologies used in vehicle manufacture, there were bound to be features of the car itself which either contributed to the injury or did not prevent it happening. The dichotomous nature of litigation did not capture this feature fully and help with the apportionment of responsibility.
5. The person responsible for the railway or vehicle would often not be the driver. (The coachman became the chauffeur, and many delivery vehicles were owned by firms.) There needed to be legal mechanisms to ensure that the victim was able to recover compensation from the major person responsible for the activity.

[11]Department of Transportation (1970), p. 6.

[12]Ibid, 122.

[13]European Convention on Compulsory Insurance against Civil Liability in respect of Motor Vehicles (ETS No. 029).

fault criteria."[14] Again, we could see a certain convergence in applying the basis of liability despite differences among them.

The convergence in the regulatory intervention went beyond tort law though. European states provided safety legislation, including administrative regulation and licensing. The mutual influence between countries was related to the similarity of problems as well as to the fact that industrialization was not a local phenomenon.[15] The second output of industrialization was harm suffered by consumers due to defective products. Mass production and the availability of products on a high scale increased the number of accidents and the prospect of the future. The sophistication of products increased fear of the severity of injuries to life and health. Moreover, consumers were unprepared to match and mitigate these risks while the manufacturers, on the other hand, had the means to reduce the risk and render the product safe at their disposal.[16] Once again, we could notice various responses across the continent, but the broader picture revealed that they usually moved toward imposing strict liability or other forms of no-fault liability on manufacturers. Eventually, a coherency in the attitude is attested by the Product Liability Directive, a legal instrument providing for no-fault liability of manufacturers.

The development of bases of liability in B&H had not occurred organically throughout history. More precisely, B&H was a part of more than one country in the nineteenth century and later. Very often, the law has been made outside B&H and brought to it. Until the Congress of Berlin in 1978, it was a part of the Ottoman Empire that exercised its rule. Since 1978, it formally remained a part of the Ottoman Empire, but the Austro-Hungarian Empire occupied it in accordance with the conclusions of the Congress of Berlin. The occupation lasted until 1908 when the Austro-Hungarian Empire annexed B&H. In the period between occupation and annexation, the Austro-Hungarian government already started with the modernization of the B&H legal order. This was a period of coexistence of Ottoman law and Austro-Hungarian law, where the latter was gradually replacing the former.[17]

Since the occupation, the Austrian Civil Code has been applied in civil law relationships, including the rules of the basis of liability. Fault-based liability acted as a default basis. Subsequent changes during the Austro-Hungarian period concerning liability rules were marked by the top-down application of law. The laws had been adopted in other parts of the empire and enforced in B&H. Hence, B&H had not had a public discussion of its liability regimes or autonomous adaptation of current rules by domestic courts. The bases of liability were simply transplanted into its legal system from a foreign law. In Yugoslavia, even before 1978 LO, the development of the basis of liability had occurred through the interpretation of the courts. Namely, in a case concerning wires of an electric pillar that fell and killed the victim's wife and daughter as well as caused the death of his

[14] Ibbetson and Bell (2010), p. 146.

[15] Ferguson (2000), pp. 78, 90–91.

[16] See Reimann (2015), pp. 250–278.

[17] See Bećić (2014).

livestock, the Supreme Court of the Federal People's Republic of Yugoslavia in 1950 decided that a tortfeasor should be held liable regardless of its fault due to the increased danger of its activity. In order to recognize a strict liability, this court invoked the established practice of lower Yugoslavian courts.[18] A discussion about developing liability law was only a part of a broader discussion of modernizing civil law. Yugoslavia had not managed to adopt a civil code during its existence. Some parts of civil law were heavily influenced by socialistic thought and thereby had not passed the test of time, especially after the dissolution of the state and the change to a democratic system of governance with a market-based economy. Legislation on inheritance and family law was very modern at the time of adoption, but it has been replaced.[19] LO, as an epitome of long-lasting legislation, survived. Rules on liability and specific rules on the basis of liability, their scope, and mutual relationship were crafted to deal with the changing landscape of society due to industrialization.

Due to late industrialization compared to developed European states who had undergone similar processes before and internal political turmoil, Yugoslavia had a range of national experiences in Europe at its disposal. LO was a modern piece of legislation at the time of adoption in 1978, which successfully reflected a societal response to these challenges. The following sections will elaborate on what selection of basis of liability ought to achieve and on the plurality of basis of liability in domestic law.

4.3 What Bases of Liability Ought to Achieve

The level of difficulty an injured party might face in obtaining compensation for an injury by AI depends based on liability they can rely on in a specific case. If a basis of liability determined by either legislators or judges is based on fault, a victim's position is harder since a tortfeasor has the right to prove lack of fault in order to shield themselves.[20] If instead, the applicable law entails the application of strict liability, there is no specific behavior of tortfeasor which has to be proved by an injured party. It only has to prove that a risk attributable to tortfeasor occurred. Article 173 LO prescribes that an injury occurring concerning a dangerous object or dangerous activity shall be treated as originating from such object or activity unless it has been proven that these were not the cause of injury or loss. Hence, either a higher or lower standard has to be met.[21]

[18] Bazala (1956), p. 272.

[19] Law on inheritance of FB&H (Official Gazette FB&H 80/2014, 32/2019); Law on inheritance of Republika Srpska (Official Gazette 1/2009, 55/2009, 91/2016, 28/2019, 82/2019); Family law of FB&H (Official Gazette FB&H 34/2005, 31/2014), Family law of Republika Srpska (Official Gazette Republika Srpska 54/2002, 41/2008, 63/2014).

[20] According to Article 158 of LO, the existence of fault is a presumption which can be contested by a tortfeasor.

[21] Karner et al. (2021), p. 11.

Selection of the basis of liability is a balancing tool in the hands of lawmakers. Depending on various criteria related to a specific thing or an activity, it is used to equal positions of tortfeasors and injured parties. A list of criteria the legislation can have in mind when deciding on this issue is not limited. As we have seen in previous sections, industrialization in nineteenth and twentieth century was marked by an increased likelihood of injuries, increased severity of injuries, and the difficult task of proving that a sophisticated machine caused an injury. Every specific piece of technology or its field of application could have its risks and threats. Some of the criteria characteristic for this area are applicable in the case of AI too.

The legislative history of LO demonstrates that a legislator used very general terms in describing what constitutes increased dangerousness or what constitutes a defect. In other words, it allowed courts to interpret general notions in accordance with the time and context in which injuries occur. As we could see in the previous section, there has already been in place a doctrine of strict liability established by the courts as a response that concerned increased dangerousness of activities, and which was related to technology. Thus, Yugoslavian courts had been capacitated to apply concepts even before they had been legislated in the entire state. The arguments concerning the economic analysis of law, although available in the European and the US scholarship and taken into consideration by some European legislators, were not decisive in Yugoslavia. Scholarship at the time expounded on some of the criteria legislators had in mind. Andrija Gams argues that strict liability has a role in protecting socialist property while fault-based liability would protect individual property.[22] Vrleta Krulj argues that both bases of liability were supposed to act as intermediaries in a socialist society until it managed to completely internalize risks and render liability law redundant.[23] Marija Karanikić Mirić notes that the aforementioned arguments were not persuasive. She emphasizes that the most decisive ones in Yugoslavia followed the line of reasoning of the European lawmakers at the time.[24] They were related to the changing technological landscape caused by industrialization. The reasons for legislating strict liability were:

1. increased dangerousness of an object or an activity for the environment;[25]

For example, compared to a horse carriage, a motor vehicle generates a much higher source of danger for passengers, pedestrians, drivers, and surrounding property.

2. the ability of the holder of the source of increased dangerousness to control the risk;

A driver of a car is in the best position to control it, compared to other passengers and pedestrians. This inference is valid provided that a car is not defective. If there is a defect, the law turns to the producer as the responsible party.

[22] Gams (1966), pp. 252–254.

[23] Krulj (1966), p. 260.

[24] Karanikić Mirić (2019a), p. 35 et al.

[25] Tasić (1939).

3. whoever profits from an activity, should be responsible for it (eius damnum, cuius commodum);[26]

Again, the driver is the person who is typically reaping the benefits of covering a certain distance with a car, provided that it is not a professional chauffeur. The same can be asserted in the case of other passengers. However, not only one criterion is decisive but rather a combination of criteria. This explains why other passengers can be treated as tortfeasors.

4. The hardship of proving fault in cases involving sophisticated technology.[27]

From the perspective of a victim, it might be excessively hard to prove the intent or negligence of a driver, especially as it would entail knowledge about technology used in the motor industry. In order to even the playing field, this requirement has been removed completely.

Article 178 LO creates a difference in the applicable basis of liability depending on the victim. If the accident occurred between two moving motor vehicles, holders are liable to one another on the basis of subjective liability. If a victim is a third party, it can rely on strict liability: "A car is a dangerous thing, so in this case the legal provisions on liability for damage from such a thing should be applied (Article 178, paragraph 4 of the Civil Obligations Act)."[28]

To determine the appropriate basis of liability for a specific accident involving AI, it is important to determine which criteria should be adopted. A separate question is whether current bases of liability, as they currently are in B&H in force, are sufficient to adequately address specific AI characteristics. These questions will be the subject of analysis in the following sections.

4.4 Plurality of Bases of Liability in B&H Law

Chapter II of LO, devoted to the torts, begins with Article 154. The title of this Article is "Bases of Liability". The LO itself, therefore, determines that there is more than one basis of liability that might be applicable. What is exactly meant under the term "bases of liability" was a subject of debate in the scholarship. Differences in the opinions were sometimes purely theoretical had did not have much to do with the application of the law. However, it is worth mentioning that this subject for a significant period of time has not been settled in Yugoslavia, not only before the adoption of LO but also in the aftermath. Vuković claims that there is only one basis for liability and that fault and causation operate as criteria for determining liability.[29]

[26] Konstantinović (1969b).

[27] Ibid.

[28] Supreme Court of Croatia, Rev. 405/99, od 22. 4. 1999. - Izbor odluka 2/1999 – 46.

[29] Vuković (1956), p. 62.

Vedriš considers a wrongful act as a basis of liability.[30] Vizner classifies regimes of liability on the basis of liability, as he understands it. He claims that LO recognizes fault-based liability, fault-based liability with presumed fault, vicarious liability, and strict liability concerning dangerous things.[31] Radišić recognized a multitude of understandings in the Yugoslavian scholarship and claimed that the reason for such disarray is the confusion between the bases of liability and conditions for liability. He claims that the confusion is not limited only to scholarship but that legislators also demonstrate a lack of uniform understanding.[32]

According to LO, strict liability and fault-based liability are two separate bases of liability. They coexist independently and do not have a mutual relationship of hierarchy. Each of them has its field of application. In Konstantinović's words, they do not act as a rule and an exception but stand rather parallelly to one another.[33] This view has been supported by other authors in scholarship too.[34] Apart from strict liability and fault-based liability, LO recognizes also a liability based on equity. However, this basis of liability does not stand on equal footing with the other two bases. Rather, it acts as a corrective mechanism that allows for mitigating undesired consequences that would occur in its absence.

Bases of liability in LO are regulated by the principle of numerus clausus. The courts cannot add a new one in the application of the law. However, as will be discussed in the following sections, the very general wording of the provisions allows for very broad interpretations, creating a potential for dealing with the challenges of AI. Such developments might occur in the future. For now, it might be argued that B&H does not have a problem with a lack of applicable basis of liability for AI. As Wagner said, although national law might not have specific or even sufficient rules on liability in certain areas of application, the general rules of non-contractual liability apply. Even if certain is not seen as increasingly dangerous, "as in other areas, fault-based liability serves as the work-horse of the liability system in protecting victims of any status or calling against harm caused by any entity or activity".[35] Of course, specific features of the applicable basis of liability are very important for the outcome of a case. If for example, an AI-driven meat grinder causes harm due to its autonomous behavior, it would still be treated under the rules of strict liability like a traditional meat grinder.[36]

Lastly, for liability to occur, only one of the bases of liability is enough.[37] The plurality of bases of liability does not entail that the requirements of each of them need to be met. In fact, strict liability and fault-based liability are mutually exclusive.

[30] Vedriš (1978), p. 199.

[31] Vizner (1969).

[32] Radišić (2004), p. 191.

[33] Konstantinović (1992), p. 1154.

[34] Machiedo (1995), p. 45 et al.

[35] Wagner (2019), p. 6.

[36] Supreme Court of FB&H, 070-0-Rev-08-000194, 23.04.2009.

[37] Karanikić Mirić (2019b), p. 274.

To use the previous example: if a meat grinder is considered an object of increased dangerousness, the strict liability rules apply and fault-based liability rules do not.

4.5 Strict and Fault Liability

Section 4.4 described the status of strict and fault liability in the civil law of B&H. They are the two foundational pillars on which the system relies. This section will elaborate on their contents, mutual relationship and how can they be an apt response to AI accidents.

4.5.1 Fault Liability in B&H

Fault liability in B&H is one of the two main regimes in LO. It acts as a default basis of liability in case there is no increased dangerousness of a certain object or an activity or if a legislator had not prescribed specifically the application of strict liability for a particular behavior. In that regard, it is a catch-all regime that ensures that any type of harmful behavior remains not uncovered. Both actions and omissions constitute behavior.[38]

4.5.1.1 Degrees of the Fault and Rebuttable Presumption of Fault

According to Article 158 of LO, degrees of fault are intent and negligence. There are no definitions of these terms in the statutory text. The legislature allowed courts to develop them. In criminal law, the intent is a default degree of fault required for criminal liability while a person can only exceptionally be liable in case of negligence. Civil liability, however, does not require a specific degree of fault for the duty to compensate to arise. In other words, the duty will exist if either intent or negligence is present. There is only one situation in LO (Article 170) in which only intent can establish a duty to compensate: when an employee causes harm to a third party, a victim can require compensation from it directly only if there was an intent on employee's side. A difference between intent and negligence is also not very significant for the scope of compensation. LO in Article 190 prescribes that harm has to be compensated to the amount sufficient to restore the material state of the person sustaining damage into the state it would have been without harm. One of the exceptions from this rule is made in case of a poor material situation of the responsible party so that payment of full indemnity would bring him into poverty. In such situations, according to Article 191 LO, courts are entitled to award

[38] Bikić (2010), p. 21.

compensation in the amount lower than the amount of harm but only if it has not been caused by intent or gross negligence. Therefore, consequences of intent and negligence, in general, are the same in terms of the existence of a duty to compensate and the amount of compensation. The differences are envisaged only exceptionally.

When fault-based liability applies, there is a default rule established in Article 154 that a tortfeasor has a burden of proof when it comes to the fault. In other words, its fault is presumed, and a tortfeasor is given a chance to rebut it. Not long after the adoption of LO, the highest court instances in Yugoslavia provided its interpretation of the meaning of this provision:

According to the rule on presumed guilt (Article 154, paragraph 1 of LO), only the mildest degree of guilt of the perpetrator (ordinary negligence) is covered. Heavier the degree of guilt (gross negligence and intent) was presumed only if so the presumption is explicitly established by a legal rule, or if from the meaning of the respect of the legal rule, it unequivocally follows. Outside of these cases, the degree of guilt is proved according to the general rules of evidentiary procedure.[39]

4.5.1.2 The Dominant Understanding of Fault Is Objective

The fault is understood as a social fact rather than the psychological status of a tortfeasor. When it is assessed, the courts do not investigate the mental state of a person. It is relevant in the assessment of one's ability to be held liable in the first place. One's inability to be held liable is assessed on a case-by-case basis. For example, the courts allow for lucida intervalla exception.[40] Legal persons have the capacity to be held liable without exceptions. When it comes to natural persons, their status depends on their age. Article 160 LO prescribes that a person of up to seven years of age shall not be liable for loss or injury. A person from seven to fourteen years of age shall not be liable for loss unless it is proved that she was mentally competent while causing the damage. A person of fourteen years of age or older shall be liable with the possibility to rebut this presumption. Article 159 LO stipulates that a person who, due to mental disease or insufficient mental development, or for some other reason, is unable to reason (i.e. mentally incompetent), shall not be liable for loss or injury caused to another if it proves so. In case there is no legal capacity of a minor to be held liable, LO provides relief through rules on vicarious liability and liability on the basis of equity. This will be elaborated on later.

The fault is rather a qualitative benchmark of a tortfeasor's behavior which comes into play only if a person can be held liable. Therefore, it should be understood as different from one's capacity to be liable in the first place. When courts assess whether there has been a fault, they compare the regular course of events and the expected behavior of a reasonable person or a reasonable businessman in such

[39] Conclusion XIV Joint sessions of the Federal Court, republican and provincial supreme courts and of the Supreme Military Court of 25 and 26 March 1980.

[40] Supreme Court of Serbia, Rev. 4115/01, 18 April 2002, Bilten sudske prakse VSS, 1/2003.

circumstances. Thus, a hypothetical behavior or a reasonable person/businessman is juxtaposed with the tortfeasor's behavior. Similarly, the fault of a professional, such as a lawyer, physician, or engineer, is assessed in a similar process. The court juxtaposes its behavior with the behavior of an abstract prudent professional. Such an understanding of fault was not legislated, but there is the long-established practice of courts based on it.

4.5.1.3 Lack of Wrongfulness

LO does not prescribe that harm has to be related to wrongful conduct. Article 16 stipulates that everyone shall be bound to refrain from an act that may cause damage to another person but omits to define characteristics of such behavior. This provision does not address wrongfulness directly. Wrongfulness does not operate as a separate condition for liability. It is related to the fault. If there is a fault, courts do not inquire whether harmful behavior was wrongful. When courts deliberate on whether there was a fault, they compare one's behavior to legitimate social expectations.[41] Wrongfulness exists when a person's behavior is not in line with legitimate social expectations. This also means that wrongful behavior does not have to constitute a breach of a legal duty, but only an established practice. If a victim had a ground to rely on such practice, the behavior of a tortfeasor that is not in line with it is wrongful and faulty.

There are different understandings of the role of wrongfulness in the Yugoslavian scholarship. Radišić notes that wrongfulness is a constitutional part of fault-based liability. He claims that wrongfulness is implied in Article 16 of LO. Such a conclusion has been reached since LO contains provisions on justifiable self-defense, vis maior and consent of a victim, which proscribe situations when one's conduct lacks wrongfulness.[42] Oliver Antić considers wrongfulness to be applicable only in case of fault-based liability and not other bases of liability as these defenses are listed in the part of the statute devoted to this specific basis.[43]

Karanikić Mirić disagrees and claims that the law does not require tortious conduct to be contrary to a statutory, contractual, or moral norm. Moreover, a tortfeasor cannot defend themselves by proving that their actions or omissions were not contrary to a statutory, contractual, or moral norm.[44] She presents another interpretation of wrongfulness as an implied duty contained in Article 16. Namely, wrongfulness is implied as not every loss is recoverable under Bosnian and Herzegovinian tort law. Types of harm that are not recoverable are the ones where the wrongfulness is not present. However, this author disagrees with this interpretation on the grounds that the limits of recoverable harm is not caused only on the basis of

[41] Ibid, 284.

[42] Radišić (2004).

[43] Antić (2007).

[44] Karanikić Mirić (2019b), p. 259.

lack of wrongfulness. It is an expression of a normative understanding of harm, i.e. that the law regulates the type of harm to be recoverable.[45]

Case law of the courts that apply LO suggests a lack of clarity in understanding this term. If there is a clear set of duties one has to meet, a failure to do so constitutes wrongfulness. In the case of legal persons of actions of government officials, the courts juxtaposed their behavior with professional standards or norms in a field.[46] However, even if one's behavior was in accordance with professional standards or norms, they can still be imposed a duty to recover harm. The courts held that there is a duty if one's conduct was not of a prudent person.[47] This understanding is in line with the requirement of Article 170 of LO whereby a legal person is liable for damage caused by an employee while working or in relation to work unless it is proved that the employee, in given circumstances, had proceeded as he should have. Furthermore, established practices of a profession, even if they are not considered to be mandatory but rather customary, have been taken into consideration in the case law.[48] Violation of rules but also of customary practices which constitute legitimate expectations is important for the assessment of fault. Notably, the courts do not distinguish fault from wrongfulness when they engage in such analysis. Baretić analyzed recent Croatian case law and inferred that wrongfulness is a necessary condition for liability, as the rules as applied by the Croatian courts. Only exceptionally, liability can be established without wrongfulness.[49] Unfortunately, such clarity cannot be asserted for other post-Yugoslavian legal systems such to a lack of comparable studies.

As wrongfulness is not central to the question of liability for AI, it will not be addressed in detail. It is likely to be more important once the clear set of duties for persons who manufacture or use AI is adopted, or when it is understood what constitutes prudent behavior. Even then, it may be argued that this question does not require an answer in order for tort law to be operational.

4.5.1.4 Causation

Along with harm, causation is necessary for every type of civil liability.[50] It presupposes a link between the harmful event and the harm that can be attributed to a person. Contrary, in order for a duty to compensate to arise, the harm must not be attributed to casus or vis maior. There is a lack of a unifying understanding of causation in Europe.[51] Similarly, there are no specific rules in LO on how causation

[45] Ibid, 258.

[46] Supreme Court of Serbia, Rev. 535/06.

[47] Supreme Court of Serbia, Rev. 2875/05.

[48] Supreme Court of Croatia, Gž 596/80.

[49] Baretić (2020), p. 628.

[50] Carbonnier (2004).

[51] See Infantino and Zervogianni (2017).

should be understood by the courts. Unlike their counterparts in various European states, the courts applying LO's rule on causation do not elaborate on their understanding of this notion and what it entails.[52] In their practice, they accepted the theory of adequate causation. This theory relies on the assessment of all potential causes of harm. Then, it discards all inadequate causes, i.e. all causes which do not lead to such harmful consequences in an ordinary course of events. Which cause is adequate is a subject of analysis in every situation. For this reason, the courts held that a certain behavior constituted a cause for harm while in other situations it did not. For example, Croatian courts in one case found that an error of a prison guard that led to the escape of the prisoner was a cause of the harm suffered by the prisoner, while in another case it was not.[53] The burden of proving causation lies on the victim.

In line with what has been elaborated on wrongfulness, it should be added that not every behavior which is in a causal relationship with harm leads to the duty to compensate. The courts investigate whether such behavior was wrongful. In other words, if there is a causal link between behavior and harm, behavior constitutes adequate cause if it can be considered wrongful. For instance, a properly applied medical treatment by physicians which failed and eventually led to harm to a patient does not qualify as an adequate cause. This is so because the treatment was applied professionally and with a sufficient degree of care and there is an inherent risk of failure which a victim has to bear.[54]

Moreover, the foreseeability of harm has a relevant role in establishing a causal link. Certain behavior can be deemed an adequate cause only if its harmful consequences could be foreseen at the time of the tortfeasor's actions or omissions. Contrary, there is no causal link and a duty to compensate if the harm was unforeseeable.[55] Harm has to be foreseeable for the tortfeasor. Even if potential harm is not usual for behavior but it was nonetheless foreseeable by a tortfeasor due to its specific knowledge or experience, the causal link can be established. In such a situation, vis major cannot be invoked.

4.5.1.5 Liability Based on Equity

As we have discussed, along with strict liability, fault-based liability operates as a pillar of the liability regime. However, LO in Article 169 prescribes that under certain circumstances fault can be supplemented with equity. Those are two situations. The first situation is when the tortfeasor cannot be held liable but there is a responsibility of another person to supervise a tortfeasor. Traditional rules on vicarious liability entail that the supervisor is liable. However, in situations when

[52] Bukovac Puvača et al. (2019).

[53] Ibid, p. 33.

[54] Supreme Court of Serbia, Rev. 2066/80, Bilten sudske prakse 5-6-/1981.

[55] Magnus (2000).

the supervisor does not have enough property to ensure compensation and the tortfeasor does, the court is entitled to order the tortfeasor to compensate. The second situation is when the tortfeasor is a mentally competent minor who is unable to redress harm. The court is entitled to oblige the parents to compensate a victim should equity so required and more particularly due to the material situation of parents, although they might not have a duty to supervise a minor. As these situations demonstrate, liability based on equity constitutes a corrective mechanism to the inadequate solutions of fault-based liability. The wording of the provisions of LO provides for a specific set of situations when this basis of liability can be applied, thereby providing its limited scope in domestic law. However, the courts have a history of creative interpretation. Maja Bukovac Puvača notes that courts applied Article 169 even when no person had a responsibility to supervise the tortfeasor.[56] For instance, when an incapacitated person without a supervisor caused harm, courts imposed on it a duty to compensate by invoking this provision.

4.5.1.6 What Are the Problems Caused by AI

Anthropocentric Concepts of Fault

It is important, at the outset, to note that the LO's presumption of fault is very favorable for a victim due to its presumption which a defendant has to rebut. This is justified because it might be very hard for a victim to prove fault in case of accidents involving AI if the behavior of humans is not the standard. As a new technology, AI has not been studied and is well-known to humans and courts. The duties of humans behind it are likewise insufficiently known. Therefore, it seems reasonable that humans who are behind AI and thereby understand how it operates should bear the burden of proving that they acted with a sufficient level of care.

On the other hand, fault liability and product liability require rethinking as well. Fault liability relies on the anthropocentric conception that cannot be easily settled with the autonomous behavior of AI.[57] Intention and negligence are not designed to cope with non-human autonomous actors. Furthermore, the benchmarks LO sets for assessing one's behavior in Article 18 are the behavior of a good person, the behavior of a good businessman, and the behavior of a good expert. Again, they operate within the realm of humans and do not require some intelligible behavior of other artificial agents.

It might be argued that such standards, as they are focused on human behavior, cannot satisfy the requirements of AI accidents. However, we do not need to hold AI liable. These standards are anthropocentric exactly because they aim at holding persons behind technology liable. They circumvent any means natural and legal persons utilize as independent agents and focus on their behavior instead. Thus,

[56] Bukovac Puvača (2010), pp. 800–801.

[57] See Eidenmüller (2019).

special standards of behavior of AI are not required, at least not at the moment. Due to the lack of knowledge in the present times, it is impossible to predict the development of this technology. Fault-based liability and strict liability, traditionally aimed at dealing with human behavior, either when they cause harm directly or through an agent, remain suitable until those changes occur.

Assessment of human behavior in AI accidents is a challenging task enough. We need to modify the meaning of the traditional concept in light of the use of new technologies, which is not going to be hard. "It will take years rather than months for the industry to cohere around a standard."[58] We can expect courts and legislators to need even more time due to the information asymmetry, especially since it is sometimes necessary to reconstruct one's duties "after the fact by the court on the basis of social beliefs about the prudent and reasonable course of action in the circumstances".[59] Standards of AI behavior are important, but not as a separate standard of behavior, but rather as a tool to assess the one of a human behind.

4.5.1.7 Raising of Standards in Order to Match AI Capabilities

A horse carriage used to be a standard in the transportation industry. Once cars became pervasive, the standard of care started being assessed with the new means of transportation in mind. They simply provided different performance in terms of safety, comfort, and speed of travel. Horse carriages became extinct from the roads, and they are used usually by enthusiasts and probably in places with less developed infrastructure and lower living standards. The standard of care has been adapted to the new technology. The benchmark of safety started being assessed with it in mind too. In those systems which do not recognize strict liability for motor vehicles, the level of duty of care in fault-based liability was set so high that it resembles strict liability. The standard of care required from drivers is set so high that it is difficult to meet and is almost always violated. In jurisdictions with a narrow range of strict liability rules, there is a common practice of bypassing these limitations by inflating the duty of care under fault-based liability, thereby improving the likelihood of victims succeeding in their claims. As we can see, even before the adoption of LO, the courts in Yugoslavia adopted strict liability as a concept in order to cope with the change.

If AI replaces traditional technologies in certain areas, the standard of behavior might be changed as well. The long-term consequences of AI on the understanding of the duty to care might be profound. This question is different from whether we should treat AI with different standards from humans. I will address this possibility below. At this point, the question is whether the two standards overlap or whether they might impact one another? Duty to care relies on whether a reasonable person or a reasonable businessman would act in a particular way in a given situation. This

[58] Robotic Rules of the Road, The Economist, in: Ibid, 121.

[59] Report, 23.

approach suffices insofar as the services are performed only by humans. Then, their behavior can be juxtaposed to that of a reasonable human. Hypothetically, if a certain set of services is performed only by AI, then a reasonable AI behavior that currently exists in the market can act as a benchmark for the assessment of care. However, if there is competition between humans and AI, the problem arises. Whether humans and AI can be held to the same standards? Abbot suggests:

Once AI becomes safer than people and practical to substitute for people, AI should set the baseline for the new standard of care. This means that human defendants would no longer have their liability based on what a hypothetical reasonable person would have done in the situation, but what an AI would have done.... Eventually, the continually improving reasonable robot standard should apply to AI tortfeasors, at which point AI should cause so little harm that the primary effect of the standard would make human tortfeasors essentially strictly liable for their harm.[60]

In theory, if AI acts along with humans and competes in performing tasks, its increasing standards will also impact how humans should act to avoid being held liable. Increased safety and quality of services performed can justify this presumption because otherwise, it is hard to imagine why we would turn from it. However, the overlap of AI and human standards of behavior should rely on the availability of AI to a wider group of consumers. If AI is available to a majority of people, AI should be the standard for humans who perform respective tasks too. Otherwise, the high standard of behavior will allow only a minor group of people to be shielded from liability. For example, if a majority of people are in a position to own or operate self-driving vehicles, its presumably increased standard of care (compared to traditional vehicles) should increase the level of expectation from all persons who operate vehicles, regardless of whether they are fueled by AI or not. On the other hand, if self-driving cars are an exception on the roads rather than a rule, the general standard of care in relation to traditional vehicles should not be impacted so long as they are not a norm.

The human standard of care in the case of traditional services should have a different impact on the standard of care in the case of tasks performed by AI. It has to operate as a minimum standard of care for AI. If AI provides less safety than humans, it does not merit being marketed. Therefore, from the outset, AI should not be provided with subsidies in the form of a lower threshold to be met. More precisely, humans behind AI need to be burdened with the level of care which is at least on the level of humans who perform such tasks without AI. Furthermore, although the human standard of care acts as the minimum, it should not remain so permanently. The standard of the behavior of humans behind AI should follow the trends in the industry. One of the reasons we employ AI is to increase safety. If the industry sets the bar higher, the duty of care should increase correspondingly. Thus, eventually, the human standard of care should ideally be divorced from that of AI as the latter surpasses the former. Due to the lack of experience, the courts might face

[60] Abbot (2020), p. 51.

problems in assessing the party's real level of care, in the beginning, i.e. there is a lack of methodology in applying fault-based liability to AI accidents that courts need to adopt. The process might be bumpy since the courts might not intend to juxtapose one's behavior to someone else's—AI to humans or humans behind AI to humans who traditionally perform corresponding tasks. This creates a lack of predictability. Thus, having human standards of behavior as a starting point, some sort of a minimum guarantee of AI's behavior would aid in overcoming this period.

Imagine if there is a collision between a traditional vehicle and a self-driving vehicle.[61] The applicable law in B&H seems to cover self-driving vehicles under the definitions of vehicles.[62] According to Article 178(1) of LO, holders of vehicles are liable based on fault. Here, we have a double problem. It would be hard to measure fault based on the standards of behavior for a self-driving vehicle. Many situations are possible. A driver perhaps had to take control at a certain point and its fault could be constituted. It is also possible that a vehicle operated completely autonomously without any involvement of its users. The courts would face hardship in trying to establish whether a duty to care has been matched. In any case, the courts should not be left to struggle with such fundamental issues. If the fault is to be preserved in case of liability of vehicle users to one another, there needs to be a clear set of criteria that could be applicable for the assessment of the behavior of self-driving vehicles. An additional problem would be to which behavior should the court compare AI's—another humans' or AI's? If there is another AI that performs the same self-driving operations such as the AI that caused harm, there is the case for using it as a benchmark. If that is not the case or the criteria are hard to determine, the courts can resort to human behavior.

4.5.1.8 Modifying Standard or Adding a New One for AI

When it prescribes how one should behave in carrying out its obligations, Article 18 of LO prescribes standards they shall be bound. Depending on the characteristics of a person, those standards require one to act with the care of a good person, a good

[61] In order to illustrate points and problems, a number of hypothetical cases presented in this chapter. These cases have not been selected randomly. In the study "Comparative Law Study on Civil Liability for Artificial Intelligence", ordered by the European Commission, authors Ernst Karner, Bernhard A. Koch, and Mark A. Geistfeld have addressed problems of AI on exactly these cases. They created hypothetical scenarios which are not unrealistic in a foreseeable future. Some of them have already happened in the real life. Having a rather bird-eye perspective, these authors have provided general remarks on how legal systems would likely deal with these cases.

Problem arising out of the hypothetical cases are likely to happen in B&H too. In order to demonstrate problems and findings related to basis of liability, I will try to apply the current law of B&H.

[62] Law on fundamentals of traffic safety in Bosnia and Herzegovina (Official Gazette 6/06, 75/06, 44/07, 84/09, 48/10, 18/13, 8/17), Article 9: "motorno vozilo je vozilo koje se pokreće snagom sopstvenog motora i koje je prvenstveno namijenjeno za prijevoz lica ili tereta na putevima, ili vuču priključnog vozila, osim vozila koja se kreću po šinama i pomoćnih pješačkih sredstava."

businessman, or a good expert. As we have mentioned, LO does not define intent and negligence. Although the opinions of scholars vary, objective standards of behavior in Article 18 are used as a benchmark for the assessment of one's care. This is especially so in the case of negligence, as intent puts focus to a greater extent on the personal characteristics of a tortfeasor. When AI is involved in an accident, the question is whether to hold humans liable under the same standards of behavior as in traditional accidents? Or an adoption of a new standard of behavior is required—reasonable AI? The answer to these two questions depends on whose behavior we assess and under what circumstances. As will be elaborated in detail in the next chapter, we need to hold humans accountable, and not AI itself. Also, if it is impossible to assess what one had to do or there is an excess in risk, strict liability is traditionally applied to cover such cases. Thus, the standards of a good person, a good businessman, or a good expert can be applied to AI accidents. They can be stretched or modified to involve specific duties humans have, but they remain to be standards for the assessment of the behavior of humans. It can be argued that this solution is not fair. In words of Karni Chagal-Feferkorn:

The difference in tort frameworks applying to human versus non-human decision-makers, however, presents horizontal inequity at its most crystalized form: even if both tortfeasors have sufficient resources to compensate the victims, and even if the cases were judged at the same instance by the same judges and were argued by the same lawyers, the inherent differences between the reasonableness standard that would apply to the human driver and the wholly different tort framework that might apply to the driverless car would render the two cases, their costs and their outcomes, very different.

However, victims can be differentiated from each other on the basis of whether the harm was caused by human or AI behavior while the system preserves coherence and justice. Here we make a distinction between them which does not affect the rights of victims based on which it is prohibited (such as whether the pest is rich or poor and whether or not it has insurance), but according to different types of sources of harm. The consequence of one's behavior might be the same regardless of the source of harm (e.g. bodily injury), but the same harm can occur due to a different number of factors. For example, bodily injury can occur during poor treatment by a doctor or in a car accident. We commonly apply different standards of behavior to tortfeasors (e.g. standard of a good professional or a good person). Just as a doctor is different from a driver (if it is not a professional) from this example, a self-driving car is potentially different from a traditional car. Also, creating a distinction between human and AI negligence standards will not detriment the position of victims of the former. Traditional damages would still be valued according to existing standards. We will only have an improvement in the position of the victims in the new type of damage. The problem may occur when we have damage caused jointly by man and AI. However, this does not have to be so if we apply procedural devices through which a victim can redress from all tortfeasors in the full amount. Joint and several liability as the more favorable standard for the victim would solve this problem. On the specific position of a victim in this process, see Chap. 6.

4.5.1.9 Creating New Duties for Humans

The contents of the duty of care for persons behind AI might be changed due to different modus operandi of AI. The behavior of humans as users might require a different understanding. An example would be the German Road Traffic Act which was reformed in 2017. It provides a user of the vehicle with automated functions to "turn away from the road and from steering the vehicle as long as she remains 'perceptive enough' to identify a need to retake control of the steering functions at any given time".[63] Thus, the duty of care is perceived differently—the duty to operate was under certain circumstances changed to the duty to monitor. There has been some criticism on account of the formulation of this duty due to a lack of clarity as to what exactly this means.[64]

Notwithstanding whether duties in the case of the German Road Traffic Act had been successfully formulated, it is clear that what is required by humans is different than in the case of traditional technologies. New duties correspond to the changing nature of AI. However, like in the German example, creating duties might suffer from vagueness. Admittedly, it is hard to precisely define new duties due to the lack of experience with AI and knowledge of its potential behavior. For this reason, it is even less plausible to try to formulate a general duty to monitor which would cover all AI applications. Simply, the scope and meaning of such duties would be hard to assess. Moreover, if a user can monitor, it does not necessarily have to be in a position to stop the operation of AI and prevent a potential accident. For example, while a user of a self-driving vehicle can theoretically monitor and take over due to its proximity to the AI's operation, a lack of proximity would prevent such possibility in the case of automated drones.

Even if we manage to overcome this problem, a general duty would entail a possibility for humans (and especially users as they are directly involved) to modify or stop AI's operation. Such a general requirement requires general AI rules, which require broader debate in society and more extensive knowledge of this technology. Shavell considers that courts themselves will not be able to adequately formulate such duties due to lack of information: "Consider, for instance, the ability of courts to formulate correct fault standards in regard to communications between vehicles to reduce accident dangers, whether sensors should be able to detect black ice, or the degree of testing that should be conducted into the structural integrity of a vehicle using a modified material".[65] It is hard to predict whether the court will face such questions as they are closely related to the existence of ex-ante safety regulations that they can rely on. Moreover, if the task is too difficult, legislators or courts might intervene and decide that increased dangerousness or other specific characteristics of a particular AI merit the application of strict liability.

---

[63] Karner et al. (2021), p. 46.

[64] Ibid.

[65] Shavell (2019), p. 11.

The Report suggests that the general duties of manufacturers and operators in relation can be formulated as:

Operators of emerging digital technologies should have to comply with an adapted range of duties of care, including with regard to

(a) choosing the right system for the right task and skills;
(b) monitoring the system; and
(c) maintaining the system.

Producers, whether or not they incidentally also act as operators within the meaning of, should have to:

(a) design, describe, and market products in a way that effectively enables operators to comply with the duties under; and
(b) adequately monitor the product after putting it into circulation.[66]

These duties might act as a roadmap for the courts and involved parties. Specific sectors where AI accidents materialize would determine their meaning and potentially modify them. So far, we can conclude that the duty to care in LO is flexible and broad enough to cover even those new duties a court might find in a specific case. If there is enough knowledge in a specific field such as self-driving vehicles, specific duties can be imposed by legislators on the sectoral level. Until that happens, the courts will be left to roam in search of the formula.

4.5.1.10 Dealing with the Foreseeability of Humans Behind AI

Because fault relies on foreseeability, it might be very hard to establish that humans behind could foresee consequences if AI acted autonomously. Rachum-Twaig suggests that lack of foreseeability is one of the main challenges AI poses for tort law as one it is hard to settle AI's autonomy and opacity with human's foresight before imposing liability.[67] Likewise, the harm caused by AI might not have been anticipated by any persons who are in any capacity involved with AI,[68] regardless of whether they participated in manufacturing or deployment of AI or they simply hold it or use it. It is important to address the question of whose foreseeability is required. As will be demonstrated in the following chapter, the traditional rule of holding only holders' or operators' liability seem obsolete in the case of AI. Under certain circumstances, foreseeability needs to be assessed also concerning manufacturers.

Foreseeability should be understood differently when AI is involved. It might behave autonomously. This is how it is marketed and one of the main reasons why

---

[66] Report, 43.

[67] See Omri Rachum-Twaig, Whose Robot Is It Anyway?: Liability for Artificial-Intelligence-Based Robots, University of Illinois Law Review, Vol. 2020, Forthcoming , Available at SSRN: https://ssrn.com/abstract=3339230.

[68] Balkin (2015), pp. 45, 52.

the idea of AI development is attractive. Foreseeability, as understood in tort law, should take into account that humans behind AI are aware of its characteristics. It ought to presume that certain autonomous types of AI's behavior, although unintended by humans, might have been predictable by them. This idea has been asserted in the Report—responsible persons should be held liable if it was predictable that unforeseen developments might occur.[69] On the other hand, when unforeseen AI behavior could not have been predicted, there should be no leeway for fault-based liability. Admittedly, this criterion is very hard to be constructed in reality. However, shielding persons who benefit from AI or who are in the best position to control at the expense of a victim seems unreasonable too. An obvious escape in such situations is to apply strict liability every time specific duties of persons behind AI are impossible to be construed. Thereby, due to the LO's presumed causation, they will bear the burden of successfully invoking available defenses. For example, a hospital uses an AI-driven surgical robot. It harms a patient during surgery by performing an incision on a wrong spot, although it has been programmed correctly by the doctors in the hospital. Provided that fault-based liability is applicable, this accident should not be considered unforeseeable. The next question is, naturally, for whom was this accident foreseeable—for manufacturers of AI or the hospital? In the 1990 case famously called Zaragoza Radiotherapy Accident,[70] the Spanish court had to decide who was responsible for malfunctioning Zaragoza Clinic's electron accelerator which caused patients' skin burns, inflamed internal organs and long-term disabilities. It established that the repair of the machine was faulty and blamed the technician who carried out the repair and the American General Electric Company (GE), who supplied the equipment and was responsible for maintenance. The difference between our example and Zaragoza Radiotherapy Accident is in the existence of a defect.

There might not have been a wrong action conducted in the case of an AI-surgical robot, as both manufacturers and hospital could conduct their tasks prudently. AI might have acted autonomously. Nonetheless, it would be unreasonable not to point a finger at any of them. Unlike in Zaragoza Radiotherapy Accident where the court could clearly establish who made a mistake, here the court has to assume who could have acted in a manner that would prevent an accident. In other words, who, of the persons involved could have foreseen the accident. The response in our example should be either-or, as a failure to assign liability due to lack of foreseeability would impair a victim.

In the case of strict liability, as we could see, the situation is different. Where the risks are increased are foreseeability hindered and unpredictable, such cases will be treated with strict liability. Accordingly, foreseeability is perceived differently (risk must be associated with an object or an activity rather than foreseeable) and this

[69] Report, 43.

[70] Zaragoza Radiotherapy Accident – 1990, available at: https://devastatingdisasters.com/zaragoza-radiotherapy-accident-1990/amp/?fbclid=IwAR13ptifQovRLaexMnT0sB7NPY75wKlTUe976Ax2UNYJAPY3JJgvBKWomNA.

problem would not exist there. In the case of fault-based liability, another solution should be made in order to cover for the novelties caused by AI's autonomy and opacity. Foreseeability should be understood to include also those unforeseen accidents which could have been predicted nonetheless.

4.5.1.11 The Principle of Integral Compensation Should Be Preserved

Because of hardship in determining fault in relation to AI, integral compensation should be appliable in all cases involving accidents caused by the autonomous behavior of AI. If determination based on intent and negligence is taken into account, victims might be worse off. LO already prescribes this as a norm. In that respect, any modifications are not required. All exceptions from this principle that currently exist allow for departure from the full compensation for reasons other than a degree of fault, which is why there is no space for their misinterpretation. Article 191 of LO relies on the poor material situation of a tortfeasor, Article 189 of LO relies on the value the object had for the person sustaining damage, Article 191 of LO relies on the fact that tortfeasors caused damage while doing something to the benefit of the person sustaining a loss, Article 192 and Article 154 of LO relies on contributory negligence and contribution of the third party. Admittedly, some of these exceptions rely also on the degree of fault of a tortfeasor. However, since they have a character of exceptions and that degree of fault is only one of the criteria if it is present at all, AI tortfeasors would not be shielded from the duty to provide full compensation.

4.5.2 Strict Liability in B&H

Strict liability provides increased liability exposure of responsible persons. As elaborated above, courts developed it even before the adoption of LO, in response to changing technological landscape at the time. Legislators have followed the lead of the courts and other European states who provided for rules on strict liability in their respective civil law codifications.

4.5.2.1 General Clause and Specific Cases

There are two main avenues European states took when it comes to the scope of application of strict liability. The first avenue consists of an enumeration of those objects or activities which are deemed to generate increased dangerousness. Then, strict liability is attached only to those persons who are in control of such objects or who are involved in such activities.[71] On accidents in relation to other objects and

[71] Karanikić Mirić (2017), p. 354.

activities which are not enumerated, strict liability is not applied. In those cases, fault-based liability acts as a basis of liability. Thus, a number of European systems use a system of numerus clausus to prescribe field of application of strict liability, while fault-based liability acts as a default basis.[72] The second avenue consists of the prescription of a general strict liability clause that applies to an unlimited number of cases. The legislator sets criteria that need to be met in order for strict liability to be applied. The courts assess whether they are met. LO follows the second avenue. Article 173 prescribes that strict liability is applicable in accidents involving a dangerous object of property or dangerous activity. What exactly those terms mean was left for the courts to decide.

B&H legislators sometimes tend to use the phrase "general regime of liability". For example, laws on a public notary in FB&H, Republika Srpska, and Brcko District stipulate that the civil liability of a notary is subject to the general regime. However, there is ambiguity as to what is a general regime of liability since, as we discussed earlier, strict liability is not an exception from fault-based liability.[73] Such phrasing is faulty and provides hardship to courts and scholarship in establishing general rules of liability specific to notary service. Moreover, the is confusion regarding whether the legislators considered notary liability to be contract-based or even quasi-contract-based.[74]

Along with the general clause on strict liability, there are a number of specific cases where legislators prescribed the application of strict liability regardless of the existence of increased dangerousness. We mentioned this specific prescription in Chap. 3. Those are accidents caused by a motor vehicle in motion,[75] product liability,[76] the liability of the state for terrorist acts, street demonstrations, or public events,[77] the liability of organizer of performances,[78] liability due to refusal to render necessary aid,[79] liability relating to a duty to conclude a contract,[80] and liability relating to conducting affairs of general interest.[81] Apart from LO, strict liability for specific objects or activities can be envisaged in other statutes. An example is the Law on Environmental Protection of Republika Srpska.[82]

[72] Karner et al. (2021), p. 33.
[73] Povlakić (2013), p. 4 et al.
[74] Ibid.
[75] Article 178 LO.
[76] Article 179 LO.
[77] Article 180 LO.
[78] Article 181 LO.
[79] Article 182 LO.
[80] Article 183 LO.
[81] Article 184 LO.
[82] Official Gazette of Republika Srpska 71/2012, 79/2015.

4.5.2.2 Dangerous Object and Dangerous Activity

Despite providing a significant leeway for court interpretation of the general strict-liability clause, LO distinguishes between dangerous objects and dangerous activity. However, it does not provide definitions of these terms or what is the reason for their distinction. Mihailo Konstantinovic, who drafted LO, provided a note explaining that objects encompass movable and immovable objects as well as those which are res in commercio and res extra commercio.[83] In decades-long practice, courts qualified many objects as dangerous, including animals. As Marija Karanikić Mirić notes, some of them are per se dangerous, while others can be qualified as such only in case of a defect that materialized after the object had been put into circulation.[84] The term dangerous activity was omitted from the first draft of LO as Konstantinovic considered it redundant.[85] However, it was accepted by the legislator and used by the courts. Like in the case of objects, some activities are per se dangerous, while others become such in specific circumstances.[86] At first, scholarship did not reach a consensus on whether there is any difference in the regime concerning dangerous objects and dangerous activities. Without going into a detailed demonstration of the variety of opinions, it can be argued that the grounds for claiming that legislators had in mind different regimes were not supported by courts. In the case law, dangerous objects and dangerous activities are treated by the same rules of strict liability with the same defenses.[87]

4.5.2.3 Presumed Causation

Unlike in the case of fault liability, strict liability provides an easier task for an injured party. Article 173 of LO is titled "Presumption of causation". As it suggests, reverses the burden of proof of causation to a responsible party. This provision prescribes that an injury or loss occurring in relation to a dangerous object of property or dangerous activity shall be treated as originating from such object or activity unless proven that these were not the cause of injury or loss. Thus, an injured party does not have to demonstrate a clear link between the specific object or activity and harmful consequences. If an object or activity is of increased dangerousness, claimants do not need to demonstrate any particular wrongful action; they only need to establish that the risk associated with the defendant materialized, without being required to prove the exact way in which it occurred.

A responsible party can be exempted from liability for one of the reasons stipulated in Article 177 of LO. First, it can prove that injury or loss took place

[83] Konstantinović (1969a), pp. 133–135.

[84] Karanikić Mirić (2019a), p. 86.

[85] Konstantinović (1969a), p. 135.

[86] Karanikić Mirić (2019a), pp. 89–90.

[87] Ibid.

due to a cause outside the object of property, whose effect could not have been foreseen, avoided, or eliminated. Second, it can prove that injury or loss occurred entirely through an act of the person sustaining injury or loss or a third person, which act could not have been foreseen by him and whose consequences he was not able to avoid or eliminate. In the case of a partial contribution of a victim or a third party, a defendant can be exempted partially if it proves so. The difference is that in of third-party contribution, the defendant and the third party and jointly and severally liable. Another difference is that the liability of the third party, in that case, is fault-based.

4.5.2.4 What Are the Problems Caused by AI

Due to the information asymmetry between developers and the rest of the population, developers can be held liable on a basis of strict liability, a basis of liability that incentivizes their more careful behavior as the only involved parties who have sufficient information to mitigate AI risks. The problem with strict liability is related to its severity which might disincentivize the improvement of the technology.

4.5.2.5 Does a General Clause with Specific Cases Suffice to Cover AI?

The General strict-liability clause is broad enough to cover accidents involving AI. The only criterion LO uses is increased dangerousness which is itself very flexible. The same applies to the notions of object and activity. Moreover, as we can see, the courts have historically interpreted the general clause very broadly and adapted it to different circumstances. What we need is for the courts to be proactive in their approach and to recognize specific characteristics of AI that constitute dangerousness. Autonomy, opacity, and vulnerability are not per se dangerous but when applied in specific contexts they might be. Also, as regulation of AI should be future-proof, courts should be given time to develop clear criteria for assessment of increased dangerousness. They will certainly depend on the future development of this technology and likely on comparative legal developments, i.e. criteria developed by foreign lawmakers. Therefore, LO does not seem to be obsolete in how it defines the general strict liability clause.

The EU Parliament's Resolution 2020 in Article 4 stipulates that high-risk AI should be subject to strict liability while Article 4 envisages fault-based liability to all other AI others to fault liability. This document defines high risk in Article 3 as "a significant potential in an autonomously operating AI-system to cause harm or damage to one or more persons in a manner that is random and goes beyond what can reasonably be expected; the significance of the potential depends on the interplay between the severity of possible harm or damage, the degree of autonomy of decision-making, the likelihood that the risk materializes and the manner and the context in which the AI-system is being used".

Such a definition was a subject of criticism. As Wagner noted, "only two aspects are relevant for whether a risk is to be classified as 'high', namely the probability of the occurrence of damage and the severity of the threatened damage".[88] LO does not share the same problems as the courts have the flexibility to adopt criteria they find appropriate. In that respect, LO should not change its fundamental formulation of strict liability and follow the lead set by Proposal 2020. Namely, Proposal 2020 employs a method of enumeration for those AI applications that can be considered high-risk. The EU Commission, according to Article 4 of this document, is entitled to change the list. "However, the courts should not be allowed to accept strict liability according to Art. 4 Apply the draft regulation to digital autonomous systems that are not listed in the annex to the regulation."[89] Such arrangement is characteristic of the likes of the German legal system where the strict liability does not operate on the basis of the general clause. LO follows the formulation of the Code Civil and there is no need for making such a fundamental change as the current one is fit for the challenges of AI and emerging digital technologies.

Also, if the legislator wants to make sure that certain areas are always treated with strict liability, it can simply add new specific cases of strict liability. LO has already made certain risks covered by strict liability explicitly, such as motor vehicle accidents and product liability. The same pattern can be applied to AI too. There are two main reasons why specific cases of strict liability would be an apt avenue in combination with the general clause. These do not and are not necessarily because the general clause cannot cover them. First, it would render the legal landscape more specific and predictable for the parties involved as well as for the courts. Second, specific provisions would allow for providing specific substantive and procedural rules concerning those risks. For example, if biometric identification is singled out, specific rules can be prescribed as well. Those could be the likes of reversal of the burden of proof or a lower standard of proof for a victim.

Specific cases of strict liability should be adopted only when the understanding of AI and risks in the specific context is mature enough to merit legislative action. Until that point, the courts ensure that even those risks will not be uncovered with strict liability if they pass the test of increased dangerousness.

Imagine a hypothetical situation under the current B&H law. A pedestrian is seriously injured in an accident with a self-driving car. Her bicycle, which she had intended to push across the road, is also damaged.[90] LO in Article 178(4) prescribes strict liability of the car users to the pedestrians and other third parties. An injured party has the right to obtain compensation from the insurance or to claim compensation from the self-driving vehicle's users. A victim would obtain compensation provided that their behavior was not illegal in the way and time of crossing the road. In other words, there must not be contributory negligence on its side. The situation is not very novel if a user had to take control over the vehicle at a certain point or perform a specific duty a failure of which caused the accident. The problem arises if a

[88] Wagner (2019), p. 556.

[89] Ibid, 558.

[90] See Karner et al. (2021). This case was modeled after the case that occurred in Arizona in 2018. See https://www.nytimes.com/2018/03/19/technology/uber-driverless-fatality.html.

vehicle performs autonomously and fails to stop before the collision. However, even in this case, due to strict liability and mandatory insurance, a victim would receive compensation, despite the law's blindness to automation or AI. Therefore, in some cases, even specific provisions on strict liability as prescribed in LO would be suitable for AI accidents and require only slight modifications. A victim would be well while the determination of the person to be ultimately burdened with a duty to compensate should be resolved.

4.5.2.6 What Constitutes Increased Dangerousness

How can a court determine whether a specific AI object or activity is of increased dangerousness? Do courts need to compare it to traditional objects and activities? This is important as it provides demarcation between the fault-liability regime and the strict-liability regime. First, the courts can employ traditional criteria for the assessment. Those would be the likes of the likelihood of harm, the extent of harm, the number of individuals at risk, and the difficulty of alleviating risk for injurer. Scholarship suggests that other criteria might be of assistance to the court, such as whether an activity is unusual and whether a party's non-verifiable precaution reduces the expected harm rather than the cost of precaution.[91] For example, both traditional meat grinders and AI-driven ones are of increased dangerousness and qualify for strict liability. Applying strict liability in product liability can also follow the same rationale.

Whether autonomy and opacity themselves are enough to constitute dangerousness? No, it should be assessed via the real risk. Autonomy and opacity are not characteristics that are per se dangerous. They can actually increase safety due to the supreme ability of AI to conduct calculations. However, in specific contexts, they create a unique set of risks that cannot be attributed to other technologies. For example, the use of AI for biometric identification or exploitation of people's vulnerabilities is per se of increased risk.[92] In such situations, it would be unnecessary for courts to assess whether AI generates increased dangerousness. They should be treated a priori as such. In fact, as was mentioned above, the general clause on strict liability in LO can be supplemented with specific cases where it applies without court interpretation. A list of specific cases should be expanded by virtue of legislative action to include such risks.

Applying fault-based liability might be problematic due to a more fundamental reason. In the case of AI, a user is potentially unable to control AI. Thus, at the time of the accident, a sufficient level of care might not have relevance to the occurrence of harm. For instance, an automated lawnmower might cut roses in a neighborhood's garden although the user-programmed it properly and also installed all required updates. A sufficient level of care would not thus provide a deterrent function, nor

---

[91] Dari-Mattiacci and Parisi (2013).

[92] See Article 5 of AI Act.

would it seem fair to treat the user liable. Moreover, even if it is possible, assessment of who was in control among the pool of potential persons and what happened renders the situation for a victim hard. As we mentioned, fault-based liability puts a burden of proving causation on a victim, while strict liability provides presumed causation. The next chapter will elaborate on the change of control over AI and its relevance for the allocation of liability. It suffices so far to say that it is closely related to basis liability insofar as it provides an argument for strict liability. Although a person in control might be distant, for example, a producer in a different country, it still might be in the best position to control AI. The rationale applicable to product liability thus applies here as well. Moreover, the lack of control of a user is manifested in the confusion around its specific duties. In other words—how can one rebut the presumption of fault if there is no specific set of duties it had to meet? This is another argument in favor of strict liability.

4.5.2.7 Limitation of Strict Liability Based on the Type of Risks

Along with increased dangerousness, this work argues that strict liability can be constituted due to other reasons, such as the difficulty of proving causation, collecting evidence material, formulating duties of operators, etc. This section will address the type of harm as another criterion, as has been briefly mentioned in 3.7. Design of liability rules. Within the realm of civil law, Wenderhost recognizes two types of risks that entitle a person to compensation. The first is functionality risks, and the second is safety risks. Functionality risks "comprise risks of the software or other product not performing properly, ie the user not getting 'good value for money".[93] An example would be a handwatch with non-functioning arrows. Safety risks encompass "all risks of harm that may be caused to people or to assets and values different from the relevant product itself."[94] An example would be a washing machine that tears clothes. While the first category of risks is regulated by contract law, the second one is subject to tort law and therefore a focus of this work. This author further classifies safety risks based on a number of criteria: 1. the type of harm caused; 2. whether the risks are caused by the free decision of a third party which was in some way instigated or facilitated by the technology or not; 3. whether the harm affects only individuals or has a broader effect on society or economy as a whole; 4. typicality of risk that a person can expect. Depending on the result, the appropriate basis of liability and appropriate defenses are afforded in each situation.

On the more fundamental level, the author argues that strict liability should be limited to physical risks and afforded only if such risks fit the matrix created based on the aforementioned criteria. Conversely, pure economic loss and social risks should be treated differently. The reason for the exclusion of these types of risk is a lack of "general duty not to cause significant immaterial harm of any kind to others

[93] Wendehorst (2020), p. 161.

[94] Ibid.

unless it is caused by qualified non-compliant conduct (such as by infringing the law or by intentionally acting in a way that is incompatible with public policy)".[95] Strict liability prescribed in the legislation is often connected with other regulatory means that ensure ax ante safety (for instance safety regulation) and ex-post swift compensation (for instance mandatory insurance). Providing strict liability for such a broad range of risks without any other general regulation in place might create many difficulties. Moreover, pure economic risk and especially social risks require a different approach. They are less traditional and more subtle. Social risks include the questions of overlap between various liability regimes. For instance, questions of breach of duties of data protection legislation, which rely on non-compliance liability, might overlap with strict liability. This might generate a conundrum hard to solve. Also, a sheer potential of harm in case of social harm and especially pure economic loss which would be dealt with strict liability might open the floodgates as injured parties would have an easier task than in case of fault-based liability.

EU Parliament's Resolution 2020 does not envisage differentiation between types of harm when it affords which types of risks ought to be addressed by strict liability. Recital 16 prescribes that the regime of strict liability it suggests should apply to the "harm or damage to life, health, physical integrity, property and significant immaterial harm that results in a verifiable economic loss above a threshold". It further clarifies that "significant immaterial harm should be understood as meaning harm as a result of which the affected person suffers considerable detriment, an objective and demonstrable impairment of his or her personal interests and an economic loss calculated having regard, for example, to annual average figures of past revenues and other relevant circumstances". Article 2 and Article 3 of the Resolution repeat the wording of the Recital 16 provision. The objections mentioned on account of such an approach merit the adoption of different provisions from what the EU Parliament proposed.

4.5.2.8 Defenses

Defenses applicable in case of strict liability are stipulated in Article 177 of LO:

(1) An owner shall be exempt from liability after proving that injury or loss took place due to a cause outside the object of property, whose effect could not have been foreseen, avoided, or eliminated.
(2) An owner of the object shall also be exempt from liability after proving that injury or loss occurred entirely through an act of the person sustaining injury or loss or a third person, which act could not have been foreseen by him and whose consequences he was not able to avoid or eliminate.
(3) An owner shall be exempt from liability only partially if the person sustaining injury or loss partially contributed to the occurrence of injury or loss.

---

[95] Ibid, 167.

(4) Should injury or loss be partially due to an act of a third person, such person shall be liable to the person suffering injury or loss jointly and severally with the owner of the object of property and shall also be bound to share the amount of compensation proportionally to the degree of his fault.

The first situation is described vis maior defense. In the case of AI accidents, it should be applied as LO requires that the cause has to be outside the object of the property. Clearly, since AI's peculiar characteristics are contained within the object that caused harm, there is no leeway for the application of this defense.

When it comes to the contribution of a third person, a user of AI can potentially rely on the erroneous behavior of manufacturers (in addition to third persons as understood in traditional accidents). However, this would be likely very hard to prove. The difficulty of proving that a manufacturer failed to behave in a required fashion impacts the user's position detrimentally. Therefore, this provision might have a limited reach in reality.

The availability of contributory negligence defense would rely on the specific situation involving AI which is to be determined on a case-by-case basis.

4.6 Product Liability

In many aspects, LO was visionary. Although adopted during the socialist regime, its main features seemed to be apt also for the capitalist market-orientated economy that emerged in B&H after 1995. Such modernity and long-term thinking of the legislators attest to the Yugoslavian endeavor to create a cornerstone of the legal regime with LO. Product liability was not an exception from such a progressive attitude of legislators. Yugoslavian statute on the law of obligations was among the first binding legal instruments in national legal orders in the European states that envisaged product liability. Even before the adoption of LO, Yugoslavian courts demonstrated increased sensibility for the increase of dangerousness generated by mass production and the high technological sophistication of the products.[96] As it has been mentioned before, they developed strict liability as a tool to deal with this issue, along with other problems of increased risk.[97]

The development of law by the courts did not occur in a vacuum. Scholarship at the time supported a position whereby a producer ought to have increased liability

[96] For example: Supreme Court of B&H, Gž. 286/78, od 11. 05. 1978., Bilten Vrhovnog suda BiH, br. 3., Sarajevo, 1978., str. 36.; "U uslovima razvijene proizvodnje i upotrebe trajnih potrošnih dobara (tehničke robe) koja svojim postojanjem i korištenjem stvaraju povećanu opasnost za okolinu, mora se prihvatiti princip objektivne odgovornosti proizvođača za štete koje korisnicima (potrošačima), ili trećim licima, nastanu uslijed nekog skrivenog nedostatka ili osobine proizvedene stvari."

[97] Krulj et al. (1974), p. 8.

for defects of the product.[98] Mihailo Konstantinovic also recognized the validity of such a position. In the draft of the LO, he envisaged product liability in Article 141: "Whoever puts a thing on the market that it has produced, which, due to a defect, of which it was unaware, represents the danger of harm to persons or things, is liable for damage that would occur due to that defect."[99]

Product liability ought to address those situations where the harm is generated by the defective product. The product has to have a defect in order for product liability to be successfully invoked. The problem is thus not a lack of conformity between what was agreed upon and what a purchaser received. Lack of conformity is addressed by LO in Article 121 which prescribes that each party of a contract with consideration shall be liable for the substantive failure of performance. Failure of performance, as envisaged in this provision includes both lack of conformity with what was agreed upon and also a responsibility of a party to protect the other party against third persons' rights and claims concerning the object of their agreement, which might exclude or restrict that party's right. Product liability should also be seen as different from the rules on substantive defects in the product (Article 478–Article 500 of LO) and the rules on warranty for the correct functioning of the object sold (Article 501–Article 507 of LO).

Article 141 of the LO draft, as written by Mihailovic, had not been translated into the final version of LO. However, the intention to provide for grounds that would expand the liability of manufacturers remained. Product liability shields not only parties to the contract involving the sale of a product that was defective. It provided extra-contractual grounds of protection whereby the manufacturer could be liable not only to the persons it negotiated and concluded a contract with but also to all third parties who suffered harm due to the defect of the product.[100]

LO formulates rules on product liability in Article 179. Based on its position in the statute, one can conclude that the rules of strict liability apply. Namely, along with other specific cases, product liability is placed as a ground for the application of strict liability. It has been singled out from the scope of application of the general clause on strict liability. Article 179 consists of two provisions that cover two situations. The first provision states: "Whoever puts on sale an object manufactured by him, which due to a defect unknown to him may cause injury, or loss to persons or property, shall be liable for injury or loss which could ensue due to such defect." The second provision states: "Manufacturer shall be liable for dangerous properties of an object after failing to take all necessary measures to prevent injury or loss, which he was able to foresee, by applying a corresponding warning, safer packaging or some other measure." Obviously, the first situation regulates product liability, and the second situation regulates the liability of manufacturers vis-à-vis dangerous products. The second situation envisaged in Article 179 relies on the foreseeability of a manufacturer who can be shielded from liability if it applies a corresponding

98 Prica (1961), p. 21.; Radišić (1972), pp. 114–117.; Cigoj (1977), pp. 113–114.

99 Author's translation.

100 Bikić (2010b), p. 59.

warning, safer packaging, or some other measures in order to prevent harm.[101] The fact that the manufacturer is not held liable for harm caused by a defective product, according to Article 179, does not mean that is not liable at all. Supreme Court of Serbia has stated that although the manufacturer might be exonerated from product liability, it can nonetheless be subject to fault-based liability.[102]

Also, Article 488 of LO provides for the liability of the seller to the buyer for compensating him for loss sustained by him because of a defect in the goods which caused damage to other property of his, in which case general rules of tort liability shall apply. Although this is a liability for defect, there are some differences compared to Article 179 of LO. First, the responsible party is the seller and not the manufacturer. Second, the applicable basis of liability is a fault. Third, with the exception of buyers, persons who suffered harm due to a defect in the product cannot rely on this provision.

LO is not the only piece of legislation that regulates product liability. The law on consumer protection of B&H,[103] which entered into force in 2006, in Article 24 stipulates that "the manufacturer will be liable for damage caused by a defect in his product in accordance with provisions of the law governing obligations in Bosnia and Herzegovina".[104] This provision does not bring any novelty. A history of consumer protection in B&H attests that the initial intention of the legislator was to create an increased level of protection for consumers compared to what was the law in force at the time. Presumably, due to the political turmoil, the consumer protection framework has never been completed. Bevanda states that it was intended for entities to adopt legislation to fill this gap. FB&H has not adopted a law on this matter yet. Republika Srpska has adopted its Law on Consumer Protection[105] but it does not provide any additional rules. In Article 34 of this instrument, it is prescribed that the manufacturer is liable for harm caused by the defect in the product under the obligation law rules in Republika Srpska. As LO is in force in Republika Srpska, it seems that this provision does not bring anything new.

Consumer protection law of B&H in Article 1 and Consumer protection law in Republika Srpska in Article 2 define a consumer as a natural person who uses products for their personal needs and the needs of their households. This means that legal persons and natural persons who use products for purposes other than their personal needs and the needs of their households are excluded from the scope of application of these instruments. Such limitation, however, does not seem to limit the reach of product liability. First, both instruments only refer to LO without providing consumers with any new right concerning product liability. Second, LO itself

---

[101] Karanikić Mirić (2005), p. 164.

[102] Supreme Court of Serbia, Rev. 368/96 od 29. oktobra 1997. godine, Zbirka sudskih odluka, kw. 23, sv. I, 102, 1999, in Ibid.

[103] Official Gazette B&H number 25, 04. April 2006.

[104] Author's translation.

[105] Official Gazette of Republika Srpska 6/2012, 63/2014, 18/2017, 90/2021.

guarantees product liability protection to all persons who suffered harm from the defective product. A list of persons entitled to compensation is not limited to natural persons and it is not limited by the purpose of use of the product.

As it is regulated within the section of LO devoted to strict liability for an object of increased dangerousness, causation is presumed and can be rebutted by the producer.[106] Such a solution is very favorable as causation might be increasingly hard for an injured party in accidents involving sophisticated technologies.[107] For example, how should causation be demonstrated when an AI system makes a decision based on flawed data it processed, when harm arises from a device whose hardware and software come from separate manufacturers due to the openness of digital ecosystems, or when a user has added software to the original equipment manufacturer's programs or altered the functioning of pre-installed software? Moreover, as there is generally no requirement or recording and tracing one's digital devices, there may be a problem with the obtainment of evidence once an accident occurs.[108]

There is no limitation on the type of harm product liability applies in LO. This is different from what PLD envisages as it limits it to specific types of harm. Suggestions made by scholarship concerning the recognition of new types of harm, such as loss of data and harm to digital content[109] can be derived by the courts from the law as it is, without the need for legislative intervention.

4.6.1 Lack of Clarity and Potential Obsolesce

Despite being visionary at the time of its adoption, LO has not changed since 1978 in the part concerning product liability. In the meantime, a significant development occurred in the EU which inevitably impacted the understanding of this field in B&H and other states that apply Yugoslavian LO. First, there has been harmonization of product liability by means of the Product Liability Directive[110] in 1985. However, directive as a type of instrument does not necessarily guarantee complete harmonization of law. Although PLD has been transposed by all EU Member States, this field remains to be divergent throughout the EU. Along with differences in the transposition of PLD, national legal regimes envisage different avenues that act as

---

106 Supreme Court of Serbia, Rev. 4206/94; Bikić (2010b), p. 58.

107 See Gifford (2017).

108 Martín-Casals (2019a, b), p. 132.

109 European Law Institute, Guiding Principles for Updating the Product Liability Directive for the Digital Age, 2021, available at: https://europeanlawinstitute.eu/fileadmin/user_upload/p_eli/Publications/ELI_Guiding_Principles_for_Updating_the_PLD_for_the_Digital_Age.pdf, 8.

110 Council Directive 85/374/EEC of 25 July 1985 on the approximation of the laws, regulations and administrative provisions of the Member States concerning liability for defective products [1985] OJ L210/29, as amended by Directive 1999/34/EC of the European Parliament and of the Council of 10 May 1999 [1999] OJ L141/20.

alternatives or supplements for obtaining compensation apart from product liability. Even though there had been an effort to introduce legislation that would harmonize the liability of service providers on the EU level as a parallel set of rules that would coexist with the PLD, the proposed directive failed to become a binding legal instrument,[111] rendering PLD the only EU binding instrument of general application dealing with the matter of extracontractual liability.

Recently, due to technological development, PLD became a subject of revision by the EU. The new understanding of product liability needs to provide answers to the questions of defective products of twenty-first century which are not covered by existing rules at all or in a satisfying manner. The aforementioned Expert Group established by the EU Commission dedicates one of its two formations to this question—the Product Liability Directive Formation. Some of the problems with product liability in LO stem simply from the lack of legislative updates. The terminology used in this instrument is very general and creates vagueness. It fails to provide clarity for courts and parties. Some of the states that succeeded LO had in the meantime amended it or provided for lex specialis statutes on product liability. Similar objections can be made on the account of PLD. This allows us to assess LO's suitability for AI accidents regarding the problems currently being discussed concerning PLD.

However, there are also certain differences. The scholarship has identified several shortcomings of PLD over issues that are not technology-related, such as the 500 euros remuneration threshold,[112] or the exclusion of property losses related to the property that in general is not ordinarily intended for private use or consumption and was used by the injured person mainly for his own private use or consumption.[113] Those will not be discussed if they are only PLD-specific and do not exist in LO.[114]

4.6.2 *Time of Placing the Product on the Market*

Article 179 of LO provides that the liability of the manufacturer is related to the moment of placing the product on the market. Scholarship deems this point in time as very important as the product has to be defective at this moment. If it becomes defective later, product liability is not applicable.[115]

---

[111] European Commission, 'Proposal for a Council Directive on the liability of suppliers of services' COM (90) 482 final [1991] OJ C12/8.

[112] Koch (2019), p. 103.

[113] Wagner (2017).

[114] Such view does not attempt to minimize B&H's obligation to align its law with acquis communitaire, as this obligation stems from the The Stabilisation and Association Agreement.

[115] Bevanda (2007), p. 33.

AI is likely to be updated over a long distance by manufacturers. The moment of putting of product on the market is not as decisive as is the case of traditional products. For example, it is possible that an AI-driven fridge was not defective at the time of sale to the buyer, but due to an erred update, it became such. Consequently, it caused all items in the fridge to become unusable.

There has been a shift at the moment until a manufacturer can extend its impact on AI. Unlike traditional products where this moment corresponds with the time of putting the product on the market, AI manufacturers are likely to continue updating the product. One might argue that not every AI does not require updates. However, due to its autonomy and opacity, manufacturers are in the best position to control it. They should be able to extend their impact over AI not only because they might want to improve the product over time, but also to provide a guarantee that they will prevent or stop undesired AI behavior. Finally, "the victim should not be burdened with proving whether a flaw in the product resulted from its original state or a subsequent update to pre-installed software".[116]

The proper solution would be therefore to change LO to reflect this feature of AI. Instead of limiting product liability to the moment of placing AI on the market, it should be extended to cover its entire lifetime. This is closely related to the notion of product.

4.6.3 Notion of Product

LO does not define a product. It also does not provide criteria whereby it can be assessed what is a product. It only mentions that it has to be manufactured by a person who will be held liable in case of harm caused by its defect. The Law on Consumer Protection of B&H and Law on Consumer Protection of Republika Srpska define the notion of product. According to Article 1 of the Law on Consumer Protection of B&H, a product is "any thing created as a result of human activity intended for consumers or it is likely to be used by consumers, delivered, whether paid or not, in progress commercial activities, and whether new, used or refurbished".[117] According to Article 2 of Law on consumer protection of Republika Srpska, a product is "any good or service that can be traded, including public services, facilities, rights, and obligations".[118] Obviously, the two definitions are different. The Law on consumer protection of Republika Srpska provides for a broader definition that covers not only things but also services.

However, due to the inherent lack of general application of consumer protection laws on legal persons and natural persons who use products for means other than

[116] Response of the European Law Institute, Public Consultation on Civil Liability Adapting liability rules to the digital age and artificial intelligence, 2022, available at: https://europeanlawinstitute.eu/fileadmin/user_upload/p_eli/Publications/ELI_Response_to_Public_Consultation_on_Civil_Liability.pdf, 10.

[117] Author's translation.

[118] Author's translation.

their capacity and their household, these definitions of product do not apply to persons who have a product liability claim based on LO. What a product means for a consumer does not have to be the case with a company that has a product liability claim. Additionally, the Law on consumer protection of Republika Srpska defines "dangerous product". A dangerous product, according to Article 2, is a product that is not safe and means products that do not meet the characteristics and standards of safe products under the law. The Law on consumer protection of B&H does not provide this definition. However, even if there was a definition applicable to the entire territory of B&H, a dangerous product does not constitute a defective product.

It would be necessary to provide predictability of law throughout B&H by means of providing the same definitions of terms. Currently, there is a lack of such clarity due to the lack of any definition in LO and the existence of different definitions in consumer protection legislation on the state level and entity levels. Lack of harmonization operates on two levels. First, definitions applicable to consumers vary in entities. What might qualify as a product in FB&H might not be in Republika Srpska, and vice versa. Second, the definition of product applicable to consumers might not apply to other victims. It would be advisable to define this notion for the entire territory and all potential victims.

Along with harmonization, an understanding of a product should pass the digital fitness check. The product should be understood as to include what has already become very important—digital content. It remains unclear how the courts would interpret the likes of software or other types of digital content. This problem is characteristic for PLD too but in a different fashion. Namely, Article 2 of PLD defines a product as movables, with the exception of primary agricultural products, even though incorporated into another movable or into an immovable. It also includes electricity in this definition. The problems with the inclusion of AI and other non-tangible content is twofold:

1. whether a product encompass a tangible (corporeal) object that incorporates AI (and other digital content)—a robot, as we named in Chap. 2?
2. whether a product encompass a non-tangible AI, so-called standalone AI?

Examples of robots are self-driving vehicles and AI-driven vacuum cleaners. An example of standalone AI is an application one installs on a phone. Both of these forms in which AI appears should be included in the notion of product. In the realm of digital technologies, the physical item might be less valuable or significant than the AI and other forms of associated digital content. Moreover, once the digital content requires internet connectivity and is periodically updated, it might be less clear-cut whether a problem with the digital content could be treated as a problem with the physical item itself".[119] In the case of standalone AI, it is clear that it cannot

[119] European Law Institute, Guiding Principles for Updating the Product Liability Directive for the Digital Age, 2021, available at: https://europeanlawinstitute.eu/fileadmin/user_upload/p_eli/Publications/ELI_Guiding_Principles_for_Updating_the_PLD_for_the_Digital_Age.pdf, 5.

fit under the notion of the product as defined in PLD.[120] It limits the scope of application to movables and explicitly excludes electricity. In conclusion, PLD should clearly define that both types of AI and other digital content should be treated as products.

The problem with B&H law is different as there is no definition of a product that would apply to all products and that all persons could rely on. A solution would to be provide a definition of the product in LO, a generally applicable instrument and not in consumer protection legislation. Such a definition should include both forms in which AI appears—robot and stand-alone. As LO's are regulated on the entity level, harmonized actions are favorable. A definition can be provided in light of the recent EU legislation on digital content and digital products. Notions of digital content and digital services, as they are defined in Article 2 of Directive 2019/770/EU[121] reflect the gist of this idea:

(1) 'digital content' means data that are produced and supplied in digital form.
(2) 'digital service' means: (a) a service that allows the consumer to create, process, store, or access data in digital form; or (b) a service that allows the sharing of or any other interaction with data in digital form uploaded or created by the consumer or other users of that service.

4.6.4 Notion of Producer

LO does not define the term producer. The wording of the first provision of Article 179 in fact omits to mention this word. Instead, it stipulates that "whoever" puts a product on the market it manufactured is liable. There are no explicit rules for product liability that would cover the situation where more than one person might be liable for harm caused by a defective product. However, general rules on strict liability as lex generali apply to product liability. Provisions contained in Article 206, Article 207, and Article 208 provide for joint and several liability of all persons who participated in the manufacturing and deployment of a product whose defect caused harm. After the injured party obtains relief from any of them, they are entitled to a right of recourse. Bevanda claims that not only a producer of the final product can be sued. An injured party can also seek redress from the manufacturer of a part of the product and deployer.[122] Bikić, on the other hand, understands that only the producer of a final product can be held liable, and not the producer of parts of the

[120] Wagner (2021), p. 548.

[121] Directive (EU) 2019/770 of the European Parliament and of the Council of 20 May 2019 on certain aspects concerning contracts for the supply of digital content and digital services (Text with EEA relevance.).

PE/26/2019/REV/1.

[122] Bevanda (2007), p.

product.[123] In any case, the liability of all producers would be strict. The finality of the product as a concept seems unviable in the case of AI because, as it has been elaborated, AI has the potential to be updated even after it leaves the possession of manufacturers and deployers.

LO envisages a very favorable avenue for a victim in case of AI accidents. This is emphasized by the opacity of AI. Namely, due to a potential lack of understanding of the defect and who of the responsible persons is liable, the victim would not have to make any deliberations. Moreover, LO in Article 208 provides a rule whereby in case it is impossible to assess the contribution of liable parties to the harm each shall bear an equal share unless equity requires otherwise in proceeding with the specific case. A recourse between potentially liable parties will be addressed in detail later. In any case, should amendments of PLD occur, lawmakers in B&H should consider whether it is important to address whether the rules of recourse are aligned with those.[124] This is especially so as it could be expected that producers, as considered in LO, could come from various countries.

Lastly, the notion of the producer should be aligned with the potential of AI to be updated, as we have mentioned before. Persons who have to provide updates on AI should be considered manufacturers too. This is also the case with persons who significantly modify used AI and place it back on the market. The lack of a problem that scholarship recognized in the case of PLD. PLD presupposes that there is a linear distribution model where, once finished and put on the market, products no longer can be impacted by producers. "PLD's definition of 'producer' is required to reflect the fact that the linear approach with a defined point at which a product is brought into circulation no longer reflects current production and distribution models."[125]

4.6.5 *Notion of Defect*

There is no definition of a product in LO. Scholarship considers that all defects can be classified as factory defects, construction defects, development defects, and industrial defects. Factory defects are the result of an error in the manufacturing process. Construction defects occur due to an error in the planning or design of a product. Development defects exist due to the lack of knowledge in science or a

---

[123] Bikić (2010b), p. 59.

[124] European Law Institute, Guiding Principles for Updating the Product Liability Directive for the Digital Age, 2021, available at: https://europeanlawinstitute.eu/fileadmin/user_upload/p_eli/Publications/ELI_Guiding_Principles_for_Updating_the_PLD_for_the_Digital_Age.pdf, 11.

[125] European Law Institute, Guiding Principles for Updating the Product Liability Directive for the Digital Age, 2021, available at: https://europeanlawinstitute.eu/fileadmin/user_upload/p_eli/Publications/ELI_Guiding_Principles_for_Updating_the_PLD_for_the_Digital_Age.pdf, 6.

particular discipline. Industrial defects are related to the lack of instructions or warnings a manufacturer has to provide.[126]

LO does not instruct courts on how they should assess whether there is a defect. The definition of a defect in PLD is determined through the reference to the standard of safety that a person is entitled to expect, measured at the time when the product was put into circulation. At this point, a distinction between flaws in AI itself and flaws in the objects controlled or powered by AI appears as significant. Issues with the objects fall under the existing definition of defects under the PLD and do not pose significant challenges. However, if defects arise due to human mistakes—such as errors in design, manufacturing, or inadequate user instructions or warnings—the liability for resulting damage should rest with the manufacturers. The question becomes more complex when no human error is involved, and the damage stems from the autonomous decision-making of AI.

Another question is how to define safety standards AI ought to comply with. PLD is silent. Traditional methods of establishing defects employed by the courts are not well suited to be applied to AI. The most common method is to compare the performance of a product with comparable products. It remains unclear whether AI should be compared to the performance of humans or the performance of other AI in similar situations.[127] This is an issue that requires the attention of lawmakers and scholars. Courts in B&H should also endeavour to adopt a test whereby defects in AI could be assessed. It is hard to establish it at the moment and the developments in comparative law should be observed.

Once the appropriate test is established, there is no need for any legislative action in B&H for it to become used by courts. An example would be to consider ethical guidelines as a matter of design. If there is a lack of conformity between AI and these rules, the courts can find such a product to be defective. Michal Cannarsa even introduces the idea of presumption of a defect in all situations that include lack of conformity with ethical guidelines.[128] Such an approach, of course, requires ethical guidelines to exist in the first place, and the development of which is a complex process in itself. Nonetheless, this might be useful as a long-term plan to establish a yardstick. Establishing defects is closely related to the applicable safety standards. As we have established before since the creation of general safety standards for AI is characterized by high difficulty which renders it unforeseeable to happen in the near future, the development of standards related to sectors where we are familiar with AI and its modus operandi is a realistic avenue at the moment.

[126] Vizner (1978).

[127] Ibid, 71.

[128] Cannarsa (2021), p. 208.

4.6.6 Defenses

There are no defenses in LO that are specific to product liability. As general rules on strict liability apply, applicable defenses are defined in Article 177 of LO.

In general, defenses are very broadly formulated and allow courts to apply to a broad category of situations. As it refers to some of the specific points related to AI and emerging digital technologies, I will below refer to specific defenses in light of this discussion.

PLD regulates defenses that can be invoked in case of product liability. We have already addressed the defense prescribed whereby a producer might not be liable if it proves that, having regard to the circumstances, it is probable that the defect which caused the damage did not exist at the time when the product was put into circulation by him or that this defect came into being afterwards. Time of putting the product on the market requires a different understanding and this novelty renders fixation of liability to a specific point in time unviable.

The most widely discussed defense in PLD is the so-called development risk defence. It stipulates that the producer shall not be liable if he proves that the state of scientific and technical knowledge at the time when he put the product into circulation was not such as to enable the existence of the defect to be discovered. This provision ought to protect producers from those events which could not be foreseen and prevented. Although PLD prescribes this defense, not all European states provide it in their national laws. Examples are Luxembourg and Finland.[129] The reason is Article 18 of PLD which allows the Member States to derogate from the development riks defense and provide in their legislation that the producer shall be liable even if it proves that the state of scientific and technical knowledge at the time when he put the product into circulation was not such as to enable the existence of a defect to be discovered. Radišić pointed out that LO classifies objects as dangerous and non-dangerous and not based on whether they have known or unknown defects.[130] As Karanikić Mirić points out, the producer cannot be exonerated from liability for harm by proving that the defect was incalculable or that it could not have been discovered at the time the object was put on the market.[131] ELI suggests that development risk defense should be thoroughly revisited in light of AI if not completely left from PLD. It argues that "the 'state of scientific and technical knowledge' would have to be specified, considering the vast expansion of (particularly online) available information as compared to the late 1970s when the PLD was first drafted".[132] It seems that LO's solution of this problem can meet the test of

[129] Karanikić Mirić (2005), p. 170.

[130] Radišić (1995), p. 142.

[131] Karanikić Mirić (2005), p. 167.

[132] Response of the European Law Institute, Public Consultation on Civil Liability Adapting liability rules to the digital age and artificial intelligence, 2022, available at: https://europeanlawinstitute.eu/fileadmin/user_upload/p_eli/Publications/ELI_Response_to_Public_Consultation_on_Civil_Liability.pdf, 21.

technological fitness. A traditional argument against development risk defense is that "whenever the injured person sues somebody other than the manufacturer or whenever he gives up his compensation claim, then product liability law fails to fulfill the deterrence function which was one of the reasons for its implementation".[133] The same objection can be made in the case of AI. The argument is even emphasized as the control over AI is expected to remain at least partially in the hands of producers even after the product is sold, as it is prone to updates. Allowing development risk defense in case of AI accidents would deteriorate the deterrent effect of tort law and potentially even the compensatory effect.

A new defense should be considered in light of AI's openness. Harm involving AI could emerge not only due to defective technology but also if it is provided with external data that is clearly unsuitable. This idea guarantees that the producer might not be liable in those situations where it has objectively undertaken all measures to prevent accidents related to its product, but it occurred due to malfunction of AI notwithstanding.[134] If externally supplied data caused the malfunction, and AI was equipped sufficiently with means to filter erroneous data which could not prevent an accident, a producer should be exonerated. As with other defenses, the producer should be appointed with the burden of proof that it was not the product/system itself that led to the injury or damage but that instead externally-supplied data did".[135] In the upcoming revision of PLD, it can be expected that the EU lawmakers will consider this proposal. This, too, should be the case with B&H lawmakers. LO should be amended to include this consideration. In theory, it is possible to interpret existing LO's defenses and include externally supplied data defense. This is supported by the finding that the courts take into account the findings that the injured party had or could have had about the existence of a defect.[136] However, the vague wording of available defenses and potential underlying lack of knowledge of the courts on the technology might render it hard to be successfully invoked by the producer. The explicit defense provided in the LO that would take into account digital technologies would not only provide certainty to producers but also instructions to the courts and injured parties.

Furthermore, a situation where more than one manufacturer provides components of digital products should be addressed for the same reasons. As we can see, there is a disagreement over whether only a final producer can be held liable or the victim can also sue producers of the components. The conundrum is even more complex when products involve AI and other digital technologies pa their parts. For instance, it is unclear whether a producer of a non-tangible AI could be treated as a producer of

---

[133] Rajneri (2005), p. 80.

[134] Response of the European Law Institute, Public Consultation on Civil Liability Adapting liability rules to the digital age and artificial intelligence, 2022, available at: https://europeanlawinstitute.eu/fileadmin/user_upload/p_eli/Publications/ELI_Response_to_Public_Consultation_on_Civil_Liability.pdf, 19.

[135] Ibid.

[136] Karanikić Mirić (2005), p. 167.

a component under Article 179 of LO. The relationship between AI and other tangible and non-tangible components, as well as the relationship of those components, remains unclear. First, as it had been suggested, all manufacturers should be treated as potential defenders. However, due to this complexity, they should be provided with a defense akin to what is intended in Article 7 paragraph (f): "The producer shall not be liable as a result of this Directive if he proves... in the case of a manufacturer of a component, that the defect is attributable to the design of the product in which the component has been fitted or to the instructions given by the manufacturer of the product". A defense that takes into account such situations, provided that it is modified to reflect changes in technology that occurred since 1985, should be adopted by the legislator in B&H. Its adoption would provide relief to the courts who would not have to struggle to fathom complex relationships that exist on the side of manufacturers and interpret them in light of vague defenses in LO. ELI suggests that the new definition should provide clarity as to what constitutes a component of a product and that producers of digital components, such as AI, should have this defense unequivocally at their disposal.[137]

4.7 Vicarious Liability

Vicarious liability treats situations where an auxiliary acts on behalf of a person who is wither responsible or in charge of it.[138] The fundamental principle behind it is described in the Latin maxim *respondeat superior, ubi commoda et eius incommode*, whereby the person in charge who extends control or influence over their agent ought to be liable for the actions of the agent. Provided that AI can be differentiated from traditional inventions that we traditionally understand as technical means used by humans, applying vicarious liability would mean that AI is more than that. Instead of means, it is perceived as auxiliary. The employment of vicarious liability would rely on the presumption that AI is functionally comparable to human labor insofar as it is empowered to conduct an autonomous decision-making process. The purpose of the application of this basis of liability would be to disallow the avoidance of liability from the principal despite the autonomous behavior of the agent.

LO regulates vicarious liability in two subsections. The first subsection is titled vicarious liability (164–169) and the second subsection is titled Liability of enterprises and other legal persons (170–172). Although the two subsections have different titles, both cover the liability of one person for the actions of another

[137] Response of the European Law Institute, Public Consultation on Civil Liability Adapting liability rules to the digital age and artificial intelligence, 2022, available at: https://europeanlawinstitute.eu/fileadmin/user_upload/p_eli/Publications/ELI_Response_to_Public_Consultation_on_Civil_Liability.pdf, 21.

[138] See PETL, Title III, Ch 6. See also Revolidis and Dahi (2018).

person. Vicarious liability operates as an exception in LO from the rule that one can be liable for its actions. A general rule is that bears individual responsibility, like in criminal law. Such liability can be fault-based and strict. Exceptionally, liability can also be based on equity. When it comes to liability for actions of other persons, LO provides it as an exception that does not exist in criminal law. A consequence of its specific status is reflected in the reduced scope of application of vicarious liability—it can be applied only when it has been explicitly prescribed by the law.

A potential value of vicarious liability has been recognized in the Report.[139] It recognizes that "the concept of vicarious liability is considered by some as a possible catalyst for arguing that operators of machines, computers, robots or similar technologies should also be strictly liable for their operations, based on an analogy to the basis of vicarious liability. If someone can be held liable for the wrongdoing of some human helper, why should the beneficiary of such support not be equally liable if they outsource their duties to a non-human helper instead, considering that they equally benefit from such delegation?"[140] Therefore, it can be argued that, despite AI's specific characteristics, it is important to consider it equivalent to agents which the law traditionally considers apt for establishing principal's liability. LO regulates liability for harm caused by mentally ill or incapacitated persons, liability for harm caused by children and minors, and liability for harm caused by employees and legal person's bodies. As it will be demonstrated, all available types of vicarious liability cannot be successfully applied to AI for different underlying reasons.

4.7.1 Liability for Children and Liability for Mentally Ill or Incapacitated Persons

Article 165 LO prescribes that parents shall be liable for loss or injury caused to another by their child. The basis of liability depends on the age of a child. If a child is up to the age of 7, it cannot be held liable. In the period from 7 to 14 age of life, there is a rebuttable legal presumption of lack of a child's capacity to reason and be itself liable. The third category regulates the liability of children of age 14 and older. There is a legal presumption of their capacity which can be rebutted.[141] The degree of a child's responsibility corresponds to the level of parents' exposure. If a child is up to the age of 7, parents' liability is strict. If a child is between 7 and 18 years of age, the parent's liability is fault-based.[142] Moreover, if a child's liability coexisted simultaneously, it is jointly and severally liable to the parents.[143]

---

[139] Report, 24 et al.

[140] Ibid.

[141] Vizner (1978), p. 689.

[142] Vedriš and Klarić (2000), p. 579.

[143] Bikić (2010b), p. 53.

Parents can be exonerated by invoking defenses available for the respective basis of liability. Also, they can prove that harm occurred while the child was committed to another person's care and if such a person was liable for loss or injury. An exception from this rule exists in an injured person proves that the child caused harm due to erroneous education and family habits.[144] Then, it can choose between suing the person who had a duty to care for a child and parents.

Mentally ill or incapacitated persons are, along with children, natural persons who cannot be liable in civil law. Just like in the case of liability for children, the law prescribes that a person who had a duty to supervise such person shall be liable for harm it causes. The liability of these persons is, unlike in the case of children, always fault-based.[145] According to Article 164 of LO, they may protect themselves from liability if they prove that they applied due control, or that harm would have ensued anyhow, regardless of applying diligent supervision.

As it has been mentioned in Sect. 4.5.1.5. Liability based on equity, parents, and persons who had a duty of supervision of minors can be held liable even if the strict liability was not applicable and their behavior lacked fault, due to the reasons of equity. Also, even the property of a child without the capacity to be held liable can be used for the same reason. Akin to liability for children, liability based on equity is applicable also in the case of mentally ill or incapacitated persons.

So, although liability based on equity creates the possibility of an incompetent person being responsible for their actions, it can only do so if an actor has the status of a person. AI does not have personhood according to B&H. Moreover, it only makes sense to burden AI with duty if it had its property, which it cannot have without legal personhood. AI cannot be qualified as a child or a mentally ill or incapacitated person. An analogy can be made with the liability of a legal entity for its bodies because they are not legal entities, but the rules on liability based on equity do not apply in those situations. They apply only in case of liability for children and mentally ill or incapacitated persons only to legal entities and not natural persons. Liability based on equity cannot, therefore, be a solution because it is provided as an exception and not an equal basis of responsibility. Despite the aforementioned practice of the courts applying LO that demonstrates flexibility in understanding equity, rules contained in the provision of Article 164–Article 169 of LO cannot be construed as including AI in the provision due to these deficiencies.

4.7.2 *Liability for Harm Caused by Employees and Legal Person's Bodies*

LO provides for the liability of legal persons for actions or omissions caused by its employees and its bodies. There is a dispute over whether liability for employees is

[144] Ibid, 54.

[145] Karanikić Mirić (2016b), p. 580.

fault-based or strict.[146] Scholarship considers that it depends on whether an employee acted as it should have in given circumstances. According to this interpretation, fault-based liability is increased. An employee has to exercise care as a good expert, a higher degree of prudence than a good person.[147] A legal person paying damages to a victim caused by an employee who acted intentionally with gross negligence shall be entitled to recover from such employee the amount paid. If there are no such degrees of fault, an employer cannot seek recourse. Furthermore, if business activities increase the risk of injury they can be considered to bear increased dangerousness, such as occupational disease, "courts tend to establish employers' liability in these cases as an instance of strict liability for dangerous activities".[148] Therefore, an employer's liability is assessed on the same or increased standards compared to the liability of an individual who is not an expert.

Bikić notes that in order for liability for an employee to be established, a few conditions need to be met:

1. a person who caused harm has to have the status of an employee;
2. harm has to be related to the work;
3. The employee failed to act as he should have in the given circumstances.[149]

There are many problems with the application of liability for employees to AI. First, AI cannot be treated as an employee. Only natural persons can be employees. Perović notes that the term employee should be construed in line with labor law.[150] In other words, there is no leeway for functional interpretation which would allow understanding of autonomous agents as employees. Second, harm should not be related to work. Since there is employee personal liability for harms that are not work-related, LO does not leave a gap. Victims can fairly easily point a finger at somebody notwithstanding what is the context in which harm occurs. The situation in the case of AI is different. It does not have free time, and it does not have voluntary actions. Moreover, it does not have personhood and property to repay the harm. Therefore, all harm caused by AI should be covered by its principal, despite the context. Finally, the phrase "given circumstances" can be interpreted broadly. It can be understood to require a comparison of the behavior of AI with other AI or other employees. This standard should be interpreted by human employees as a benchmark, and it should be raised over time to reflect AI's expected improvement. Due to the vagueness of this standard and other mentioned problems, liability for employees is inoperable in AI-caused accidents.

A legal person can also be liable for harm caused by its bodies in connection to performing its functions, regardless of whether they are composed of individuals or a group of persons. Akin to the case of an employee, a legal person can seek recourse

[146] Karanikić Mirić (2016b), p. 581.
[147] Ibid.
[148] Karanikić Mirić (2017), p. 356.
[149] Bikić (2010b), p. 58 et al.
[150] Perović (1980), p. 520.

from a person who caused harm intentionally or with gross negligence. As Vedriš and Klarić note, the reason why LO posits liability of legal persons for harm caused by its bodies under the section on vicarious liability is that, *in ultima linea*, liability for harm would be attributed to a specific natural person who acted with a legal person's body.[151] Other interpretations would be unfeasible as bodies of legal persons are not persons themselves and thereby cannot be held liable. This interpretation of the liability of natural persons for actions and omissions of its body renders the application of AI non-feasible.

Moreover, rules on liability for employees and bodies apply only if the legal person is the principal. This solution is therefore not comprehensive as it would not solve a situation where a natural person is involved as principal.

4.7.3 Liability for Animals

Animals are functionally equivalent to AI for many reasons. Humans can impact and dictate their behavior. They are nonetheless autonomous. One cannot expect that an animal will act exclusively in accordance with instructions.

What is also important is that animals are not a new phenomenon in civil law. Codifications around the world have rules on keeping animals, and the relationship between people vis-à-vis animals. Those include liability for harm animals cause to persons. LO does not regulate this issue explicitly. Courts have applied general rules of liability to establish a specific regime for animals. It should be noted that vicarious liability is not applicable here, mainly due to the same reasons it cannot be applied to AI. However, the relationship between a human and an animal resembles the relationship between a principal and an agent. Yugoslavian courts apply rules on strict liability to animals.[152] As they do not have personhood, they are considered rather an auxiliary of a person who is held liable. All animals are a source of increased dangerousness for persons who have a duty to supervise, and they are liable without regard to fault. There is no difference between domesticated and wild animals. Courts held that a reindeer[153] as well as a pig[154] merit strict liability. As Karanikić Mirić notes, animals are considered to bear increased dangerousness as long as they are alive, and sometimes also after their death.[155]

Furthermore, the courts held that the mere fact that an animal is hard to control by the person who had such a duty is enough to establish strict liability.[156] Clearly, they have established that increased dangerousness can be interpreted as including

[151] Karanikić Mirić (2016b), p. 581.

[152] Supreme Court of Slovenia Gž. 11/1966 and Gž. 1148/58.

[153] Supreme Court of Slovenia, Ips 142/1980 i 143/1980.

[154] Supreme Court of Serbia, Rev. 3454/2004.

[155] Karanikić Mirić (2016a), p. 161.

[156] Supreme Court of Serbia, 3393/92.

problems of control. Animals can move autonomously and as such, they were considered to pose an increased threat to their environment.

There seem to be many parallels between the treatment of animals with the treatment of AI. Just like animals, AI acts autonomously and can become better over time in what it does. However, it seems excessively burdensome to apply strict liability in all cases including AI. Unlike animals, AI is a human creation. The black box has been created by humans and over time, it can be better understood by humans. We may understand the modus operandi of AI on the most fundamental level better than animals because we design it. Even though human interaction with animals has occurred for millennia, arguably we have not mastered it as accidents involving animals occur in modern times. Clearly, there are rules on how to keep persons and property around animals safe and even how to train animals, but our understanding has never become so profound that we can be sure an animal is going to behave in a desired way without exceptions. On the other hand, since we are at the beginning of applying AI in certain fields, we can predict and regulate its behavior by imposing specific duties on persons who can impact it. At least, we may have a better chance than in the case of animals. Perhaps our capability to do so is currently limited, but in specific sectors where AI is applied, the goal of understanding and controlling AI may be reachable. By setting strict liability for AI in stone, we are heading towards a belief that this goal cannot be reached. Lastly, an argument about incentivizing innovation should not be forgotten. This is also where a parallel with animals does not stand.

The exclusive application of strict liability to animals is not very spread in Europe. In other European regimes, an owner or a keeper would be subject to fault-based liability. Commonly, owners or keepers of the animals can prove that they took all reasonable measures to avoid the occurrence of the loss caused by the animal.[157] LO is very strict in this respect. Being subject to strict liability, a defendant can only invoke a limited set of defenses. Extending the application of liability rules for accidents caused by animals in B&H does not have to follow the logic domestic courts utilize in the establishment of the basis of liability. A problem of causation is also non-existent as there is a presumption of fault an owner or a keeper has to rebut, which is not the case with all European regimes.

While the logic of understanding AI as human auxiliaries just like animals seems sound, an absolute application of strict liability is excessive and should be reduced to a fault in situations when the threat to AI's environment is insignificant and our understanding of AI and the duties of humans behind it is clear. A search of those situations is valuable, if for no other reason, than for the sake of stimulating innovation.

---

[157] Response of the European Law Institute, Public Consultation on Civil Liability Adapting liability rules to the digital age and artificial intelligence, 2022, available at: https://europeanlawinstitute.eu/fileadmin/user_upload/p_eli/Publications/ELI_Response_to_Public_Consultation_on_Civil_Liability.pdf, 31.

4.8 Non-Compliance Liability

Non-compliance liability refers to those cases when harm arises from the pure lack of compliance with some established rule. This regulatory technique is common in the classic tort law that deals with the assessment of one's behavior. Rather, in case of lack of compliance, a person is automatically held liable. Moreover, the exact amount of damage does not need to be established. An example of non-compliance liability is prescribed in Article 82 of GDPR. It stipulates that:

(1) Any person who has suffered material or non-material damage as a result of an infringement of this Regulation shall have the right to receive compensation from the controller or processor for the damage suffered.
(2) Any controller involved in processing shall be liable for the damage caused by processing which infringes this Regulation. A processor shall be liable for the damage caused by processing only where it has not complied with obligations of this Regulation specifically directed to processors or where it has acted outside or contrary to lawful instructions of the controller.

Non-compliance liability for AI performs a significant role. It can be used in all those situations where the activities are undertaken were per se prohibited. In other words, for non-compliance liability to exist in the first place, there would need to be a specific set of duties that persons who are participating in the development, deployment, or use of AI need to obey. Before this type of liability becomes operable, technical standards need to be adopted for a particular application of AI. Furthermore, certain policy choices should be made as well, such as whether a complete ban on the use of AI for biometric identification should be instituted. Thereby, we might expect non-compliance liability to become an important piece of the regulatory puzzle once later, but not at the outset where the fluidity of the field and lack of agreement on many issues, even the most fundamental ones, is pending.

Once the rules have been established, a person can claim compensation merely due to the lack of compliance, without the need to prove any specific harm suffered. Akin to GDPR, the notion of harm should not be limited to material or immaterial harm. This would be in line with what LO prescribes.

4.9 Contractual and Extracontractual Liability

Imagine a situation where a person purchased a home appliance containing a latent defect. In a couple of days, the device induced a fire damaging the buyer's apartment. A buyer has a contractual claim as the product was defective. The next question is whether it can cumulate contractual with a non-contractual claim for other harm suffered. Legal regimes around Europe provide different answers to this question. English law, German law, and Austrian law allow for the cumulation of the contractual and non-contractual basis of liability.[158] On the other hand, French law explicitly bars one to pursue two different types of claims by imposing a doctrine known as non-cumul. This question is important for AI accidents as well. Imagine if there is an accident involving a home appliance that operates on the basis of AI. The problem would be even extended to the question of whether and how AI's autonomous and unpredictable behavior could oblige manufacturer and seller based on the contract with the purchaser. For the sake of having timely and complete compensation, it is important to have the position of the injured party preserved at the level it used to be in traditional accidents.

LO does not explicitly provide an answer to this question. There is a disagreement in both scholarship and case law, especially when there is an additional statute that regulates a certain profession. The two dominant positions in scholarship are opposite. The first one is called the theory of individual liability, whereby a person can be liable on basis of either breach of a contractual obligation or tort rules. The second one argues that they can be cumulated.[159] Case law demonstrates that the courts also did not establish a firm position, according to the survey conducted by Milica Panic.[160] The Supreme Court of Croatia held that harm caused by a dentist consisting of fracture of a patient's mandibula is contractual and not contractual harm.[161] This author concluded the position of this court was not undisputed by other courts who applied LO. Contrary, Slovenian law allows patients to cumulate contractual and tortious liability.[162] In the example of medical law, it can be argued that contractual liability is a default, whereas it can be supplemented by tortious liability provided that a service provided by a party is not explicitly included in the contract.[163]

Differences between the two approaches are important.[164] Contractual and tortious liability provides the different scope of the right to the claimants. First, contractual liability presupposes a clear set of duties parties agreed upon. A party is liable if there has been a failure in its performance. Tortious liability, on the other hand, is a breach of a duty stipulated in Article 16 of LO whereby one has to refrain from behavior that can cause harm to others. LO itself provides rules for each type of liability in separate sections. Article 262–Article 269 of LO regulates contractual liability and Article 154–Article 209 regulates tortious liability. A responsible person

[158] Zammit (2002), pp. 49–66.

[159] Morait (2010), p. 419.

[160] Milica Panić, Ugovorna odgovornost za štetu, Zbornik radova Pravnog fakulteta u Nišu br. 81, 375.

[161] Supreme Court of Croatia Rev - 2156/1991.

[162] Jereb Tilen, "Odgovornost i osiguranje odgovornosti lekara - sa akcentom na slovenaĉko pravo—, u: Jovan Slavnić, Jasna Pak (urs), Promene u pravu osiguranja Srbije u okviru evropskog (EU) razvoja prava osiguranja, Udruţenje za pravo osiguranja Srbije, Beograd 2011, 348.

[163] Strnad Igor, Civilnopravni vidiki odgovornosti v zdravstvu in prikaz sodne prakse, Podjetje in delo, br. 5, Gospodarski vestnik, Ljubljana 2002, 840.

[164] Notably, Article 269 of LO stipulates that rules on tortious liability will apply to contractual liability subsidiarily.

in tort law can be any natural person who is 14 years and older provided it can understand its actions. It can also be a natural person who is from 7–14 years of age. A responsible person in the case of contractual liability can be only the person who can enter into a contract. With a few exceptions, the main rule is that only a person who is 18 years old can do so. Second, different rules on the statute of limitation apply. Statute of limitation applicable to tort liability commences simultaneously with the moment when a duty to compensate becomes due. According to Article 186 of LO, this is the moment of the damage taking place. Statute of limitation for contractual liability commences when a contractual obligation is due.

Further difference concerns the scope of compensation. Tortious liability does not offer any limitation besides what has been addressed. On the other hand, According to Article 266 of LO, contractual liability exposes a liable party only to the harm which at the time of entering into a contract should have been foreseen as a possible consequence of the breach of the contract, having regard to facts known to him at the time or which should have been known to him. A further difference in the scope of damage concerns immaterial harm. While it is clear that tort law guarantees compensation for both material and immaterial harm, the situation is not well-settled for contractual liability. Case law demonstrates that courts have divergent positions. There are examples when courts held that contractual liability covers only material harm.[165] Parties in a contract can shape the amounts of compensation by virtue of the contract. It can be expanded to cover risks with a higher or lower amount of compensation than what the courts would establish, or liability can be limited or completely excluded. Such agreements are not present in case of tortious liability, except when the injured party waives its rights.[166]

The problem with LO and lack of clear rules on non-cumul has been addressed by Croatia. As a state that succeeded LO from Yugoslavia, it amended it, *inter alia*, to settle this ambiguity. It expanded contractual liability to include immaterial harm.[167] Providing the same rights to the injured parties regardless of the type of liability would functionally equalize their positions. Nonetheless, this is not the situation with B&H. It seems that LO needs to be amended in this respect. Until that happens, it is most reasonable to argue that a victim should be able to claim compensation based on tortious liability irrespective of the source of the tortfeasor's duty. The courts would, by virtue of championing this position, make a strong statement in favor of equalizing injured parties. As LO is silent on this matter, such interpretation would not be against the black letter of the law and it would rather support the lack of discrimination of persons who suffered harm.

[165] Supreme Court of Croatia Rev - 985/88, in: Petar Klarić, Odgovornost za neimovinsku štetu zbog povrede ugovora o organiziranju putovanja. Zbornik Pravnog fakulteta u Zagrebu, 2006, 56.

[166] Silvija Petrić, Odgovornost odvjetnika za savjet i mišljenje Zb. Prav. fak. Rij. (1991) v. 31, br. 1, Suppl., 23–49, 2010, 29.

[167] Marko Baretić, Pojam i funkcije neimovinske štete prema novom Zakonu o obveznim odnosima, Zbornik PFZ, 56, Posebni broj, 461–500, 2006.

Moreover, complications that can arise from the influx of AI to traditional accident cases could further deteriorate the positions of those who claim compensation. When a self-driving vehicle autonomously decides to depart from the road and hit a wall, what is the position of all passengers? Whether liability of any potentially responsible party is contractual or tortious? The answer needs to be developed over time and, as it has been stated many times, it requires a deeper understanding of the underlying technology and how it operates in reality. However, this question should not bother or prevent a victim from pursuing its rights.

References

Books

Abbot R (2020) Reasonable robot. Cambridge University Press

Antić O (2007) Obligaciono pravo. Službeni glasnik

Bikić A (2010) Naknada štete. Sarajevo

Cannarsa M (2021) Civil liability and new technologies. In: Tridimas T, Durovic M (eds) New directions in European private law. Bloomsbury Academic, p 208

Carbonnier J (2004) Droit Civil, Tom 2, Les biens, Les obligations

Cigoj S (1977) Odgovornost proizvajalca za škodo po produktu. Ljubljana

Ferguson N (2000) The European Economy, 1815–1914. In: Blanning TCW (ed) The nineteenth century: Europe 1789–1914. Oxford University Press

Hondius E (ed) (2010) Development of medical liability (Cambridge University Press, 2010) 8.10. In: Ibbetson D, Bell J (eds) Comparative studies in the development of the law of torts in Europe, 6 vols. (Legal doctrine, medical liability, product liability, relations between neighbours, technological change, traffic and railways). Cambridge University Press, Cambridge

Ibbetson D, Bell J (eds) (2010) Comparative studies in the development of the law of torts in Europe, 6 vols. Legal doctrine, medical liability, product liability, relations between neighbors, technological change, traffic and railways. Cambridge University Press

Infantino M, Zervogianni E (eds) (2017) Causation in European tort law. Cambridge University Press

Karanikić Mirić M (2016a) Građanskopravni tretman životinje u štetnom događaju. In: Karanikić Mirić M, Davinić M, Vuković I (eds) Životinje i pravo. Pravni fakultet Univerziteta u Beogradu, p 161

Karanikić Mirić M (2016b) Prilog razumevanju pravila o solidarnoj odgovornosti imalaca motornih vozila. In: Lilić S (ed) Perspektive implementacije evropskih standarda u pravni sistem Srbije, vol 6

Karanikić Mirić M (2017) General clause on strict liability in comparative perspective. In: Milisavljević B, Jevremović Petrović T, Živković M (eds) Law and transition, collection of papers, p 354

Karanikić Mirić M (2019a) Objektivna odgovornost za štetu. Službeni glasnik

Karanikić Mirić M (2019b) Postjugoslovenski "život" pravila o vanugovornoj odgovornosti u Srbiji. In: Možina D (ed) Razvojne tendence v obligacijskem pravu: Ob 40-letnici Zakona o obligacijskih razmerjih, p 274

Karner E, Koch AB, Geistfeld AM (2021) Comparative law study on civil liability for artificial intelligence. European Commission

Konstantinović M (1969a) Obligacije i ugovori: skica za zakonik o obligacijama i ugovorima. Pravni fakultet u Beogradu

Konstantinović M (1969b) Obligaciono pravo. Beleške sa predavanja
Konstantinović M (1992) Osnov odgovornosti za prouzrokovanu štetu. Pravni život 9–10
Krulj V (1966) Reč u diskusiji, Građanska odgovornost. Institut društvenih nauka, Belgrade
Krulj V et al (1974) Osnovne polazne koncepcije, u obliku Prijedloga za donošenje zakona o obligacijama I ugovorima, Nacrt Zakona o obligacijama I ugovorima (kao radni material) Beograd
Machiedo D (1995) Osnov odgovornosti za prouzrokovanu štetu, Građanska odgovornost – Referati i diskusija sa Simpozijuma održanog 11. i 12. februara 1966. godine u Beogradu. Redakcija: S. T. Aranđelović. Beograd
Magnus U (2000) Causation in German law. In: Spier J (ed) Unification of tort law: causation. Kluwer Law International, Hag – London – Boston, p 65
Martin-Casals M (2019a) Causation and scope of liability in the IoT. In: Lohsee S et al (eds) Liability for artificial intelligence and the internet of things: Münster Colloquia on EU law and the digital economy IV. Nomos, p 206
Martin-Casals M (2019b) The borderlines of tort law. Intersentia
Morait B (2010) Obligaciono pravo
Morgan J (2017) Torts and technology. In: Brownsword R et al (eds) The Oxford handbook of law, regulation and technology. Oxford University Press
Perović S (1980) Komentar Zakona o obligacionim odnosima
Radišić J (1972) Garancija za trajan kvalitet i odgovornost za štetu od stvari s nedostatkom. Institut za uporedno pravo, Beograd
Radišić J (1995) Odgovornost proizvola~a neispravne robe, u: Komentar Zakona o obligacionim odnosima, glavni i odgovorni urednik Perović Slobodan, knjiga I, "Savremena uprava", Beograd
Radišić J (2004) Obligaciono pravo, Opšti deo, sedmo izdanje. Nomos, Belgrade
Rajneri E (2005) Interaction between the European Directive on Product Liability and the former liability regime in Italy. In: Fairgrieve D (ed) Product liability in comparative perspective. Cambridge University Press, p 80
Reimann M (2015) Product liability. In: Bussani M, Sebok JA (eds) Comparative tort law: global perspectives. Edward Elgar Publishing, Cheltenham
Revolidis I, Dahi A (2018) The peculiar case of the mushroom picking robot. In: Corrales M, Fenwick M, Forgó N (eds) Robotics, AI and the future of law. Springer, p 69
Vedriš M (1978) Opći dio građanskog prava po Zakonu o obligacionim odnosima. In: Goldštajn A (ed) Obvezno pravo. Zagreb
Vedriš M, Klarić P (2000) Građansko pravo
Vizner B (1969) Građansko pravo, drugo prerađeno i dopunjeno izdanje, Rijeka
Vizner B (1978) Komentar Zakona o obligacionim odnosima. Zagreb
Vuković M (1956) Obvezno pravo, Knjiga I, Uvod, odgovornost za štetu I ostale vanugovorne obaveze. Školska knjiga, Zagreb
Wagner G (2017). In: Habersack M (ed) Münchener Kommentar zum Bürgerlichen Gesetzbuch: Band 6: Schuldrecht: Besonderer Teil IV (7th edn, CH Beck) § 1 ProdHaftG
Wagner G (2019) Robot liability. In: Lohsee S et al (eds) Liability for artificial intelligence and the internet of things: Münster Colloquia on EU law and the digital economy IV. Nomos
Wagner G (2021) Haftung für Künstliche Intelligenz – Eine Gesetzesinitiative des Europäischen Parlaments. ZEuP 545, 556, available at: https://beck-online.beck.de/Dokument?vpath=bibdata%2Fzeits%2Fzeup%2F2021%2Fcont%2Fzeup.2021.545.1.htm&anchor=Y-300-Z-ZEUP-B-2021-S-550#FNA32

Articles

Balkin MJ (2015) The path of robotics law. Cal Law Rev Circ 6:45

Baretić M (2020) Protupravnost kao pretpostavka odštetnopravne odgovornosti u hrvatskom pravu. Zbornik Pravnog fakulteta u Zagrebu 70(5)

Bazala B (1956) Odgovornost za štetu prouzročenu pogonom cestovnih motornih vozila, Naša zakonitost. God. 10, 3, 4 and 5

Bećić M, Primjena Medželle u postosmanskoj Bosni i Hercegovini. Godišnjak Pravnog fakulteta u Sarajevu, LVII – 2014

Bevanda M (2007) Odgovornost za štetu izazvanu neispravnim proizvodom u hrvatskom i bosanskohercegovačkom pravu, Zb. Prav. fak. Sveuč. Rij. (1991) 28(1):xxx-xxx

Bikić A (2010b) Posebni slučajevi objektivne odgovornosti, Godišnjak Pravnog fakulteta u Sarajevu LIII:45–61

Bukovac Puvača M (2010) Zahtjev pravičnosti kao temelj obveze naknade štete bez odgovornosti. Zbornik Pravnog fakulteta Sveučilišta u Rijeci 31(2)

Bukovac Puvača M, Mihelčić G, Marochini Zrinski M (2019) Uzročna veza kao pretpostavka odgovornosti za štetu u europskim nacionalnim pravnim sustavima, praksi Suda Europske unije i Europskog suda za ljudska prava. Godišnjak Akademije pravnih znanosti Hrvatske X(1)

Dari-Mattiacci G, Parisi F (2013) Liability rules: an economic taxonomy. In: Bussani M, Sebok A (eds) Comparative tort law. Edward Elgar, Cheltenham (Forthcoming), Amsterdam Law School Research Paper No. 2013-09, Amsterdam Center for Law & Economics Working Paper No. 2013-01

Eidenmüller H (2019) Machine performance and human failure. J Bus Technol Law

Gams A (1966) Reč u diskusiji, Građanska odgovornost. Institut društvenih nauka, Belgrade, pp 252–254

Gifford GD (2017) Technological triggers to tort revolutions: steam locomotives, autonomous vehicles, and accident compensation. J Tort Law 11:71

Karanikić Mirić M (2005) Odgovornost za razvojne rizike. Anali Pravnog fakulteta u Beogradu LIII (2)

Koch AB (2019) Product Liability 2.0 – mere update or new version? In: Lohsee S, Schulze R, Staudenmayer D (eds) Liability for artificial intelligence and the internet of things: Münster Colloquia on EU law and the digital economy IV. Nomos

Povlakić M (2013) Odgovornost notara za prouzrokovanu štetu u obavljanju notarske službe. Foundation Public Law Centre

Prica R (1961) Odgovornost za štetu od proizvoda. Pravni život, Br. 4., Beograd

Shavell S (2019) On the redesign of accident liability for the world of autonomous vehicles (September 2019). NBER Working Paper No. w26220, available at SSRN: https://ssrn.com/abstract=3450246, 2

Tasić Đ (1939) Odgovornost za rizik. Arhiv za pravne i društvene nauke, Belgrade

Wendehorst C (2020) Strict liability for AI and other emerging technologies. J Eur Tort Law 11(2)

Zammit ED (2002) Does the 'non cumul' rule exist in our civil law? Id-Dritt 18:49–66

Chapter 5
Allocation of Liability

5.1 Introduction

In the previous chapter, we discussed fault-based liability and strict liability with various modalities as they exist in LO. Bases of liability are probably the key question concerning the establishment of an appropriate liability legal framework. As a very nuanced and multilayered issue, depending on how it is set, the applicable basis of liability generates different, and sometimes undesirable, incentives to involved actors. It was impossible to examine the appropriateness of bases of liability without reference to how liability should be allocated in the first place. However, some of the fundamental settings around the allocation liability were omitted. This chapter is devoted to this very question. The reason why allocation of responsibility is treated separately lies in the fundamental change of the basic presumption on which tort law traditionally relies. Peculiar characteristics of AI render it sometimes uncontrollable by anyone, while, at other points, it is the manufacturer instead of the user who determines its operations.

At the outset, it is necessary to identify the main principles which determine who should be a liable party. Those are the control of an object or an activity that caused harm and the benefits one has from it. These are the main considerations behind how lawmakers assigned liability among various persons that come into play. This brief introduction to the main principles of allocation of liability is predicated on the separation between the person and the object or activity that directly causes harm. When a person directly commits wrong or uses a certain tool for such purpose, the question of assigning liability for the exact action is clear. The underlying moral principle can be aptly formulated as "If you break it, you pay for it".[1] However, when a certain intermediary exists between a person and the harm, the problem arises. This question is not very new. Clearly, the law has dealt with situations where another person acted within the boundaries of agency relationship on behalf or for

[1] See Schroeder (1997).

N. Muftić, *Artificial Intelligence and Tortious Liability*, European Union and its Neighbours in a Globalized World 21, https://doi.org/10.1007/978-3-031-86453-7_5

the benefit of another person. Moreover, even when there was not a person but other proxies such as animals or even sophisticated technological tools such as motor vehicle that caused an accident, the law found a way to assign liability. To better understand AI accidents, it is necessary not only to discuss these main principles of allocation of liability, but their correlation and perhaps even a hierarchy between them should be established since they might point to different persons in certain cases. Typically, unlike with traditional products where control completely shifts from manufacturers once the product leaves the factory, the latter are likely to remain in a position to provide updates and monitor that AI operates as intended. In line with their extended control, the role of owners and users is likely to be limited. Such a change in control should be reflected in how responsibility for AI should be allocated.

The range of potentially liable parties is discussed further. It stems from manufacturers, owners, operators, and users. The differences between these categories of persons are often very subtle yet important. For instance, one can be an owner and user, but it cannot be considered an operator. The demarcation between various roles in which a person can appear is significant from the perspective of alignment with the principle whereby liability is allocated. Moreover, from the perspective of the economic analysis of law, efficient allocation of liability requires an understanding of possibilities a person has vis-à-vis AI. Due to the change of control, it is likely that the burden of liability should be increasingly born by manufacturers. This, however, does not mean that there are no arguments in favor of the liability of owners and users. First, they indubitably enjoy benefits from AI, either directly through the services they perform or indirectly, through the benefits third parties enjoy. Moreover, they can obtain a certain degree of control in some situations.

After examining allocation with respect to persons, the these principles should be applied to the rather peculiar idea—to hold AI itself responsible. This idea, albeit radical, received significant attention in the scholarship and by lawmakers. For instance, even the EU Parliament at one point considered it to be an avenue worth pursuing in order to get out of the liability conundrum. The legal personhood of AI, as the most obvious variation of this idea, will be a starting point. To hold AI responsible might also mean a recognition of certain rights and duties of AI without recognizing it as a person, thereby establishing its in-between status. Although there are some strong arguments in favor of establishing such rules, they are outweighed by counterarguments. Holding AI responsible allows an escape from the unpopular decision on how to allocate responsibility for harm that was caused by the autonomous behavior of AI without anyone else's error. If AI has any duties, there are pertinent philosophical and ethical problems of dealing with human creations who have their separate cognition as with holders of rights and duties. Moreover, even if this problem could be overcome (for instance, corporations as holders of rights and duties are also created on a fiction whereby human endeavors can be separated from their personalities), there are at least two significant practical problems. First, the separation of AI and humans around it shields them from liability. There would be no incentive to improve it over time or to act prudently more than it is necessary at the bare minimum. Second, how is AI supposed to cover losses it causes? In other words, who is supposed to contribute to AI's assets, and what happens after that pool has become insufficient?

Furthermore, there are situations where more than one person merits being held responsible for AI's actions. There is a problem of having acceptable agreements between various actors who can be a defendant in a lawsuit. Theoretically, they can agree in a contract to allocate liability by their own volition. The same is possible between manufacturers and buyers. Due to an imbalance between the powers of the said actor, there is a likelihood that some of them would assume burden in a socially unacceptable. The problem of protection of consumers is clear and they require protection. The small companies who contribute to the manufacturing process should deserve protection too. A big company, due to its power, can allocate a liability burden on a small company (who, for instance, can only produce a small piece of a very complex robot).

Lastly, there is a problem of intermediated risks. These are situations where AI acts as a recommender to humans who decide upon the action and eventually execute it. There is a very recent case law by the European Court of Justice concerning traditional products (newspapers). However, it is unclear what would be the reasoning of this Court regarding AI (and other digital products). The Court omitted to address the fundamental questions regarding intermediated risks and instead decided based on the differentiation between products and services and whether PLD is applicable in those cases. In the future, it would be interesting to investigate whether the employment of criterion of the functionality of a product could aid in overcoming this problem with respect to AI. This question, however, is beyond the scope of this book.

5.2 Traditional Allocation

Probably the most common situation in practice is when a person's behavior causes harm. This might be the reason why B&H legislator uses terms such as tortfeasor or a person who causes harm to regulate liability relationships to set general rules of liability. There is no doubt that a person whose behavior caused harm should be held liable and this will not be discussed further. The problem arises when a certain auxiliary causes harm. That can be either a person, an animal, or a tool. Then, the situation is not so clear because we do not have a direct relationship between one's behavior and harmful consequences. Law has dealt with such situations and established criteria whereby one can be held liable. Civil law is not the only field of law that recognizes such relationships. Criminal law also holds that a person can be found guilty if their auxiliary committed a crime, provided that all requirements have been met.

Below, this work examines the most relevant arguments that are used to allocate civil liability of a person for the actions of its auxiliaries. They are formed as principles, a set of values that determine specific rules. One should bear in mind that principles of allocation of liability need to be aligned with general goals of tort law—compensation, deterrence, and arguably efficient allocation of costs.

This work follows the findings of The Report. It suggests:

While existing rules on liability offer solutions with regard to the risks created by emerging digital technologies, the outcomes may not always seem appropriate, given the failure to achieve:

a fair and efficient allocation of loss, in particular because it could not be attributed to those:

- whose objectionable behaviour caused the damage; or
- who benefitted from the activity that caused the damage; or
- who were in control of the risk that materialised; or
- who were cheapest cost avoiders or cheapest takers of insurance.[2]

Accordingly, principles of control of AI, eius damnum, cuius commodum, objectionable behavior, and cheapest cost avoider are addressed in the following subsections.

5.2.1 Control of AI

Control of AI should not be understood as control of traditional objects. Any object is not prone to being under the absolute control of humans. They might act differently than humans intend. However, the predictability of behavior of traditional things is high, provided they are not defective. Contrary, the behavior of AI is not necessarily controllable and predictable to the same degree. Those who manufactured it and who operate it have an impact on it. Perhaps in different ways and to a different extent, but in any case, their impact is higher than that of anybody else. Resolution 2020 in Article 3 provides a definition of control:

Control means any action of an operator that influences the operation of an AI-system and thus the extent to which the operator exposes third parties to the potential risks associated with the operation and functioning of the AI-system; such actions can impact the operation at any stage by determining the input, output or results, or can change specific functions or processes within the AI-system; the degree to which those aspects of the operation of the AI-system are determined by the action depends on the level of influence the operator has over the risk connected with the operation and functioning of the AI-system.

Control of AI should be the primary guiding principle for assigning liability to a person. There is a growing consensus on this issue in scholarship. The EU

[2]Report, 34.

Parliament, too, considers it to be the primary argument to focus civil liability claims against the person in control of AI.

This argument goes in hand with what economic analysis of law designates as the cheapest cost avoider. In the economic analysis of law, the process of allocation of risk is related to the notion of efficiency. Risk is attributed to the party who can prevent or control risk in the most efficient way, or, in the way which induces the least amount of costs, compared to other potential parties. A person who is in a position to be efficient is the one who can control the risk better than others. Cheapest cost avoider will be addressed separately below.

The degree of control one asserts over AI can vary depending on the specific application and sector in which it is being used. Sometimes, more than one person can assert control. For instance, while manufacturers determine the basic functionality of self-driving vehicles, users might knowingly provide it with instructions in order to harm the third party. We may agree that there should be no responsibility of the user for this accident as the self-driving vehicle had to be designed to refrain from harmful actions despite the user's instructions. However, even if there is no user control at all, there is an argument in favor of its responsibility.

5.2.2 *Eius Damnum, Cuius Commodum*

The principle of holding someone else than the person in control is also not the new one. Attribution of responsibility to persons who do not necessarily have control but who enjoy benefits of certain activity is in fact very old.[3] It acts as an explanation for vicarious liability, situations where a principal cannot completely control the behavior of another person, but nonetheless has a certain interest in it. For example, an employer is liable for the actions of an employee since its actions aim at providing benefits to it. LO in Article 170 recognizes this principle as it limits the responsibility of the employer only to the harm which occurred within the scope of the employee's work. Despite the lack of control, the principal has to monitor the system by allowing who is allowed to use it,[4] installing updates, selecting data it can process, and refraining from misuse.

However, it is important to establish priority ranking between control of AI and eius damnun, cuius commodum. The two principles might point to completely different (set of) persons, especially in the case of AI. Obviously, even in the case of vicarious liability, they are present and important. While an employer enjoys benefits arising out of the actions of its employee, it is in the best position to control it as their relationship entails that the principal provides instructions and goals of the agent's actions. In the case of AI, both manufacturers and users might assert control,

[3] Zweigert and Kotz (1998), p. 630.

[4] Janal (2020), p. 194.

depending on the specific case. At the same time, it can be argued that they both enjoy benefits, either through obtaining revenues or a particular service AI provides—manufacturer through the price received for the product and the user due to the particular application of AI. The situation with this principle is not different from traditional products. Rather, change of control of AI acts as the main consideration that entails different allocation from before. As it has been mentioned, manufacturers should be the primary bearer of a duty to compensate a victim for harm if AI caused it autonomously.

However, this does not mean that eius damnum, cuius commodum should completely be abolished in AI accidents. After all, benefits for all persons who either manufacture, own, or use AI cannot be neglected. This principle can operate as a subsidiary of the principle of control. It can justify the victim's claim against all those persons who had no control of AI at the time it caused harm. Nonetheless, since they enjoyed benefits, a victim should be allowed to institute a claim against those persons too. Think of a smart irrigation system. If it autonomously decides to apply excessive amounts of water and cause flood at the neighbor's field. The risk of autonomous behavior was clearly beyond the control of the system's user. It could have only been controlled by its manufacturers. It is likewise obvious that the user's plants obtained watering by the system. In such cases, a victim should be allowed to institute a claim against both manufacturers and users and receive full compensation from any of them. However, since control was solely in hands of manufacturers, users of the irrigation system should be allowed to recourse.

If we accept that eius damnum, cuius commodum can act as an addition to the principle of control, it is important to note what benefits should be considered sufficient for establishing one's duty to compensate? We have previously seen that all persons enjoy benefits of AI, either directly such as owners of the field that is supplied with water by a smart irrigation system, or indirectly through receipt of purchase price or rent. For purposes of liability, it would be sound to limit eius damnum, cuius commodum to only those benefits that are directly related to the object or activity that led to the accident. The inclusion of indirect benefits has the potential of opening floodgates against manufacturers or even deployers as they also received certain consideration for their services. A line must be drawn somewhere. Lawmakers had this problem in mind in the EU. This is the reason for the 500 EUR liability cap provided in the previous version of PLD. Allowing the unlimited reach of this principle can alter the fundamental goals of tort law. Its reach should include only operators as liable persons because they are the ones who enjoy benefits but they also might assert a degree of control over AI. For instance, if two passengers travel to work by a self-driving vehicle that causes an accident due to its autonomous behavior that cannot be attributed either to the passengers or a manufacturer. Clearly, a manufacturer should be the ultimate cost-bearer as it is the only one who asserts control. The removal of the liability cap from PLD is a step in this direction.

The application of eius damnum, cuius commodum would allow differentiation between passengers who can act as a defendant. The passenger who could be considered an operator is the one who provided inputs to a self-driving vehicle. On the other hand, a person who was merely present in a vehicle without any interaction with it should be protected. The application of eius damnum, cuius commodum to owners of AI is interesting as well. This is the case when they are not the same person as manufacturers or operators and users. The owner's liability should not exist as it cannot affect AI's behavior.

A limited number of potential defendants is problematic for another reason which is, though, not specific only for the accidents involving AI. If a victim can claim compensation only from the users or only from the manufacturers, it can create a judgment-proof problem. It refers to the situation where a potential defendant cannot pay fully for the harm although the judgment against it has been rendered. Summers noted that the existence of a judgment-proof problem renders fundamental goals of tort law unobtainable.[5] If a person is aware that the judgment against it does not mean the claimant can actually receive compensation, there is a lack of deterrent effect of tort law. Likewise, a victim will remain unsatisfied. "Consequently, the judgment-proof problem is of substantial importance, since if the injurers are unable to pay fully for the harm they may cause, their incentives to engage in risky activities will be greater than otherwise."[6]

Lastly, from the perspective of the victim, it is important that a defendant is easy to be identified. This point has already been mentioned in a different phrasing before. A person who is at the scene when the accident occurs is likely to be the most easily identified, along with manufacturers. However, there might be several manufacturers involved and the victim might not know how to identify them. Also, it might not be obvious whether manufacturers of operators or users of vehicles should be blamed. In other words, who of these persons made a mistake in performing their duties? For these reasons, sophisticated situations must not be left to the victim to deal with, at least when it comes to the identification of a defendant. One of the reasons that determined the EU Parliament to propose holding operators of AI liable lies in the fact that it "considers that due to the AI-system's complexity and connectivity, the operator will be in many cases the first visible contact point for the affected person".[7]

Therefore, although control of AI should act as a primary criterion of attribution of liability, there is a principle-based justification as well as a practical set of reasons for holding more than one person responsible based on the limited application of eius damnum, cuius commodum.

[5] Summers (2020), p. 95.

[6] Kovac (2020), p. 88.

[7] Resolution 2020, Recital 10.

5.2.3 Objectionable Behavior

What is control for strict liability, objectionable (and avoidable) behavior is for fault-based liability. The understanding of one's responsibility is predicated on a clear set of duties. If a person complies, their behavior will not lead to harm. Alternatively, even if the harm occurs, a person should not be responsible as it met its duties. After all, tort law does not aim to provide compensation for all losses a person suffers.

Strict liability employs control as the main criterion in order to enhance the response to increased dangerousness. When this is not the case, fault-based liability is applicable. Accordingly, the criterion of control is replaced with the criterion of objectionable behavior of a person. In the case of AI, two points can be stressed. First, due to the lack of predictability, opacity, and autonomy of this technology, strict-based liability is likely to play an increasingly important role. These characteristics prevent regulators from being able to ascertain and prescribe specific duties of persons involved. They will thus be inclined to focus on the risks rather than on specific behavior. Second, due to the change of control, the focus will is likely to be increasingly on manufacturers than users. In the case of B&H law, manufacturers' liability is always strict-based. Moreover, even if users/operators are being held liable, current case law in B&H suggests that the courts may hold them liable based on strict liability as they do with owners/keepers of animals. Such an approach has been criticized in Chapter 4. However, until it changes, we may assume that criterion of control will be more likely applied to AI as they are autonomous entities that should be controlled by persons in charge.

For these reasons, objectionable behavior as a criterion for allocation of liability is likely to play a less important role than in the case of traditional accidents.

5.2.4 Cheapest Cost Avoider

Cheapest cost avoider is a criterion employed in the economic analysis of law for purposes of allocating liability to the party who will suffer least among the range of potential holders of liability. In theory, this person will have trouble to provide safety and prevent accidents from occurring, but compared to the range of other persons it is in the best position to do so. Throughout this work, employment of the cheapest cost avoider criterion has been mentioned as it constitutes orthodoxy in deliberations on liability.

Cheapest cost avoider argument corresponds with control. Calabresi also argues that there is a difference between the cheapest cost avoider and the best cost avoider. This means that "moral evaluations of the activities involved enter into the decision",[8] Best cost avoider is concerned not only about what is the most efficient way

[8] Calabresi (1970), p. 241.

to attribute liability but also about considerations that are not market-based. It should be noted that the cheapest cost avoider is not necessarily the same person who manufactures or uses a certain product. It is also possible that a victim can be the cheapest cost avoider.[9] However, in the case of AI, the main consideration in favor of having a certain group of people liable is related to their ability to control it. Shavell explains this with the example of self-driving vehicles:

The major rule of tort liability that we apply to reduce road accidents concerns, of course, the fault of the driver. But this rule will be irrelevant when there are no drivers in active command of their vehicles. If an autonomous vehicle speeds or strays from its lane, the explanation for that event will not involve a driver. That driver fault will be made moot in the contemplated world might suggest that society should turn its attention toward liability of manufacturers of vehicles.

The previous quote discusses fault of the driver as the major rule, although the liability of a driver in B&H is mainly strict. This difference the applicable standard, however, does not change the main point which remain—the driver and her behavior is in focus. In the case of traditional motor vehicles, a party who was behind the steering wheel is in the best position to prevent accidents from happening, i.e. the costs it may incur by doing so are lower compared to other parties. In the case of self-driving vehicles, this may not be the case. Imagine if a self-driving car hit a pedestrian. Provided it operated autonomously, a person who provided instructions on a specific destination and other details of the journey is not the one who decides on specific actions of the vehicle. In other words, it is not in a position to alter the operations of the algorithm that governs the vehicle. If a pedestrian suddenly shows up in front of the car, a person in the car may not be able to stop it. Consequently, in the previous example, the person who is in the best position to control AI is the one who manufactured it or the one who has to update and monitor it. In this chapter, we refer to such person as a manufacturer as an umbrella term for all of the aforementioned.

The cheapest cost avoider criterion, therefore, corresponds with findings of the control.

5.3 Relationship Between Bases of Liability and Responsible Persons

It is hard to determine a responsible party as many potential actors come into play. Manufacturers, operators, holders, users, or AI itself could be held liable for a harmful event, and there are arguments to support each of the choices. For instance, control of the risk might be a criterion (manufacturers and operators), benefits of use

[9] Ibid, 221.

(manufacturers, operators, and users), or autonomy of the technology (AI itself). The most striking choice discussed in this respect would be to hold AI liable, either as a separate legal person,[10] or an entity that holds a certain amount of property for purposes of compensation.[11] This is predicated primarily on autonomy and self-learning capacity of AI. However, the idea of holding AI liable seemed to be received unfavorably both in the legislative process[12] and in the scholarship.[13] Apart from the conceptual problems with underlying legal doctrines, the complexity and opacity of AI might create difficulties for the tortfeasors at the redress level.[14]

The previous chapter expounded on the basis of liability. It determined the burden one has to bear in order to prove that it suffered harm, as well as the burden defendant, has in deflecting the claim. The question closely related to this one is who should be liable on the appropriate basis of liability. The two questions are intertwined to the extent that the basis of liability cannot be determined without having a specific role person performs in mind. For example, it would make no sense to hold anyone but the manufacturer responsible for defects in the design of the product. Since its position puts it in a control over the manufacturing process, and due to the increased likelihood of the occurrence of harm, product liability is based on strict liability. This is supposedly the reasoning of LO drafters and legislators. However, the relationship between the basis of liability and the person who should be burdened with the duty to compensate a victim is not clear in all situations. As we have seen, the most troublesome problem is the occurrence of autonomous behavior of AI that no one could predict. In such circumstances, there is a hardship in establishing who is to be blamed.

Of course, the law as we know it now does not recognize a situation where it is unclear who should be responsible. The law, at least on paper, is clear on who is responsible as well as in establishing situations when no one should compensate a victim. When a dilemma occurs, it is based on a vague factual background of the case rather than on the lack of a choice made by the legislators. For instance, the law is clear that accidents caused due to vis maior cannot be attributed to any person. The difficulties arising in practice is in establishing what events constitute vis maior.

However, AI merits rethinking current choices. Not all risks relevant for liability deserve to be treated by traditional rules due to the fact that occasionally no one can predict them nor prevent them. The relationship between the allocation of liability and the applicable basis of liability should recognize this. A position of a defendant, no matter who it is, can be more or less favorable depending on the basis of liability

[10] Schirmer (2019), p. 131.

[11] van den Hoven van Genderen (2021), p. 21.

[12] EU Parliament had mentioned in before in the Resolution on Civil Law Rules on Robotics from 2017, but the idea has been abandoned in the Resolution on a Civil Liability Regime for Artificial Intelligence from 2020.

[13] For example: Eidenmüller (2019); van den Hoven van Genderen (2021).

[14] The Report, 32.

and available defenses. For instance, should a user be held liable based on strict liability without any defenses designed specifically for AI (see 4.6.6. Defenses)? As Chap. 3 repeatedly stipulates, this work argues that the law should be risk-sensitive and balance the burden between the injured party and a tortfeasor based on the characteristics of the risk. Manifestation of this regulatory choice would be to apply a specific basis of liability to a specific person, but only if it takes into consideration the nature of risk.

Furthermore, rules on strict liability, apart from product liability, apply to users and owners in LO. There is a technical problem of applying them in the case of manufacturers, although they are the ones who are likely to continue to assert control of AI even after the product is in the hands of the third party. The problem lies in the fact that "national jurisdictions are almost exclusively about the strict liability of the owner or other long-term deployer of a device".[15] A shift in the fundamental rules on the addressees of strict liability would require more than a mere twitch in the current legislation. This is also the problem with LO. While it recognizes a strict liability for producers in case of product liability, the remainder of the provisions on this basis of liability is devoted to other addressees. The scholarship made several objections to LO, mainly due to its obsolescence, as has been mentioned previously in this work. However, there were no fundamental changes of the 1978 text in B&H (unlike other Yugoslavian successor states) due to reasons that are probably not the product of a different legal understanding of civil law, but rather due to political gridlock. Consequently, requiring legislators to consider the amendments that would take what is perceived in common parlance as a futuristic and far technology seems like a Don Quixote struggle.

5.4 Potentially Liable Parties

It is hard to determine a responsible party as many potential actors come into play. Manufacturers, operators, holders, users, or AI itself could be held liable for a harmful event, and there are arguments to support each of the choices. For instance, control of the risk might be a criterion (manufacturers and operators), benefits of use (manufacturers, operators, and users), or autonomy of the technology (AI itself). The most striking choice discussed in this respect would be to hold AI liable, either as a separate legal person,[16] or an entity that holds a certain amount of property for purposes of compensation.[17] As AI possesses certain autonomy and a significant cognitive apparatus, the problem of allocation of liability puts into perspective a liability of the technology itself, an unusual position for human creations. Apart from

[15] Wendehorst (2020), p. 174.

[16] Schirmer (2019), p. 131.

[17] van den Hoven van Genderen (2021), p. 21.

the conceptual problems, the complexity and opacity of AI might create difficulties for the tortfeasors at the redress level.[18] The solution should aim to hold the ones who can impact future behavior of AI liable, as they are the cheapest cost avoiders.[19]

If data used by AI caused the accidents, some of the potentially responsible parties should be liable nonetheless. They are the ones who had to predict that data can be of different features as well as the ones who can alter AI and prevent future accidents. As it will be argued, manufacturers are the first ones in the line of responsible parties. The exception from this rule should be made in case of malicious actions of users who provided erroneous data in order to induce harm or who failed to install updates suggested by manufacturers. Even in that case, the "blame the data" argument should not be available.[20] In the absence of an external breach, users who provided data should be liable. As John Villasenor puts it: "The malicious user would bear responsibility, as potentially would the company for failing to design the system to be more robust against this sort of manipulation."[21] In other words, there should be no situation where there is no one to be held responsible.

This section will elaborate on the range of potentially responsible parties. It will address the liability of AI itself. This is a radical yet very popular idea in scholarship. However, I consider it to bring more harm than good, as will be demonstrated below. This idea will be elaborated first since the main focus should be on the allocation of responsibility between manufacturers and users.

5.4.1 *Holding AI Responsible*

Deliberation on the appropriate allocation of liability is typically limited to persons involved. Those are natural and legal persons. Even the inclusion of legal persons was a departure from the attribution of responsibility to humans. It is a truism that companies and other legal persons are held liable for their actions although their actions are in fact actions of humans who operate on their behalf in some capacity. If we allow such a departure from the clear-cut rules of having humans behave responsible for the consequences of their behavior, can we perhaps make another exception for AI?

History attests that various categories of humans and their associations that had not been treated as a person later gain that status. Examples are slaves, women, and

[18] The Report, p. 32.

[19] In order to recognize a multitude of actors who might be involved in the process of development of AI, a distinction between backend and frontend operators had been suggested by the Expert Group. The EU Parliament's Resolution of 2020 accepted it. See European Commission, Report from the Expert Group on Liability and New Technologies – New Technologies Formation, Liability for Artificial Intelligence and other emerging digital technologies, pp. 39–42.

[20] John Villasenor, Products liability law as a way to address AI harms, available at: https://www.brookings.edu/research/products-liability-law-as-a-way-to-address-ai-harms/.

[21] Ibid.

companies. Each of these categories is either humans or human creation. In the case of slaves and women, the process of emancipation was not intellectually challenging to be understood although, in reality, the struggle involved enormous sacrifices and great numbers of victims. However, both of these categories are humans, with human characteristics and human reasoning. Even in the case of companies, the ones who ultimately make and execute decisions are humans. Although there might be other reasons for treating legal entities as separate persons from humans who participate in their operations, such as the protection of humans from personal liability, it is always possible to trace any company behavior to humans and explain it to other humans. In all these examples, we can recognize free will, reason, and self-awareness that is attributed to humans, either directly as in the case of natural persons or indirectly as in the case of legal persons. However, some scholars argue that exploring different avenues is worth trying. As Teubner formulates is: "Private law is therefore faced with a choice: Either it gives autonomous software agents an independent legal status and treats them as responsible actors, or there is an increasing number of "accidents", without anyone being responsible for them."[22]

Furthermore, not all persons have always had the same rights, and some do not have them at present too. It is well-known that women and people of different racial and ethnic backgrounds have been impaired for a long period of history, which is a problem that humankind is attempting to overcome more or less successfully. Nowadays, not all persons have the same set of rights. Apart from differentiation on the basis of nationality (and related rights such as the right to vote), there is a difference between legal and natural persons. B&H (and that of former Yugoslavia) private law and scholarship differentiate between the scope of the capacity of legal and natural persons. Legal persons are allowed to conduct in a certain way only if their actions fall within previously approved areas. All other actions that fell outside this limited number of areas are not permitted. On the other hand, the opposite rules apply to natural persons. They are allowed to behave in any desired way and engage in activities in any area unless such behavior is explicitly prohibited. Such a diversity between how persons are treated attests ability of law to adapt to a variety of circumstances and peculiar characteristics of phenomena it attempts to regulate. "The concept of personhood is an abstract concept; neither the natural person, nor the artificial person is more real than the other. Both of their legal personalities are based on the fact that they retain a particular bundle of rights and duties."[23] Perhaps AI might be situated under the same umbrella too.

This section will elaborate on three specific ideas. The first is the introduction of legal personhood for AI. Just like in the case of corporations, it can be argued that AI is another case of non-humans that merit to be treated as complete people who can

---

[22]Teubner (2018), pp. 106–149, 109, available at: https://papers.ssrn.com/sol3/papers.cfm?abstract_id=3177096.

[23]van den Hoven van Genderen (2018), p. 36.

make decisions on their own behalf. This idea is very radical not only from a legal perspective. There are important philosophical considerations behind too.[24] The idea of electronic personhood for AI gained a lot of attention in scholarship in the last decade idea that aimed at treating AI as something more than an object. The following two ideas do not suggest treating AI as persons but nonetheless suggest providing certain rights and duties. Two ideas that will be presented in this respect are the idea of treating AI akin to slaves in ancient Rome and the idea of applying the German concept of Teilrechtsfähigkeit.

5.4.1.1 Electronic Personhood

A task of allocating liability between various persons who in any capacity manufacture, own or use AI is very hard. The lawmaker needs weigh between opposite and persuasive positions. The appeal of holding AI itself liability would be an escape from a hard policy choice as none of the persons would be liable. According to this idea, AI would be treated as a separate person who is itself liable for the harm it causes as it operates with less or no human control compated to traditional human inventions and conducts a separate decision-making process. "AI would have a separate pool of assets from its manufacturers and users and this would be used when the duty to remunerate harm it created arises. This would not be a first time the lawmakers recognize certain human creations as separate entities. An example are corporations. AI's capacity to independently or autonomously interact with third parties could make the argument for granting it separate personhood even more compelling than for legal entities, which always have humans making decisions behind the scenes. In 2017, the EU Parliament found this idea attractive. It included in in the Resolution on Civil Law Rules on Robotics.[25] This documents proposes:

> creating a specific legal status for robots in the long run, so that at least the most sophisticated autonomous robots could be established as having the status of electronic persons responsible for making good any damage they may cause, and possibly applying electronic personality to cases where robots make autonomous decisions or otherwise interact with third parties independently.

It, however, this idea failed receive unanimous support in the scholarship and the expert community. First, philosophical and ethical considerations of recognizing electronic entities as persons fired the debate about the status and understanding of humans and their peculiarities in modern societies." It is suggested, as Horst Eidenmüller pointed out, that the introduction of electronic persons might create disturbance as the current concepts of personhood are anthropocentric and not suited for electronic entities such as AI.[26] Furthermore, even if understood as a pure

---

[24] See Kurki (2019).

[25] European Parliament Resolution of 16 February 2017 with recommendations to the Commission on Civil Law Rules on Robotics (2015/2103(INL)) [2018] OJ C252/239 (Resolution), paras 49ff.

[26] For further discussion see Eidenmüller (2019).

liability question in isolation from broader negative implications, other potential problems exist. If an electronic person is deemed responsible, it needs a pool of assets in order to provide compensation to injured parties for the harms it creates.[27]

Assets of the AI as a separate person requires further deliberation. How will they be established and maintained? "Manufacturers or users or a third party inevitably ought to provide at least initial assets which will be used for the compensation and a certain method of maintenance of assets needs to be used, such as some sort of initial capital or mandatory insurance. If manufacturers or users will bear the cost of establishing and maintaining the assets of an electronic person, then why is there a need for a separate legal person at all? For instance, insurance can be purchased even without the existence of an electronic person. Also, the question of whether manufacturers or users ought to bear the cost of establishing and maintaining the assets of an electronic person since they might re-allocate any lawmaker's rule through the freedom of contract."[28]

A creation of separate person can cause even more problems. For perspective of manufacturers, this is an apt chance to be relieved. Just like corporations can shield natural persons from risk exposure, AI as an electronic person can shield manufacturers (and users). The problem with limiting exposure is in how it impact incentives. In other words, provided they may not be requested to pay once a harm has been done, they may have no incentive to improve AI's safety and consequently to reduce the risk of harm.[29] Separate assets of the electronic person could be seen as a liability cap for the parties who have to provide them. In other words, granting electronic personhood could allow manufacturers to avoid accountability, as they might be less inclined to invest effort in ensuring product safety due to their limited or non-existent liability. Holding the electronic entity responsible would not drive improvements in its performance, as its capacity to learn and evolve depends solely on its programming. As previously discussed, deterrent effect as one of the important considerations would be undermined.[30] Moreover, as discussed previously, it would be hard to settle AI with law created for humans. New 'standards of "conduct" [...] in order to hold them liable individually, which could hardly be brought in line with negligence standards for humans'[31] would have to be adopted.

Although the idea of electronic personhood was championed by the EU Parliament in the Resolution of 2017, it has been completely rejected in the 2020 Resolution. Such a shift in the approach should be welcomed due to various problems inherent in this idea. B&H legislator should not consider it too, at least for the time being.

---

[27] Schirmer (2019), p. 131.

[28] Ibid, p. 15.

[29] Schirmer (2019), p. 57.

[30] Schirmer (2019).

[31] Koch (2019), p. 115.

Despite many problems with granting AI status of a legal person, some authors consider that there are very useful pieces that can be extracted from this idea. Perhaps AI should not be a person, but nonetheless can be awarded some rights and duties. As Ryan Calo describes it, AI can be treated by "a new category of a legal subject, halfway between person and object"[32]

5.4.1.2 Analogy with Slaves

There is also an idea whereby AI that would resemble the status of slaves in the Roman Empire. An American mathematician and philosopher Norbert Wiener has in 1950 compared robots with slaves: "the automatic machine, whatever we may think of any feelings it may have or may not have, is the precise equivalent of slave labor."[33] The idea was further developed with reference to some historical examples. Most notably, it builds on how Romans differentiated human beings and the set of rights and duties they attributed to them accordingly. As Esposito notes, "no human being was a person by nature – not as such. Certainly not the slave, but not the free man either: before he became a *pater*, that is, a legal subject, he still had to pass through the status of *filius in potestate*, which reflected the fact that, in the changeable dispositive of the person, since human beings arrived into life from the world of things, they could always be thrust back into it".[34] Some people at the time, therefore, were not considered human beings for a long time, nor did they have human rights.

However, even then, the law recognized their difference from objects and animals. Although they could not own property or enter into contracts as Roman citizens, their intelligence, ability to be autonomous, and needs entailed separate treatment. They had the possibility of having a peculium though, to have and hold a certain amount of property as their own private property that their masters allowed them to spend or use as their own. This device acted as a shield to slave masters. Typically, they could be sued for the actions of their slaves as they are considered to be their property. Peculim protected them as their liability was limited to the amount of property covered by it. Robert van den Hoven van Genderen sees the relationship between the slave and their master and the relation between the slave and society as a whole as "more than instrumental. The slaves could perform a legal representative position, independent legal transactions and could appear as a witness in court. Moreover, the slave could be declared a "free man" by their master (manumission). This was not strange because at that time, on a population of one million people in Rome, there were 400,000 slaves. The position of the slave may be similar to the position of the robot in a future society although declaring them "free men" as in the Millennium Man might be a step too far. Maybe robots could also hold peculium in

---

[32] Calo (2015), p. 549.

[33] Wiener (1950).

[34] Esposito (2012), p. 79.

the sense of a 'financial resource to be used without human control'."[35] Not only peculium acted as means for limitation of master's liability. If a slave caused harm, its liability was limited to the slave's value. Consequently, instead of compensating a victim, a master could simply surrender the slave.[36]

Treating AI analogous to slaves in ancient Rome brings many advantages. First, the problem of granting personality would be avoided. Ethical and philosophical considerations would not be applicable as AI would constitute a person. Rather, it would be an entity without personhood which peculiar characteristic merit having a certain group of rights. Second, the problem of solving accidents caused by autonomous and opaque AI behavior would be avoided. Traditional liability regime always tends to allocate responsibility to a certain person or a group of persons. It uses different criteria that are not easily compared, and which mutual relationship might depend on the personal sensibility of the one who applies the law. Treating AI as a slave would depart from such reasoning and recognize that certain accidents are essentially different and therefore require different solutions.

The analogy between AI and slaves has the potential to provide wrong incentives to persons who act in the development and deployment of technology. Roman law treated slaves as something specific, differentiating them from animals. Arguably, the treatment of slaves concerning exposure to liability of them and their masters benefited masters in the first place. Devices such as peculium and the ability of a master to surrender a slave essentially gap its liability. It provides that there is no incentive to control the behavior of a slave. Of course, regardless of their treatment under the law at the time, slaves were human beings with cognition, consciousness, and features of all other humans. As such, they cannot be considered as being capable of being understood by their masters. Humans are complex entities that do not operate linearly and often in an understandable fashion. Unlike them, albeit opaque and sometimes even capable of being better than humans in performing tasks, AI is a human creation. In the long run, we might be able to understand it and this option, notwithstanding its current potential unforeseeability, should not be abandoned. Moreover, since humans create it, AI is capable of being changed. Slaves do not have such capacity. Shielding persons who participate in the manufacturing of deployment of AI means that we essentially give up on providing incentives to them to render AI better.

Providing AI with duties and sanctions is problematic for another reason. The law would have to be drafted with an incentive to AI in mind, instead of those of humans. This objection can be made for all ideas that aim at the imposition of liability on AI. Tort law aims at providing incentives to the addressees in order to reach the goals of efficient compensation and prevention of future accidents. One of the fundamental changes in civil law since the times of the Roman Empire was the abolition of physical punishment for civil wrongs. Compensation in property is the sole sanction for one's behavior in the law of B&H. This type of sanction provides an incentive to

[35] van den Hoven van Genderen (2018), p. 46.

[36] Revolidis and Dahi (2018), p. 69.

natural and legal persons to stop behaving in a certain way as well as guarantee to the victim that their suffering will be compensated. If we accept that artificial organizations who operate differently should be responsible, how can we be sure that the law provides appropriate incentives? Casey and Lemley dealt with this issue. They argue that the law needs to incentivize that "algorithms are modified to include sanctions as part of the risk-reward calculus"[37] and that "if the AI is self-learning, we may never know who is to blame".[38]

This position merits to be criticized. AI is not a simple and uniform entity that operates in accordance with the rules intelligible to lawmakers. It would be hard to create a unique set of rules that would be appropriate for a variety of contexts where it operates and techniques behind AI. Given the changing nature of AI, it may be hard to design the rules that account for the possibility of change and yet provide appropriate incentives. What would be incentives for AI in the first place? Can they be coded? How the legal rules designed to be understood by AI should look like and whether such endeavor is possible in the first place? These questions are pending. Instead of targeting AI, the law should burden persons behind it with a duty to compensate. To do otherwise would mean to shield persons behind it through some form of limited liability and not provide them with incentives to render products better and safer over time.

5.4.1.3 The Idea of Teilrechtsfähigkeit

Another idea of a limited legal capacity has been introduced by Schirmer.[39] He introduces a theory whereby the existing legal concept of Teilrechtsfähigkeit would be applied to AI. Originally, Hans-Julius Wolff introduced this concept. He expounded earlier idea of Eugen Ehrlich.[40] Essentially, the concept refuses to accept that the question of personhood can be presented in binary form. It recognizes that entities can have different statuses that would cover a range of rights and duties and not only a specific set of rights and duties that are characteristic for humans or legal persons. Therefore, this is not necessarily a binary question. An extension of a German concept of Teilrechtsfähigkeit has been proposed as a suitable solution to overcome the problems with attribution of AI with liability duties. It would provide it with "a status of partial legal subjectivity based on certain legal capabilities"[41] which would be limited to specific rights and obligations needed for the performance of its tasks. This concept bears similarities with how slaves were treated in ancient

[37] Lemley and Casey (2019), p. 1367.

[38] Ibid, 1353.

[39] Schirmer (2019).

[40] Ibid.

[41] Schirmer (2019), p. 140.

Rome—more than objects and less than humans. Both ideas can be illustrated by the example of a jar and resemble the Yugoslavian scholar understanding between legal personhood of natural and legal persons:

For a person, the jar is full, in principle persons can have all rights and obligations the law has to offer. This does not mean, of course, that they actually do have all those rights and obligations. But there is a presumption in their favor that persons have a legal capacity not only in the abstract but also with regard to specific rights and obligations. Thus, there is an urging need for justification whenever certain rights and obligations are excluded from persons. Taking candy out of a jar presupposes a defense. For subjects with only partial legal capacity it is a different story. They start off with an empty jar. Candy is placed into the jar only with respect to their specific functions. Again, this does not mean that the glass will always stay at that level. But each new candy placed into the jar has to be justified. In other words, the burden to justify the allocation of legal capacities is the exact opposite—legal personhood deals with subtracting, while Teilrechtsfähigkeit is concerned with adding rights and obligations. And those different starting points make a huge difference.[42]

Unlike Roman slaves, Teilrechtsfähigkeit is not an outdated idea. It is used in modern legal orders. German law recognizes some sort of holder of rights and duties in a company even before it has been registered (Vorgesellschaft). If it does not require registration, German law recognizes it as a subject of rights and duties (Rechtsform sui generis).[43] It demonstrates that it has its place in modern considerations of legal personhood. B&H entities company law prescribes that person establishing a legal person are themselves, holders of rights and duties, until registration of the company. Once it has been registered, a company takes replaces them. This is a form of overcoming the rule of ultra vires, as the company needs to have premises for its office, utilities such as electricity, water, etc. Furthermore, the Law of Civil Procedure of B&H's entities allows for non-persons to be treated as such for purposes of a specific civil procedure. For example, governmental bodies are not legal entities, but they can represent the state if the matter falls within its purview.

Many considerations need to be taken into account in a debate over providing rights and duties to AI. This issue highly surpasses the scope of this work. For the purpose of regulation of liability (which, admittedly, can hardly be individualized from other fields of law), the same objections can be made like in the case of electronic personhood and analogy with slaves. Shielding persons behind AI from responsibility can have detrimental effects on the fundamental goals of tort law. Problem with separate assets of AI is present too.

[42] Ibid, 13.

[43] Mocanu (2022), p. 7.

5.4.2 Manufacturers

Compared to traditional products, manufacturers will be able to exercise more control over AI. Their control will not stop at the moment a product leaves the factory. It will continue as long as the product is being used according to the instruction by the users. As they are the ultimate party among the available pool of persons who can control AI, they should bear the burden of compensation. Moreover, it can be stipulated that manufacturers should be liable in every situation when an accident occurs and users are not liable, provided that the accident has been predictable.

Economic analysis of law supports this finding. The manufacturer is likely the cheapest cost avoider. It is in a position to alter the way AI operates. In fact, it is probably, the only one who can actually do so. This is especially so "in the case of a closed software system that prevents third parties, including the user, from tampering with the algorithm that runs the device".[44] This finding excludes all other parties to be held liable because otherwise the goal of deterrence would not be met.

LO does not recognize the tortious liability of manufacturers except when harm has been caused by the defective product. As the previous chapter demonstrates, the product liability framework in LO, although broader than in the case of PLD, is very vague. It requires additional specification of the used terminology. Moreover, it requires rules on the relationship between the liability of manufacturers and the liability of users to be clarified. If control of AI is the governing rule that justifies holding manufacturers liable, benefits of the use of AI and its potential misuse are what justifies the liability of owners and users. An attempt to clarify this relationship can be found in the 2020 Resolution. It distinguishes between backend and frontend operators. Article 3 provides a definition of these terms. "Frontend operator means any natural or legal person who exercises a degree of control over a risk connected with the operation and functioning of the AI-system and benefits from its operation. Backend operator means any natural or legal person who, on a continuous basis, defines the features of the technology and provides data and an essential backend support service and therefore also exercises a degree of control over the risk connected with the operation and functioning of the AI-system."

In the remaining part of the document, it stipulates joint and several liability of frontend and backend operators for harm. Article 12 of the 2020 Resolution addresses how their contribution should be determined. Namely, it employs a "degree of control the operator had over the risk connected with the operation and functioning of the AI-system" as a criterion. Clearly, the very meaning of control and especially its expression in degrees is very vague.

Even the way in which the backend operator has been introduced is vague. Article 3 (d) stipulates that the notion of the operator' encompasses both "the frontend and the backend operator as long as the latter's liability is not already covered by

[44] Ibid.

Directive 85/374/EEC". In other words, the 2020 Resolution is not applicable as long as PLD is. If a person is considered to be a producer under PLD, the general liability regime envisaged in the EU Parliament's recent document is not applicable. Such circumstances might severely curtail the reach of the 2020 Resolution. PLD envisages the strict liability of a producer, but it used to limit it in many ways. Probably the most notable limitation is the 500 EUR liability cap. The liability cap had been removed with the updates, but the new version still has deficiencies, such as the limitation of damages to privately used property, death or personal injury, and data loss. Whether a manufacturer can be considered an operator in a concrete case would depend on the interpretation of this provision.[45]

Wagner considers that Resolution wrongly addresses operators as responsible parties should be manufacturers due to their ability to control AI. He notes: "But why, of all people, are the users of these systems chosen as the subjects of liability? … manufacturers have more responsibility than was the case with traditional products. The reason for this is simply that the user largely loses his influence on the "behavior" of the system, while the manufacturer gains influence."[46] However, this was hardly the intention of drafters of the 2020 Resolution. As Wendehorst explains, differentiation between backend and frontend operators might be a convenient way to formulate a manufacturer's liability.[47] Namely, the duties of manufacturers should correspond to the ones of a backend operator. Such formulation, if made adequately, would allow for the application of current law to manufacturers, without the need for fundamental changes of the text. This reasoning is applicable to LO as well. Liability rules focus on the user of a thing rather than its producer, with the exception of product liability. Change of paradigm that AI brings would require separate rules in LO or the creation of an entirely new set of liability rules. Defining producers as backend operators and (some) users as frontend operators would allow lawmakers to circumvent the difficult process of amending general rules that are decades-long in use.

It is also important to differentiate between various potential manufacturers. For instance, in the case of the robot, it is possible that a manufacturer only participated in the creation of hardware or another component that did not cause a defect. A manufacturer of a robot might be completely unrelated to AI as it only provided sensors for external data collection. Furthermore, it is also possible that the defect might not be related to AI but in the way, it has been integrated into the hardware. There is a myriad of potential situations.[48] It is necessary to be able to establish who made a mistake that led to harm. A clear set of tasks among manufacturers as well as a possibility to trace back their actions would ease the problem. Under B&H law, all manufacturers can be held jointly and severally liable for harm caused by the product. While such a solution is favorable from the perspective of the victim, it

---

45 Zech (2021), p. 12.

46 Wagner (2019), p. 556 (author's translation).

47 Wendehorst, (2020), p. 176.

48 Revolidis and Dahi (2018), p. 75.

generates other problems that concern the possibility of having one defendant liable for potentially great amounts of damage. B&H law does not recognize liability cap akin to 500 Euro cap in the former version of PLD. A participant in a manufacturing process who supplies less relevant components might be burdened with a high amount of harm without any actual relationships with the harm. Regardless of its right of recourse, a duty to compensate harm it did not cause can render it insolvent. This issue and corresponding issues will be addressed in 5.5. Holding one than more actor responsible.

Holding manufacturers liable is justified from the perspective of eius damnum, cuius commodum principle. After all, although an irrigation system provides water to the crops of their owner, manufacturers are the ones who benefited from receiving the purchase price for the system. Their benefit might be indirect, but it is apparent. Furthermore, manufacturers are likely to be in a better position to defend themselves than users, in case of disputes that require an understanding of AI and reasons for its behavior. Manufacturers are likely to have "better access to the facts helping to prove (or disprove) the defect"[49] as well as to interpret them in a persuasive way that would be sound before the court. The problem of access to data by other parties than manufacturers is very important. In the first place that would be a victim who might need them to prove its claim, but also users who might be defendants in a case. This question will be addressed separately in the next chapter.

5.4.3 Owners

Owners are a category of persons related to AI that do not necessarily have any control of it. In theory, they can be the same person as manufacturers or users, but for the purpose of this work, it is apt to treat them as separate persons. For example, one person bought an AI-driven mown lawn machine. It rented it to his friend in order to trim its yard. A friend operated it but it failed to program it correctly. As a consequence, the machine cut and destroyed a field of tulips that belonged to its neighbors.

Unlike manufacturers and users, owners' mere connection to it is through the legal relationship. Of course, an owner may benefit from the exploitation of AI. For instance, it can rent it to another person. Therefore, there is a lack of control but a presence of eius damnum, cuius commodum. The following question is whether such a setting merit extending duty to compensate to an owner. Unlike many questions that are novel due to AI characteristics, this one is traditional. The owner of an AI is not different from the owner of traditional things. Case law suggests that courts that apply LO employ the criterion of control of a thing or an activity as an exclusive one for establishing liability.[50] Even when there was no

[49] Koch (2019).

[50] Supreme Court of Croatia, Rev-382/85 od 3.4.1985.

control, in reality, the courts are entitled to burden a person with a duty to compensate a victim if it had a duty to assert it. For example, this is the essence of vicarious liability, situations where a principal cannot control the behavior of its agent who acts independently, but where it nonetheless benefits from it. The analogy with animals is not applicable, at least in the case of LO. As it has been discussed in the previous chapter, animals are not considered to be agents but rather objects in the liability law of B&H. Owner is liable due to the fact that it had to take care of its objects rather than the fact that it has benefits of keeping an animal.

5.4.4 *Operators/Users*

At the outset, terms operators and the user should be differentiated from one another. Their meaning can overlap, but they can also be different. Both terms refer to persons who employ AI in order to satisfy some needs to theirs. The difference is in the control they assert. For example, an operator of a self-driving vehicle is a person who provides inputs to AI on the destination, desired route, etc. A user is a person who is a passenger in such a car but who does not necessarily provide instructions to it. In other words, operators influence specific behavior of AI while users might not. What has been said about owners applies to users too. For the same reasons, they should be held liable if the harm caused by AI occurs only when they were in control of AI. If users were not in control, their liability should be limited to misuse of AI. For instance, they might use it contrary to the instruction, or they might provide it with polluted data, or they might fail to install available updates.

Differentiation between users and operators has practical significance in some jurisdictions.[51] Motor Insurance Directive[52] in Article 12 stipulates that the insurance has to "cover liability for personal injuries to all passengers, other than the driver, arising out of the use of a vehicle". If a vehicle is self-driving, a driver might not be in control of it anymore. Consequently, an injured driver could not avail of strict liability in some jurisdictions such as Austria and Germany. Instead, it would have to pursue the claim based on fault liability.[53] Clearly, the current provision is predicated on the understanding that a driver had influence over the behavior of the vehicle. This is what separated its position from other passengers. Self-driving vehicles militate against such a rule as the driver is likely to be on par with other passengers in terms of control. The same problem might appear in B&H. Law on Mandatory Traffic Insurance of the Federation of BiH in Article 22 and Law on

---

[51] Karner et al. (2021), p. 74.

[52] Directive 2009/103/EC of the European Parliament and of the Council of 16 September 2009 relating to insurance against civil liability in respect of the use of motor vehicles, and the enforcement of the obligation to insure against such liability [2009] OJ L263/11.

[53] Karner et al. (2021), p. 74.

Mandatory Traffic Insurance of Republika Srpska in Article 22 stipulate that the owner of a vehicle has to enter into a mandatory insurance contract that covers harm suffered by third parties, passengers, and their property. Both instruments fail to define the term passenger. However, they in Article 2, respectively, define the term driver as a person who operates a vehicle. Admittedly, it is possible to creatively interpret the term driver and claim that in the case of self-driving vehicles there might be no driver at all. However, in order to avoid uncertainty, legislative action that would settle this question is desired.

An operator is a person who instructs AI on how to perform specific tasks. The term operator used in this section corresponds to the term frontend operator in Sect. 5.4.2. Manufacturers. In line with the 2020 Resolution, the operator's impact on AI behavior can occur on different levels. Based on this criterion, this document recognizes backend and frontend operators. Latter ones are what traditional law considers to be an operator—a person who determines the actual and specific operation of AI. As it has been mentioned, the 2020 Resolution stipulates joint and several liability of backend and frontend operators. The Report suggests that liability between backend and frontend operators should be borne by "the one who has more control over the risks posed by the operation. While both control and benefit are decisive for qualifying a person as operator, the benefit is often very difficult to quantify, so relying only on benefit as the decisive factor for deciding who, out of two operators, should be liable, would lead to uncertainty."[54]

The demarcation between the liability of backend and frontend operators seems like a difficult task. Provided the general rules apply, the courts might have a hard time in establishing who had more control and who, ultimately, should bear the costs. In order to avoid this problem, the legislator should step in whenever it is possible and create a clear set of duties of backend and frontend operators. The risk of autonomous AI behavior, provided that all involved persons acted prudently, should be borne by the backend operator as the cheapest cost avoider.

5.5 Holding More Than One Actor Responsible

Aa s position of the victim should be in focus there should be no doubt on who is a potential defendant. In other words, those actors who control and/or benefit from technology should bear a duty of compensating the injured party if an accident occurs. From a position of an injured party, a range of potentially liable parties provide for a selection and lack of risk of insolvency of a defendant. A principle of functional equivalence between accidents involving AI and traditional accidents should be followed. This is a concept used in The Report whereby victims should have the same level of protection as in the case of traditional technologies.[55] This

[54]The Report, 41.

[55]The Report, p. 34.

problem can be mitigated by various devices such as insurance or compensation funds. More on this issue in the following chapter.

Ideally, manufacturers and users will be held liable for the harm. Who should be liable in a specific situation should depend on whether a user behaved prudently and not misused AI. If the answer to this question is affirmative, we should turn to the relationship between manufacturers and users. First, in the process of manufacturing, there is potentially a number of actors who provide different parts or improvements to AI or a product to which it is embedded. As Wagner notes, all actors who can be considered manufacturers typically have an agreement that concerns the harm of a product. "The obvious tool for re-allocation of the costs of liability within one of the groups is a contractual agreement. Modern standard supply agreements among the members of the manufacturer group, i.e. end-producers and component suppliers of different layers routinely include clauses that provide for the allocation of the costs of product recalls and other costs caused by defective components."[56]

The problem of allocating costs by a means of agreement has a potential problem. Due to an imbalance of power during negotiations, it is possible that not-so-influential actors might agree to terms of an agreement that put an excessive burden on them. Imagine a small company from a developing country that supplies a complex robot with a component. The main manufacturer of the said robot is a multi-billion company that is well-established on the market. When they arrange their relationships by means of a contract, it is unlikely that the small company would be able to negotiate a fair share of liability exposure, especially if a component it supplies can be found elsewhere.

The situation is even more complex if owners and users are to be held liable along with manufacturers. As we mentioned, there is a strong argument in favor of the liability of both manufacturers and users. Regulation of their mutual relationships is prone to the power imbalance even more so than in the case of transactions between the small company and a multi-billion company from the previous example. Buyers will enter into agreements with sellers of AI, usually without technical knowledge and legal education to be able to understand the risks they are undertaking. Provided they share the position of liable parties with manufacturers, they might be exposed to boiler plate clauses whereby the majority of exposure would be borne by them. This scenario is undesirable. In the B&H context, consumers need statutory protection from such situations. Legislation should reflect the change in the rules on allocation of responsibility. The new rules should take into account that users must be able to identify their share of liability relatively easily and in a reliable way. Legislation should be of general application, and not applicable to only a set of users. For example, consumer protection legislation would deny many users this protection, such as small and medium enterprises. A problem with providing different product liability standards for consumers and other injured parties in B&H, as has been demonstrated in the previous chapter, should be avoided.

[56]Wagner (2019), p. 32.

If harm occurred due to the unforeseeable but unpredictable behavior of AI, a choice on the ultimate liable party should be made. This concerns only those situations where harm cannot be attributed to any persons who either manufactured or used AI. For example, if an AI-driven drone hits and destroyed installations on the utility pole, should its manufacturers or owners, and users be liable? An injured party should have the possibility to institute a claim against any of them, but who should be able to have a right of recourse? This is a fundamental policy choice that, being such, should not be left to be decided by contractual means. As it has been stipulated before, freedom of contract might not provide just solutions but rather imposition of agreement that a more powerful party prefers. For this reason, legislators should make this choice. Those who can exert control should bear the burden. They are the cheapest cost avoiders and the ones who can change the design of AI to prevent a similar event from occurring in the future. Those are in the first place manufacturers.

References

Books

Calabresi G (1970) The costs of accidents: a legal and economic analysis. Yale University Press

Esposito R (2012) Immunitas. Einaudi

Janal R (2020) Extra-contractual liability for wrongs committed by autonomous systems. In: Ebersband M, Navas S (eds) Algorithms and law. Cambridge University Press, p 194

Karner E, Koch AB, Geistfeld AM (2021) Comparative law study on civil liability for artificial intelligence. European Commission

Kovac M (2020) Judgement-proof robots and artificial intelligence a comparative law and economics approach. Palgrave Macmillan

Kurki AJV (2019) A theory of legal personhood. Oxford University Press

Revolidis I, Dahi A (2018) The peculiar case of the mushroom picking robot. In: Corrales M, Fenwick M, Forgó N (eds) Robotics, AI and the future of law. Springer, p 69

Schirmer J-E (2019) Artificial intelligence and legal personality: introducing "Teilrechtsfähigkeit": a partial legal status made in Germany. In: Wischmeyer T, Rademacher T (eds) Regulating artificial intelligence. Springer

Schroeder HC (1997) Causation, compensation, and moral responsibility. In: Owen GD (ed) The philosophical foundations of tort law. Oxford University Press

Summers J (2020) The Case of the Disappearing Defendant: An Economic Analysis. University of Pennsylvania Law Review, in: Mitja Kovac, Judgement-Proof Robots and Artificial Intelligence: A Comparative Law and Economics Approach, Palgrave Macmillan, 132:145–185

Teubner G (2018) Digital personhood? The status of autonomous software agents in private law. Ancilla Iuris, pp 106–149, available at: https://papers.ssrn.com/sol3/papers.cfm?abstract_id=3177096

van den Hoven van Genderen R (2018) Do we need new legal personhood in the age of robots and AI? In: Corrales M, Fenwick M, Forgó N (eds) Robotics, AI and the future of law. Springer

Wagner G (2019) Robot liability. In: Lohsee S et al (eds) Liability for artificial intelligence and the internet of things: Münster Colloquia on EU law and the digital economy IV. Nomos

Wiener N (1950) The human use of human beings. Eyre & Spottiswoode, Houghton Mifflin

Zweigert K, Kotz H (1998) Introduction to comparative law, 3rd rev. edn. Clarendon Press, Oxford

Articles

Calo R (2015) Robotics and the lessons of cyberlaw. Cal Law Rev 103:513
Eidenmüller H (2019) Machine performance and human failure. J Bus Technol Law
Koch AB (2019) Product Liability 2.0 – mere update or new version? In: Lohsee S, Schulze R, Staudenmayer D (eds) Liability for artificial intelligence and the internet of things: Münster Colloquia on EU law and the digital economy IV. Nomos
Lemley AM, Casey B (2019) The University of Chicago Law Review, Remedies for Robots
Mocanu D (2022) Gradient legal personhood for AI—painting continental legal shapes made to fit analytical molds. Frontiers in Robotics and AI
Wendehorst C (2020) Strict liability for AI and other emerging technologies. J Eur Tort Law 11(2)
Zech H (2021) Liability for AI: public policy considerations. ERA Forum 22:147–158

Chapter 6
Position of an Injured Party

6.1 Introduction

Previous chapters addressed several issues that are generated by AI. From the most fundamental ones, such as the definition of this technology, over the assessment of its characteristics through the lenses of tort law, to the proper balancing between just and pragmatic considerations in applying a basis of liability to a specific person, each chapter was focused on a specific problem. At the outset of this work, a number of potential avenues have been present as choices between favoring important, yet sometimes opposed interests. An injured person can be seen as a person at whose expense technological progress should occur as it creates higher overall benefits for society. If the regulation is overly protective of victims, innovation may be stifled and people who are capable of bringing progress may leave the country or jurisdiction. On the other hand, favoring innovation without sufficient care for collateral harm it creates to consumers of new products (but also other types of harm, which are not always treated by tort law, such as psychological or environmental harm), is not the way to imagine the future.

Occasionally, what would each of the avenues mean for injured parties was explored along with the impact on the incentives to the responsible parties.

However, a comprehensive perspective of an injured party should an accident occur has not been provided. When one is faced with an accident, there is a number of mutually related factors that a person who suffered harm needs to take into account in order to assess its position. Sometimes, unlike what Jhering suggests, it might not be worth it to pursue a claim since the suffered harm was too low. It is also likely that a victim may face hardship in identifying a person against whom it can win or enforce a judgment. There is a consensus in scholarship that AI detrimentally affects the position of injured parties compared to traditional accidents. Authors claim that the increase of technical sophistication of this technology spurred with its autonomous behavior that cannot often be explained further disincentivize their

N. Muftić, *Artificial Intelligence and Tortious Liability*, European Union and its Neighbours in a Globalized World 21, https://doi.org/10.1007/978-3-031-86453-7_6

position. The exact position, of course, depends on several factors, such as the sector in which the accident occurred and degree of victim's education in law.

This chapter examines some of these problems. By focusing on the position of an injured party after the accident occurs—it compares it to the position of a party in a traditional accident, i.e., when a non-autonomous and completely explainable technology was involved in an accident.

It examines the problem of increased exposure to the harm of victims as a reason that was used in history to enhance their position when the degree of protection offered by the law seemed too low. When this problem occurred, the legal system responded by providing substantive and procedural rights to victims and duties to tortfeasor in order to even the playing field in the court proceedings as well as to foster compensation even in the absence of the court epilogue. Then, specific problems in relation to AI. Those are increment of administrative costs that may be borne by the victim in order to have a successful claim, standard of proof a victim has to meet and who has to prove what, the problem of establishing causation, insurance and compensation funds, and joint and several liability. Each of these problems relates to others yet merits to be elaborated separately as they portray a deteriorating position of the injured party in the process of accessing justice and obtaining remuneration. A victim may expect to face AI in all spheres of life. The potential limitless application of this technology renders the range of potential injuries high. Second, personal data expected to be even more important than it is nowaday. We may expect to have harm related to the use of personal data by AI accordingly. Third, due to the complexity of technology, a victim is likely to have a hard task of proving harm and linking it to the specific person or a set of persons if traditional rules on causation are applied. As an interim solution, the courts can act as a regulator who employs an understanding of a victim of an AI accident as a weaker party in order to interpret LO in a way that evens the playing field for the parties with the opposite interests in the court proceedings.

All three considerations will probably increase the costs of the proceedings for the victim. It will have to avail of expert witnesses. It will have to pay in advance for all the costs it incurs in the evidentiary phase of the proceeding. In case of partial success, it may not be able to recover the costs of representation due to inherent problems with B&H civil procedure law.

The problems with causation stem from factual and legal reasons. The factual reason is composed of multiple reasons why the harm occurred which the victim (or anyone) may not be able to discern. Legal reasons are grouped around the standard of proof and the burden of proof. This chapter elaborates on why the standard of proof as it is in present in LO should not be amended. It is not formulated strictly and it should remain that way. Case law demonstrates that the courts in B&H (and Serbia as neighboring country where LO is also in force) demonstrated sensibility towards different problems concerning causation and employed LO's formulations to solve them. If anything, it should be clarified that the courts will not follow the strict rules on the standard of proof in the case of emerging digital technologies. The burden of proof requires more attention. A victim has to be able to obtain data in order to prove their claim. This is one of the reasons why logging by design should be obligatory for all AI. LO already recognizes adverse inferences as a way of dealing with parties who fail to deliver the required information. Reversal of burden of proof, and often suggested measure, already exists in case of strict liability and its reach will thus depend on how courts interpret the notion of increased dangerousness. A clarification of adverse inference would be a step forward.

A certain set of auxiliary tools that ease the victim's position are insurance, compensation funds, and joint and several liability. All these devices are operable in B&H. Insurance and compensation funds sometimes even operate together in a multi-layered system of compensation. The victim is protected with the deep pocket of insurance companies despite whether the tortfeasor intentionally caused harm. In designing insurance for AI, companies should be able to monitor AI in order to prevent reckless behavior of insured persons who may feel free not to care about their behavior due to insurance. Logging by design is helpful.

Lastly, tools set to provide relief to the injured party should be considered. Those are the procedural tools such as the reversal of burden of proof and reconsideration of standard of proof, and the tools which enable easier compensation such as insurance and compensation funds.

6.2 What Are the Problems Caused by AI?

Previous chapters addressed the impaired position of an injured party in case of AI accidents, especially compared to traditional accidents. The adversity is at least threefold. First, the range of potential injuries is high as AI is potentially applicable in all spheres of life. It might provide medical treatment to a patient as well as assess the value of the real estate. It may cause harm to one's reputation by adversely leaking information on the internet and rejecting one's job application. While regulation (especially sectoral one) might mitigate risks to a certain degree, there has never been a clear demarcation between what sectors can AI penetrate. Admittedly, this question received attention with the AI Act and it is currently being debated, at least in Europe. However, in the likes of B&H, where there is a lacuna in the governmental response as well as public debate, this problem is hardly going to be solved any time soon. As we have seen, the problem of increased exposure to risk is not a novel one. Product liability is a specific type of strict liability that has been developed in Yugoslavia to deal with exactly those risks. Second, there is the increased importance of data. Of course, this characteristic cannot be attributed only to the way AI is operating. Data is vital for many emerging digital technologies since it acts a cornerstone of industries that operate within this sphere.

However, any one of these technologies should not be treated in a vacuum. They are likely to interact, exchange data and other inputs relevant for providing services to persons. When it comes to AI, there are specific problems that arise with the way it processes data. This issue is not the focus of this work though. The importance of data in the digital economy surpasses the question of liability and touches upon some of the fundamental values upon which western societies rely, such as privacy and even one's right to freely choose those who will run the government at the elections.[1] The importance of data for AI is high, as we elaborated before, and those who develop it are not going to give up on its collection and processing. In the words of Peter Norvig, chief scientist at Google: "We don't have better algorithms than anyone else. We just have more data."[2]

Third, the position of injured parties in the proceedings in the aftermath of an accident is changed in the procedural sense. As we have seen previously, there is a problem of identifying the responsible party. As the EU Parliament 2017 Resolution stipulates: "whereas under the current legal framework robots cannot be held liable per se for acts or omissions that cause damage to third parties; whereas the existing rules on liability cover cases where the cause of the robot's act or omission can be traced back to a specific human agent such as the manufacturer, the operator, the owner or the user and where that agent could have foreseen and avoided the robot's harmful behavior". Or, as the 2020 Resolution stipulates, "the potential victims of harm or damage are often not aware of the operation".[3] There is also a problem of predictability of the basis of liability to be applied as well as how the courts can assess the behavior of humans with respect to AI. Whether fault-based or strict liability should be applicable and what they exactly mean is yet to be developed. Other procedural problems are addressed in this chapter.

Furthermore, a victim might face a number of practical problems too, such as insolvency of the responsible party, its bankruptcy or a long time required for a decision of Bosnian and Herzegovinian court decisions to be adopted and enforced. Its position would often depend on whether it can obtain compensation without court proceedings.[4] As a norm, a victim is better off if a responsible person had a (mandatory) insurance policy. A second avenue is an out-of-court settlement. There are no statistics in B&H on the number of accidents where the compensation is achieved by the activities of the insurance companies and through out-of-court settlements. It can be plausibly assumed that a significant part of cases ends up in court. This chapter will mainly discuss the latter portion of accidents.

More specifically, the problems this chapter addresses, each in a specific section, are related to the position of an injured party should the court proceedings occur. The reason for focusing on this part of the accidents is an increased vulnerability of a victim in an accident. Imagine if a responsible party had an insurance policy that covers harm it causes to third parties. A victim would be (likely completely) compensated and better off than in a case of the court proceeding. The same applies to an out-of-court settlement. A victim would be able to recover its losses easier than before the court, at least in terms of time and money it would not have to spend.

---

[1] For example Facebook–Cambridge Analytica data scandal.

[2] Google's 'Infringenovation' Secrets, Forbes, 3 October 2011, available at: www.forbes.com/sites/scottcleland/2011/10/03/googles-infringenovation-secrets/#78a3795430a6.

[3] Recital 11.

[4] Alternative dispute resolution mechanisms will not be discussed as they are not mandatory nor common in B&H.

Furthermore, a position of an injured party in the court proceedings is reflected in the interaction between the responsible party and itself in general. For instance, if an injured party is aware that it cannot obtain evidence in order to prove its claim, there would be a lack of incentive to pursue a court avenue.

Likewise, a responsible party may be reluctant to settle out of court if it is aware of the injured party's hard position in the court proceedings. In the case of harm covered by mandatory insurance, the weak position of the injured party may impact the price of insurance. "The less foreseeable a system is, however, the less willing insurance companies are likely to be to offer insurance at reasonable premiums."[5]

Assessment of an injured party's position in the court proceedings is contingent on a number of factors. Some of them depend on the applicable substantive law. This has been, more-less, covered in the previous chapters. The following sections will present how these legal devices may operate in action from the victim's perspective, for better or worse. Substantive law should not be divorced from procedural law for this purpose. Jointly, they shape a position of a party in the proceedings. Clearly, they would be hard to demarcate from one another. For instance, the rules on strict liability are considered to be substantive. However, B&H legislator nonetheless provides for procedural consequences if it is applicable in the case. Those are the likes of presumed causation and joint and strict liability. Further, there is a justification for the protection of specific categories of injured parties. Not all of them are impaired to the same degree nor do they have the means to protect themselves equally. As we mentioned on several points in this work, the fundamental principle of equality of parties is changed by AI and other emerging digital technologies. The scholarship has recognized it a long time ago and the lawmakers followed the lead. The EU has been a global standard-setter.

The 1975 Council resolution observed that the new market conditions, such as an increased abundance and complexity of goods and services, have shifted the balance between suppliers and customers in favor of the former. According to the Council, such an accentuated imbalance resulted in the need to keep consumers "better informed of their rights and protected against abuses".[6] Shortly after, in the second consumer program of 1981, further factors were mentioned that transform the relationships between market participants, including the "new data processing and telecommunications technology".[7,8]

B&H adopted its consumer protection legislation (which, unfortunately, has not been updated in order to follow recent developments in technology and best regulatory practices). Such differential treatment is justified by evidence of the imbalance between the parties, which leads to the need for solutions favoring the 'weaker'

[5] Hubbard (2014), p. 486.

[6] Council resolution of 14 April 1975 on a preliminary programme of the European Economic Community for a consumer protection and information policy [1975] OJ C92/1.

[7] Council resolution of 19 May 1981 on a second programme of the European Economic Community for a consumer protection and information policy [1981] OJ C133/1.

[8] Jabłonowska et al. (2018), p. 10.

party. Some injured parties are, however, weaker than the others. This is the case with consumers. While AI has the potential to adversely impact the opposition of injured parties in general, they are likely to be more impacted than the others. However, in the case of B&H, this may not mean so much, as consumer protection legislation refers to the general rules of liability, i.e. LO.

6.3 Consideration of a Weaker Party as Interpretive Lenses

LO provides very generous protection to the victims of accidents compared to previous limitations of PLD. In fact, in can be argued that PLD became closer to LO after the amendments as it removed compensation cap of 500 EUR, provided for reversal of burden of proof (is some situations) and expanded meaning of its terms such as product and defect. Definitions of a product, a defect, or specific product liability defenses are not provided in the text of LO. In the case of fault-based liability and strict liability, standards provided in LO are vague and thereby flexible for interpretation. Increased dangerousness of an object or an activity or a reasonable person as a benchmark for a tortfeasor's behavior is completely left to the courts understanding. While previous chapters advocate for certain legislative changes, they also stipulate that the current framework is capable of being adapted for the challenges posed by AI.

For that to be achieved, the court is invited to be proactive. Rather than to be blind to the rapid changes in the technological landscape that surround us, they may use LO as a tool in their hands to foster transition to an AI-present world. Specifically, in the interpretation of the current LO, the courts should bear in mind that the ambiguities should be interpreted in a way that provides the same degree of protection of victims of AI as it does of victims in general. The Report recognizes that this in as one of the failures of the current law—to provide "a coherent and appropriate response of the legal system to threats to the interests of individuals, in particular, because victims of harm caused by the operation of emerging digital technologies receive less or no compensation compared to victims in a functionally equivalent situation involving human conduct and conventional technology".[9]

A search of functional equivalent can operate exactly as lenses through which the court sees the cases involving AI. Whenever this technology is involved in an accident, the courts can interpret the broadly defined notions in LO in favor of providing the counterbalance for altered positions of involved parties. As Glen Hodgson put it:

> The most appropriate public-policy response to disruptive technology is to recreate a level playing field in as many ways as possible so that neither status-quo businesses nor disruptive forces gain an arbitrary advantage.[10]

[9] The Report, 5.

[10] Hodgson (2019), p. 18.

In the absence of specific provisions that would regulate AI, the courts in B&H are authorized to do so. Moreover, as the historical development of strict liability and product liability attests, such practice would not be seminal. The courts in Yugoslavia have previously responded to the deteriorating position of injured parties even before legislators. We should remind ourselves that strict liability has been applied even before it has been legislated in LO.

Moreover, technological neutrality is embedded in the current legislation in B&H. This statute has the general scope of application which intentionally provides leeway to the courts for adaptation. Just like it covers electrical telegraph, it should also cover AI. The trend of applying existing legal concepts to new technological phenomena is not new or AI-related. In the EU, the main legislative role model after which B&H drafts its legislation as well as case law[11] recognizes this as a regulatory principle. Bonn Ministerial Conference, held in 1997, adopted as one of the principles that "general legal frameworks should be applied on-line as they are off-line".[12] The clearest expression of this principle, as Andrej Savin claims,[13] has been made in the 2006 UN Convention on E-Commerce.[14] This document aimed at establishing equivalence for documents and signatures in the electronic environment. It stipulates that functional equivalence "an analysis of the purposes and functions of the traditional paper-based requirement with a view to determining how those purposes or functions could be fulfilled through electronic-commerce techniques".

Koops note that "if the effects of a technology are regulated rather than the technology itself, the regulation will usually establish functional equivalence between "off-line" and "on-line" technologies".[15] Reed claims that this idea in its essence is an endeavor to expand the rules that regulate physical work to the digital world.[16]

Despite being recognized by the EU rule makers, there is a lack of consensus on what is the reach of this principle. This is especially so in B&H, where the scholarship on the intersection between law and technology is underdeveloped. This section does not attempt at providing a standing on the meaning of this principle in abstract. It is certain, however, that it permeates legislative actions as well as decisions of the courts at least in the EU if not beyond. The application of a generalized set of rules to AI requires a deep understanding of this technology, as it has been described in Chap. 3. The problem lies in the fact that new technologies

---

[11] Law on competition of B&H (Official Gazette B&H 48/05, 76/07, 80/09) in Article 44 even allows for direct application of the Court of Justice of the EU case law and decision of the EU Commission.

[12] Principle 22; Conference held on the 6–8 July 1997, available at http://europa.eu.int/ISPO/bonn/Mindeclaration/ifinalen.html.

[13] See Savin (2019).

[14] UNCITRAL Model Law on Electronic Commerce with Guide to Enactment 1996 with additional Article 5 bis as adopted in 1998, available at http://www.uncitral.org/pdf/english/texts/electcom/V1504118_Ebook.pdf.

[15] Koops et al. (2006), p. 83.

[16] Reed (2012), p. 106.

may require a change of basic rules on which the legal framework is predicated. This section does not attempt to argue that courts should make decisions that imply policy choices. Rather, when there is an equivalence between the effects of well-known technology and AI, their treatment by the courts should have the same effect under LO in terms of the application of general norms. This is so in terms of burden each party bears in the proceedings. Unquestionably, AI renders the position of injured parties harder than it used to be. In such cases, the courts may recognize that there is a functional equivalence between AI and other technologies.

Moreover, functional equivalence might be interpreted as requiring a comparator in the existing world to be implemented. For instance, it may be argued that an old phenomenon and a new phenomenon have similarities and hence, they should be treated by the same set of rules. This is questionable in the case of AI. In nothing else, it gained popularity as a unique technology that is like no other else. The functional equivalent can be found in the previous actions of the courts. If they were willing to apply strict liability to cars as a new phenomenon that replaced horse carriage, they may do the same for AI. Different natures of AI risks would allow for different treatment, especially since the courts are enabled to apply it due to the general wording of the applicable LO rules. After all, providing an even field in order to respond to changing circumstances would be in line with one of the fundamental ethical principles recognized by ancient Greeks and formulated Cicero - Iustitia suum cuique distribuit. Should the courts in B&H accept that AI in both stand-alone and embedded format is a product, strict liability would apply to the producer(s). Consequently, a victim would be relieved from the burden of having to establish causation as it is presumed. The number and scope of available defenses will be curtailed too, compared to fault-based liability.

This work repeatedly claims that legislators should step in and clarify ambiguities in the existing liability framework. Until that happens, the courts can act as an interim regulator who employs an understanding of a victim of an AI accident as a weaker party in order to interpret LO in a way that evens the playing field for the parties with the opposite interests in the court proceedings.

6.4 Increment of Administrative Costs

Court proceedings in B&H are regulated by the statutes on civil procedure of the entities and Brcko District. Each of them stipulates that they include expenses incurred during the proceedings or in connection therewith[17] as well as remuneration for work of attorneys and other persons whose right to remuneration is envisaged, such as expert witnesses.[18] The rule on the ultimate cost-bearing is that the party that

[17] Article 383 of Law on Civil Procedure FB&H, Article 383 of Law on Civil Procedure Republika Srpska, Article 117 of Law on Civil Procedure Brcko District.

[18] Article 384 of Law on Civil Procedure FB&H, Article 383 of Law on Civil Procedure Republika Srpska, Article 118 of Law on Civil Procedure Brcko District.

has lost the litigation in its entirety shall cover the winning party's costs. Likewise, if the party was partially successful, the court may, depending on the success in the proceedings, order each party to cover its costs, or one party to cover a proportionate part of the other party's costs.

There is an inherent problem with the implementation of the rule distribution of costs in case of partial success. As the text of the statute suggests, the courts have discretion over distributing costs when a tortfeasor did not completely win in the proceedings. Currently, the case law on tortious liability suggest that courts interpret this provision differently. The problem arises when the court considers the distribution of costs to be contingent on the percentage of the claim expressed in terms of money. If the duty to compensate has been established by the court, but not in the amount requested by the tortfeasor, the court may consider it as a partial success and distribute costs of the proceedings between the parties. To illustrate the problem, consider the case[19] before the Cantonal Court of Tuzla, a court of the second instance in the Federation of B&H. It concerned tortious liability and rules of LO were applicable. In the part of the decision that deliberated on the appellant's claim that the first court distributed costs of the proceedings erroneously, this court held:

> Contrary to the stated position of the first instance court regarding the success of the parties in the dispute, this court finds that the fact that the plaintiff originally filed a claim in the name of the plaintiff damages the total amount of 54,000.00 KM, that is his success in the dispute, and given the amount awarded to the name of the damage by this judgment of a total of 13,442.00 KM, 24.89%, while the success of the defendant is 75.11%. In the repeated procedure, the plaintiff claimed the total amount of 29,760.00 KM in the name of damages, so it is his success in the dispute 45.16%, and the success of the defendant 54.84%, all in terms of the provision of Article 316, paragraph 2.[20]

The problem is that sometimes the amount of harm cannot be calculated in terms of money. For instance, there might not be a conclusive statement of the expert witness on the value of the damaged property, or various expert witnesses might offer different views of the same situation. Some forms of harm are by their nature incalculable, i.e. immaterial harm. Ultimately, the courts determine the amount a defendant has to pay. Consequently, if the percentage of the amount to be paid determines the allocation of costs, the courts can by their discretionary appraisal of harm burden a victim with the costs despite its success in the proceedings.

In case of immaterial harm, the Court of B&H reasoned[21] that the success in the proceedings should not determine the allocation of costs: "The principle of success in the dispute, applied by the first instance court, there is a place in disputes for compensation of material damage, which cannot be equated with a fee which represents satisfaction and the amount of which is not known at the time of submission lawsuits. Therefore, the plaintiff's appeal rightly indicates a misapplication of the material rights, but not for the stated reasons of changing the

[19] Cantonal Court of Tuzla, 126 0 P 142724 21 Gž 2, 10.05.2021.

[20] Author's translation.

[21] Court of B&H, S1 3 P 0 16700 16 Gž 2, 03.06.2016.

value of the dispute, but for reasons listed in the reasoning of the second instance decision."[22]

The existing case law seems to be conflicted with the understanding of this problem adopted at the Panel for Unification of Judicial Practice in Civil Field, which was attended by representatives of the Court of Bosnia and Herzegovina, the Supreme Court of the Federation of B&H, the Supreme Court of Republika Srpska and the Court of Appeals of Brcko District on January 30, 2014. They concluded that in the case when the defendant disputed the basis of the claim in its entirety, due to which only the costs of the litigation were incurred, the plaintiff may be awarded the costs of the litigation in full, regardless of the amount requested and awarded.

This problem, although not specific for AI, has the potential to create the same impact in litigation involving AI as well. By the way it operates, it can be described as having a chilling effect on the injured party who might not seek to obtain compensation in court proceedings. Unfortunately, this is not the only problem that exists in the current civil procedure law of B&H with the potential to generate the same effect. For example, the length of litigation proceedings is often excessive which has been recognized by the European Court of Human Rights as a violation of Article 6 of the European Convention of Human Rights.[23] The enforcement procedure is also of very limited efficiency, rendering the fact that an injured party obtained decision only a half-way success.[24]

Another problem, specifically relevant for AI lies in the fact that a victim as a tortfeasor has to cover the costs of the proceedings in advance. That is, irrespective of the outcome of the proceedings, one might assume its costs in advance. Again, this is general norms B&H civil procedure law. In proceedings that involve sophisticated technologies, it is plausible that participation of an expert witness will be necessary and expensive evidence might be necessary. Consequently, a victim who does not have sufficient funding might be diverted from claiming compensation. The change of the rules of civil procedure that would alter existing rules might undermine the entire structure of the current law, which is, operable and fair. Rather, a specific set of rules might be adopted only in relation to this technology. "Emerging digital technologies should come with logging features, where appropriate in the circumstances, and failure to log, or to provide reasonable access to logged data, should result in a reversal of the burden of proof in order not be to the detriment of the victim."[25] Thereby, the costs of obtaining evidence for a victim would be foreseeable and limited. It could know where to look for evidence and what would be costs of obtainment as well as costs of interpretations by an expert witness.

---

[22] Author's translation.

[23] Some of the recent cases include: Dorić v. Bosnia and Herzegovina, 68811/13, 2017; Škrbić and Vujičić v. Bosnia and Herzegovina, 37444/17 i 75271/17, 2019; Hadžajlić v. Bosnia and Herzegovina, 10770/18, 2020.

[24] See more at: Vodič: Suđenje u razumnom roku, Constitutional Court of B&H, 2021, available at: https://www.ustavnisud.ba/uploads/documents/vodic-sudjenje-u-razumnom-roku_1611845149.pdf.

[25] The Report, 4.

Moreover, an additional burden to a responsible party who is not a manufacturer would not be imposed. A victim would bear the costs of obtainment and interpretation of evidence. Manufacturers would have a duty to embed logging features in AI, and the duties of operators would be to log data and to provide access to data in case of an accident. The latter duty is not a new one in B&H, though. Laws of civil procedure already envisage that one party might use a document which is in possession of another party: "Where one of the parties proposes a document in evidence which he asserts is in the possession of another party, the court may grant an order for the possessor of the document to produce it within a prescribed time limit."[26] Furthermore, The Report's suggestion on reversal of the burden of proof can to a limited extent be found in current B&H's civil procedure law. It envisages that "when a party refuses to comply with the court's order to produce a document or denies the possession of the document, the court shall, taking into consideration all the circumstances, determine the inference to be drawn from such conduct".[27] Although the reversal of the burden of proof is not mentioned, adverse inference acts as a solid incentive to the responsible party not to refuse to provide access to logged data.

Although there is a lacuna in case law concerning tort cases involving AI, scholarship suggests that the number of experts to be consulted and the duration of proceedings might be increased. The increase of costs of the proceedings might be increased accordingly. Consequently, attorneys who receive compensation on the basis of contingency fee structure might be disincentivized to take a risk and accept such cases.[28]

6.5 Causation

Depending on the applicable basis of liability, a victim has a different set of tasks to meet in order to receive compensation. One of the fundamental differences lies in causation. We have seen, strict liability means that the causation is presumed. It is enough to prove that there was a risk concerning a dangerous object of property or dangerous activity. The burden of proof then shifts, and a defendant has to rebut the presumption. The same standard is applicable in the case of product liability and, as we could see, by means of court interpretation, in the case of liability for animals. In the case of fault-based liability, a victim has to establish a connection between tortious acts and harm as consequence.

One of the main reasons for debates on whether the current liability framework suffices in light of the emergence of AI is related to the question of causation. We could previously see how causation operates in B&H tort law in Sect. 4.5.1.4.

---

[26] Art 135 Law on Civil Procedure FB&H.

[27] Ibid.

[28] Ibid.

Causation. In case of strict liability, causation is presumed and can be rebutted by the producer, whereas the burden of proof is borne by the victim in case of fault-based liability. The differences between fields of application, sectors, and what are the underlying relations between all involved parties may create specific problems there. All the aforementioned factors have potential to change the situation and create a specific set of circumstances that are not present anywhere else. A huge number of scenarios requires that a clear demarcation between cases where fault-based liability and strict liability is applicable. Furthermore, complex relationships between manufacturers, deployers, owners, and users additionally render the situation even more sophisticated for victim, especially in case of fault-based liability as it may be required to identify specific person as a defendant.

Seeking redress within complex value chains, such as the car manufacturing industry, has been commonplace for many years, and existing laws regarding liability seem largely fit to also deal with AI technologies. However, while in many cases this tried-and-tested approach to liability will work, there may be times when it fails. Untangling the causal strands of who was responsible for what can be tricky even in human-only situations; this can become far more difficult as complex algorithms with various human touchpoints are added. There is a growing concern over how best to ensure that end-users of complex AI systems are adequately protected if there are so many contributing factors to what happened (including potentially even the autonomous actions of a machine) that responsibility becomes diffuse, and it is hard to reliably assign blame for problems.[29]

The potential number of scenarios relevant to causation is high. Karner and Koch note that the problems might arise on at least for levels:

First, "the AI itself may have malfunctioned. However—and this distinguishes AI systems from other technologies—it may have worked as intended, but nevertheless produced an undesired outcome due to its self-learning abilities and the capability of adapting its behavior to new challenges".[30] This has been covered in the previous chapter as well as in scholarship that deals with AI. Those are situations where a human is not directly responsible for the misconduct of AI.

Second, "AI systems embedded in hardware may cause harm due to flaws of the hardware itself, or due to its AI features, or because the latter caused the former to fail. Identifying what exactly initiated the process ultimately leading to the victim's loss is thereby complicated even further".[31] This is the case where the performance of AI is impacted by external, yet directly, connected components. For example, sensors for the detection of moving objects in an AI-driven lawn mower are defective and it caused AI to perceive an animal that belongs to another person as a plant that needs to be cut.

---

[29] Google, Perspectives on Issues in AI Governance, 27, available at: https://ai.google/static/documents/perspectives-on-issues-in-ai-governance.pdf.

[30] Karner et al. (2021), p. 24.

[31] Ibid.

Third, "the operation of AI systems is influenced by human conduct, be it by their users, by content providers, by their manufacturers, or by software or hardware component producers, or by third parties".[32] This set of reasons has been covered extensively in the previous chapter. The number of errors in operation is unlimited—from mistakes in the phase of programming, lack of providing necessary updates, or failure to use AI in an envisaged way. The more actors are involved, the harder is to establish a connection between actions and consequences.

Fourth, "implementations of AI systems often significantly rely on an interaction with other technology, often themselves AI-based".[33] Given that they operate in a digital ecosystem, there is a chance that complex interactions blur the picture.

The aforementioned reasons may occur simultaneously, effectively rendering access to justice very hard for the victim. Such complexity should not fall on the back of victims. Along with the traditional vulnerability of victims in comparison to sophisticated entities who may be sued, an inherent lack of knowledge and the ability to impact and improve AI renders their position even harder. Therefore, a standard of proof, as well as the burden of proof, should be adjusted. Of course, the problem is different depending on whether strict liability or fault-based liability is applicable.

6.6 Standard of Proof and Burden of Proof

The EU law had not traditionally regulated the problem of the standard of proof and the burden of proof. This has been changed partially with the updates to the PLD. They provide for the presumption of defectiveness when a defendant is breach of the obligation to disclose evidence and for the presumption of causality for typical damages if defectiveness has been established. The interpretation and application of these rules remain in the hands on the Member States as this directive rests on national procedural rules"[34] Therefore, understand the law, it will be necessary to consult the national legal regimes of Member States once they take over the updates of the PLD.

As a norm, national legal systems deal with the problem of causation. This is especially evident in situations where it is uncertain that there was only one event that caused the accident. While joint and several liability is the predominant device used throughout Europe, there are important variations. Karner and Koch note that in Denmark, France, Italy, and Spain, in order for persons who participated in the concurring event that led to harm to be held liable, they need to act jointly.[35] Other jurisdictions, such as Belgium, understand causation as to mean cause essentielle.

[32] Ibid.

[33] Ibid.

[34] Bertolini (2020), p. 58.

[35] Karner et al. (2021), p. 38.

There is also the preponderance of the evidence as a standard in place.[36] It requires that there was more than a half of certainty that a specific event caused harm. Furthermore, some jurisdictions apply an all-or-nothing approach, allowing full compensation or no compensation at all, depending on whether the standard of proof has been met. Other jurisdictions include proportionate liability that nuances between several alternatives or cumulative contributions to the harm.[37] Proportionate liability, as it exists in Austria, recognizes differences between various contributing factors, thereby failing to treat cases in a binary fashion. In the words of Jaap Spier: "One could argue that there are hardly compelling reasons to make a choice either way whose interests should prevail. In this reasoning, the idea of fairness should depend on the merits of every single case and to some extent also tradition. More specifically, one might say that it is far from obvious that the different heads of damages, of or liability—in particular strict, vicarious, mere fault or grave fault—are to be treated similarly. One could also imagine that the magnitude of the harm, the number of tortfeasors, or of victims might play a role."[38]

We already addressed the applicable theory of causation in B&H law. At this point, it can be added that Mihailo Konstantinovic understood causation to mean the only direct connection between actions and consequences. He stipulated that as a rule, a tortfeasor is liable only for harm that would not occur without their actions. Limitation of liability to direct consequences operates as a means of protection of tortfeasor. Exceptionally, indirect consequences of their actions might lead to harm, and the tortfeasor would be liable for those too. He provides two examples. The first is an example of a person who coerces another person to enter into a vehicle. If an accident occurs during the time when they were located in the vehicle while there was a collision with another vehicle, Konstantinovic considers the person who coerced another person to be liable. This situation can be distinguished from a situation where one person persuades another person to enter into a train, and the train later participates in an accident. In the first case, the previous behavior of tortfeasor qualifies it to be liable for indirect consequences. In the second one, it does not. The second is an example of a person who is suffocating due to the actions of another person. The responsible person would be liable also for the harm that might be potentially suffered by a third person who attempts to save the suffocating person.

In reality, however, understanding of causation in the case of court which applies LO is flexible. They do not strictly take into consideration only the relationship between actions and their consequences but also other factors, such as the purpose of liability, foreseeability of harm, the scope of harm, as well as other theories of causation. After all, LO failed to strictly regulate how the courts should interpret the notion of causation, providing leeway for interpretation that would be in line with the fundamental principles of civil law. This is also a means whereby the courts may provide a nuanced view on causation. By flexibly applying different theories of

[36] Ibid.

[37] Ibid.

[38] Spier (2005).

causation on a specific and often unique set of facts, they may achieve what proportionate liability aims at. The standard of proof should not be altered by legislative means at this point. After all, a tradition of B&H courts, like courts in many jurisdictions is to adapt standards of causation to a specific problem before them. Although it might be hard to be formulated in a general rule, the standard of proof can be adapted to the challenges of AI as the amount of case law grows.

Another problem is that at the moment, we do not know how to change it by means of statute. If victims are in a harder position than in traditional cases, what is the proper avenue to take? Instead of dealing with the standard of proof, the focus of legislator should be rather on who has to prove what. Naturally, when a strict liability (and product liability) is available, there is no question. The rules of LO on presumed causation provide a favorable position to the victim. When a fault-based liability is applicable, certain amendments should be considered.

Alteration of the burden of proof with various possible modalities might ease the victim's position while, at the same time, provide not an excessively hard task for potential defendants. Availability of information does not necessarily mean that the burden of proof will not be heavy for a victim. This problem has been recognized as "the single most difficult steppingstone to receiving compensation for damages"[39] by the EU Commission.

A number of measures known in comparative law can be used, such as the likes of res ipsa loquitur theory, whereby the occurrence of harm is enough for the inference of negligence. As I identified before, devices with similar effects include lowering the standard of proof,[40] the application of prima facie evidence,[41] judicial presumptions,[42] and adverse inferences of the failure of manufacturers or users to produce evidence in their control about the harmful event.[43] As mentioned before, The Report even suggests a reversal of the burden of proof of causation and fault[44] if the victim faces "disproportionate difficulties or costs"[45] and if the defendant is in a much more favorable position to provide proof.

Adverse inferences are the clear favorite in the spectrum of possible avenues due to the reason that it is already available in the general rules on civil procedure. However, the application of this device makes sense only if there is data available to the defendant. For these reasons, logging by design should be a mandatory feature of every AI. While LO provides for such regime, it requires clarification whereby a

---

[39] Report from the Commission to the European Parliament, the Council and the European Economic and Social Committee on the application of the Council Directive on the approximation of the laws, regulations, and administrative provisions of the Member States concerning liability for defective products (85/374/EEC), 5.

[40] For instance, liability law in the medical sector employs some of these measures. See Koch (2011).

[41] Martin-Casals (2019a, b).

[42] Ibid.

[43] Report, 51.

[44] Ibid, 49–55.

[45] Ibid, 6.

failure of a responsible party to provide data shall mean that court shall conclude as a victim who sought the data claimed. The current law does not prevent such interpretation. For the sake of clarity, a further clarification of adverse consequences would be desirable.

As Frank Pasquale writes, the opacity of AI is not a mono-causal phenomenon.[46] Admittedly, the reasons for opacity can be unpredictable behavior that is incomprehensible, and which cannot be explained. However, opacity can also come from a lack of availability of data. The latter reason can be mitigated by mere disclosure. Unavailability of data to the injured party can be a product of legal arrangements that exist between manufacturers, owners, and users, such as contractual terms. Transparency of AI, besides empowering injured persons to yield success in obtaining compensation, also creates broader societal benefits—"AI openness to spur innovation in access to data and explanation that could transform the next wave of scientific development".[47] Of course, consideration should be provided to the interests of manufacturers to have their technology protected from competition. Transparency might jeopardize it and they should be provided with protection, such as in camera review of data by an expert witness or confidentiality duties imposed on persons who received access to the data.

A special problem is whether data obtained from AI is explainable. While transparency entails that one can obtain data, it does not guarantee that it will be comprehensible. A variety of techniques used in crafting AI, some of which were briefly mentioned in Chap. 2, attest that there will hardly be a single AI expert that can be invoked by the court to interpret data. According to the civil procedure rules in B&H, a person who requires that expert witness acts has to suggest a specific person to the court and cover its expenses in advance. How can one be sure that a specific AI expert has knowledge in specific AI techniques and in a specific sector to be qualified to complete the task? This remains to be a question that requires clarification.

Lastly, once the right person is selected, there might be cases when it is uncertain what caused the specific accident—unexplainable AI behavior or errors in manufacturing or operation. In such circumstances, a specific basis of liability will aid. Presumed causation, inherent for strict liability, will act in the victim's favor. On the other hand, if fault-based liability is applicable for an operator, a victim can still avail of product liability. "For example, a countertop AI-enabled slow-cooker could foreseeably exceed its heat setting and increase risk of fire in a consumer's home. Disclosures of representative explanations along with process and technology details could be useful to demonstrate that the manufacturer has reasonably implemented appropriate technical steps to avoid injury."[48] If they fail to demonstrate so, product

[46] See Pasquale (2016).

[47] Tschider (2021), available at: https://ilr.law.uiowa.edu/online/volume-106/legal-opacity-artificial-intelligences-sticky-wicket/.

[48] Ibid.

liability (in other words, strict liability in B&H legal order) comes into effect and provides a victim with a favorable outcome.

6.7 Insurance and Compensation Funds

Chapter 3 already addressed the role of insurance and compensation funds are as part of the broader regulatory puzzle around AI. It emphasized its role in providing incentives to reduce risk, moderate levels of harmful activities, and provide safety for injurers and certainty for victims. It elaborated on how European societies, including B&H's one, are used to employing mandatory insurance for a certain set of activities, such as mandatory vehicle insurance, and insurance for medical professionals. Compensation funds too are not a novelty in Europe and B&H. In Bosnian and Herzegovinian context, a compensation fund is employed as a mechanism that ought to cover residual risks from mandatory vehicle insurance. An owner of a vehicle has to obtain insurance that covers costs to third parties. If for a number of reasons elaborated in Chap. 3, an injured party is unable to avail of insurance, it has a compensation fund at its disposal. Admittedly, an injured party does not have guaranteed complete coverage of all risks covered by insurance and compensation funds as some accidents are left out. However, B&H legal system has a longstanding experience with the combination of insurance and compensation funds in a multi-layered system in order to provide relatively reliable compensation to the victims.

Insurance as a means of achieving various policy goals has soared with the development of strict liability in Yugoslavia. In the era of expanded liability that covers harm caused without fault, the insurance industry was developing in parallel with the changes in tort law. Moreover, legal theory considers the duty of an insurer to compensate an injured party to be equal to the duty of a responsible person. It acts as a limitation of the insurer's duty in quantity.[49] Likewise, if an injured person failed to institute a claim or if a responsible person simply unknown, the insurer's duty will not come into effect. There is also an opinion in the scholarship whereby the duty of a responsible party cannot be treated as equivalent to the duty of an insurer due to the differences such as limitation of the insurer's duty by the covered amount.[50]

Since the EU has already harmonized the rules on the mandatory insurance scheme for vehicles by virtue of the Motor Insurance Directive, there is significant experience on the part of Member States that would facilitate the adoption of such mechanism for AI. Mandatory insurance aims at preventing risk of the insolvency of the tortfeasor and facilitating compensation of a victim. For damages not covered by mandatory insurance, a fund that would cover the residual losses might be

[49] Karanikić Mirić (2011).

[50] Petrović Tomić (2020), p. 83.

introduced. 2017 Resolution[51] also supports this position. Mandatory insurance in theory also help responsible parties as it limits their risk exposure. "Just like mandatory insurance, the concept of a fund that would supplement mandatory insurance is not new as it already exists in Member States' national legal systems. Consequently, a risk of having an unknown mechanism in a compensation scheme is reduced. Furthermore, since society reaps the benefits of technological progress, compensation funds could perhaps be used to cushion the transformation risks in the development of our transforming society.[52] The issue of who ought to bear the cost of mandatory insurance and who ought to contribute to the fund does not have a clear answer at present. However, since one of the main goals of the technological advancement is to create lawless machines that perform tasks better than humans, or at least with a lower number of errors, the price of insurance and the contribution to the fund ought not to be high as the occurrence of tortious events is expected to be diminished.

Insurance and compensation funds are favorable for the victim as they often render resolution of sophisticated and costly legal questions unnecessary. They eliminate the need for litigation between the victim and a responsible party (or even an insurance company). Case law of B&H suggests that the insurance company is obliged to compensate a victim for suffered harm even when the insured persons intentionally caused harm. Only after the victim is compensated, the insurance company has the right of recourse from the responsible persons concerning the entire amount of damage, interest compensation, and associated costs.[53] In the case of the compensation fund, the victim who cannot obtain compensation from the insurance company has the right to initiate administrative proceedings in order to receive payment. Unlike litigation, these proceedings are free of costs such as court fees and the victim can relatively easily obtain compensation if it can present documents attesting that the tortfeasor is unknown or that it does not have insurance. Both mechanisms favor the victim compared to litigation. The problem is, as Chagal-Feferkorn notes, that "the less foreseeable a system is, however, the less willing insurance companies are likely to be to offer insurance at reasonable premiums".[54] As this chapter observes the problems from the perspective of a victim, this risk will not be addressed further.

Another important consideration from the victim's perspective, although it is not related to the position of an injured party in the court proceedings, is the safety insurance and compensation funds provided for responsible persons. As Shavell notes, liability insurance reduces incentives of injurers to reduce risk since the harm of their activities will be covered by the insurance company. If a person is aware that the insurance company will cover the accidents that arise out of their activities, they are more likely to be carefree than if they have to provide out-of-pocket

[51] Resolution of 2017, paragraph 59.

[52] Ibid.

[53] Supreme Court of FB&H, Gvl–9/03 od 26.8.2003.

[54] Chagal-Feferkorn (2020), p. 486.

compensation. Insurance allows them to allocate and spread the risk of loss. From the victim's perspective, quick and reliable compensation is not better than no harm in the first place. If insurance provides for both avenues, the victim is not well off. Shavell notes that the problem of excessive engagement in risky activities and lack of care of insured persons can be mitigated if an insurer can monitor their activities and adjust the terms of an insurance contract in response to their behavior.[55] This is an additional argument for logging by design. Apart from victims who can avail of the data in litigation administrative proceedings, insurance companies can use it to assess the behavior of insured persons. 2020 Resolution also recognizes it:

> Insurance can help guarantee that victims receive effective compensation and pool the risks of all insured persons. One of the factors on which insurance companies base their offer of insurance products and services is risk assessment, based on access to sufficient historical claims data. A lack of access to, or an insufficient quantity of, high-quality data could be a reason why creating insurance products for new and emerging technologies is difficult at the beginning. However, greater access to, and optimizing the use of, data generated by new technologies, coupled with an obligation to provide well-documented information, would enhance insurers' ability to model emerging risk and to foster the development of more innovative cover.[56]

Nataša Petrović Tomić stipulates that the goal of deterrence can actually be fostered by insurance. "For understanding the preventive role of liability insurance, it is crucial that it is not comprehensive, i.e. that it does not cover the entire scope of liability of the insured, and therefore that it does not bring into question the preventive function of liability. Very prominent elements of the prevention of liability risk (insured's obligations, excluded damages, coverage limit, the *bonus-malus* system, contraction of self-adherence, etc.) make liability insurance not only an instrument of protection but also an efficient means of preventing high-risk business practices."[57] However, if a person who is in the best position to control the risk of autonomous AI behavior that causes harm to third parties are operators, and among them manufacturers in the first place, limitation of the insured amount may have undesired effect on their activities. After all, we should not be punishing innovators who did not act recklessly even if the mistake occurred. From the victim's perspective, it seems more important that the compensation is timely and complete than to use tort law to impact the responsible person's behavior by potentially ineffective means. After all, the first goal of tort law in B&H is to provide compensation to a victim and only then to prevent future harmful activities. For these reasons, incomplete insurance coverage would not be productive means to enhance the victim's position.

Insurance should be compulsory in sectors where the harm is increased and where the likelihood of its occurrence is higher. Again, this is traditional reasoning around Europe as well as B&H. Motor vehicle insurance is a stellar example. In B&H, it is

---

[55] Ibid.

[56] Resolution 2020, Recital 21.

[57] Petrović Tomić (2020), p. 88.

mandatory and covers accidents where fault-based liability and strict liability are applicable. To remind a reader, fault-based liability is applicable if an accident involves colliding with moving vehicles, while strict liability is applicable if a vehicle harms third parties. A compensation fund acts as an additional safety net. Such a scheme seems like a well-oiled machine that regularly yields favorable results for injured persons. With slight modifications, it can be applied to AI-powered vehicles. In other sectors where the exposure to harm becomes increased, this scheme can be replicated. Of course, the need for compensation funds might not exist if liability insurance sufficiently mitigates the risk. For example, if the use of autonomous drones becomes prevalent to the same degree as cars are in present times, there is a strong case for mandatory insurance. The need for compensation funds should be contingent on the gravity of the injured party to identify the drone that caused the harm, a responsible party, as well as whether data on the accident are easy to obtain. If the logging by design feature is integrated into a drone, this task might not be too hard. The additional layer of protection would be overly burdensome and redundant.

A compensation fund can substitute mandatory insurance in certain situations. "Absent adequate statistically relevant data, risks might be hard to define and assess, and a generalized duty to insure might have a strong technology chilling effect."[58] A compensation fund can replace insurance in such cases, provided that there is a limitation of exposure of persons who have to contribute to the fund.

6.8 Joint and Several Liability

Due to the various problems elaborated in this work, primarily the gravity of identifying responsible persons and the judgment-proof problem, the ideal solution for accidents involving AI would be to hold responsible parties jointly and severally liable. An injured party should have a clear situation when it comes to selecting its defendant. "The question of who bears responsibility for the accident, be it the driver who drove too fast, the owner keeper who failed to afford proper maintenance of the car, the shop owner whose repairs were deficient, or the manufacturer who failed to meet the required standard of safety, is not a concern of the victim."[59] It should not need to be involved in potentially layered relationships between natural and legal persons who may appear on the side of a tortfeasor. A one-stop-shop solution would render the victim's position predictable.[60] This could be achieved by allowing it to select whoever is available among manufacturers and users. Naturally, responsible parties need to have a right of recourse, and parties in the interest of efficiency ought

[58] Bertolini (2020), p. 14.

[59] Wagner (2019), p. 71.

[60] Report, 58.

to be "incentivized to make contractual arrangements for tort claims in advance".[61] The Report also advises joint and several liability of manufacturers who produce different components of a "commercial and technological unit" who "cooperate on a contractual or similar basis".[62]

The Report suggests that individuals who do not control AI are excluded from the group of jointly and severally liable parties. Since cooperation among manufacturers is required "on a contractual or similar basis," it implies that component manufacturers who are unaware of or do not collaborate with other component manufacturers are not subject to joint and several liability. In open digital environments, such as cases involving unbundled components assembled by the owner of an AI-based digital ecosystem, it is unlikely that all manufacturers involved are aware of such cooperation in each instance. Including AI users in the group of jointly and severally liable parties and removing the requirement for cooperation "on a contractual or similar basis" would strengthen the position of injured parties. 2020 Resolution champions this approach by prescribing joint and several liability of backend and frontend operators.

The application of LO would allow the use of joint and several liability. In the words of the Court of Sarajevo Canton: "For the harm caused by several persons together, all participants are jointly and severally liable so that the debtor of the joint and several obligations is liable to the creditor for the entire obligation, and the creditor may demand its fulfillment from each joint and several debtors until this obligation is fully fulfilled."[63] To keep the victim away from the complex set of relationships that may exist between persons behind AI and per se sophistication of technology, harm caused together can be understood to include frontend and backend operators. Clearly, an ambiguity of the meaning of what constitutes harm caused together requires regulatory intervention.

Another justification for joint and several liability is a potential difference in the amount and availability of assets held by persons form whom there are reasons to be held liable. Simply, the victim is better off if a potential defendant is a solvent as there is a guarantee of compensation if it wins in a dispute. In the US, where the common law tradition of courts allows them to depart from the written law, scholarship recognized that "deep pocket jurisprudence is most likely to occur when (a) the victim is truly innocent and therefore highly sympathetic, or the damage is done to the environment; (b) the injuries or contamination are severe; (c) the true wrongdoer is unavailable for the litigation, does not have sufficient funds to pay the claim, or would not be able to address the problem on a large-scale basis; and (d) the risk of harm was arguably foreseeable to the defendant."[64]

Imagine if an owner, who operated an autonomous chainsaw is bankrupt. A victim would, despite obtaining favorable judgment, be paralyzed. We previously

---

[61] Ibid.

[62] Ibid.

[63] Court of Sarajevo Canton, 65 0 Ps 022929 09 Pž, 23.9.2011.

[64] Schwartz et al. (2018), p. 404.

described this phenomenon as a judgment-proof problem. In present times, B&H is struggling with traditional cases where a judgment cannot be enforced properly. In the Municipal Court in Sarajevo, the average workload of judges and professional associates who were in 2018 assigned to the executive division of the courts with the highest amount of cases was 107% of the prescribed norm. Shockingly, only three professional associates worked in 2018 in the Municipal Court in Sarajevo, where the volume of cases is the highest, in that year achieved very high values of the annual norm, namely: 450%, 396%, and 609%.[65] The problem of judgment-proof defendants deserves to be addressed in B&H in general, and the deep-pocket considerations act as an avenue in case of AI accidents due to legitimate reasons for placing the burden on a range of persons due to their control and benefits from AI.

Lastly, there is a problem of unbundling. AI might divorce hardware from the software of multiple hardware and software components. A person who buys AI-driven hardware might be able to decide what software it wants. It may also decide to update hardware with another hardware component. A user may have more freedom than ever before in optimizing their device and adjusting it for its specific needs. A similar line of reasoning can be applied to a combination of noncorporeal AI. As a consequence, one manufacturer may not control the entire device or even be the sole creator of its corporeal and incorporeal components.

The updates of the PLD envisage that "economic operators" should be held liabile. This notion includes the manufacturer of a product or a component, and in the case of a manufacturer of a product or a component established outside the Union, and without prejudice to the liability of that manufacturer the importer of the defective product or component, the authorised representative of the manufacturer, and where there is no importer established within the Union or authorised representative, the fulfilment service provider. Also, any natural or legal person that substantially modifies a product outside the manufacturer's control and thereafter makes it available on the market or puts it into service shall be considered to be a manufacturer. If an economic cannot be identified, distributor of the defective product can be held liable, or, under certain circumstance, an online platform that allows consumers to conclude distance contracts with traders.

These provisions should prevent situations where the victim has to investigate whether the accident was caused by defective hardware, defective software marketed by the supplier of the original software, software manufactured by a third party and added to the device by the user, or by other modifications made by the user after the acquisition of the device. This burden may deter many victims from bringing suit and may seriously undermine the success even of meritorious actions.[66]

Joint and several liability can also help in these situations. Only on the level of recourse, potentially responsible parties should be able to settle the question of responsibility among them. This is an additional argument in favor of logging by

---

[65] See Povlakić et al. (2021).

[66] Wagner (2019), p. 49.

design. AI devices should record evidentiary data that can be used in the recourse proceedings. In LO, the problem of identifying who should be treated as a producer is not solved by the black letter of the law. As mentioned in Chap. 4, its provision can be interpreted as including a producer of the component as a producer under product liability rules. The question is whether unbundled components should merit the same treatment? At this moment, it can be stipulated that the answer should take into account the gravity of the position of a producer of an unbundled component in the recourse proceedings. Logging by design features of AI might allow for easy recovery, thereby enhancing argument in favor of joint and several liability.

Another important consideration is the nature of the relationship between unbundled components. Although users determine whether to connect them, there should be rules provided by manufacturers on what components are complementary and how to connect them. A user should not be expected to be an AI expert who can make an informed choice between a range of potential options on the market. If there are clear rules that are respected by the users, there is an additional argument in favor of joint and several liability. Needless to say, producers of unbundled components should have a duty to create such rules.

How B&H law might approach the problem of unbundling can to some degree be predicted on the basis of existing scenarios. Marija Karanikić Mirić[67] notes that the case law of Serbian courts that applied rules on liability for motor vehicles rejects claims that one operator of a motor vehicle was not responsible by proving that the operator of another motor vehicle caused the accident.[68] While an operator might be completely correct, this circumstance should not be a concern of a victim. This is an interpretation of Article 177 paragraph 3 of LO that prescribes the following:

> An owner of the object shall also be exempt from liability after proving that injury or loss occurred entirely through an act of the person sustaining injury or loss or a third person, which act could not have been foreseen by him and whose consequences he was not able to avoid or eliminate. Furthermore, paragraph 4 of Article 177 prescribes that should injury or loss be partially due to an act of a third person, such person shall be liable to the person suffering injury or loss jointly and severally with the owner of the object of property and shall also be bound to share the amount of compensation proportionally to the degree of his fault. The understanding of Serbian courts is supported by the scholarship:

> Operators of collided motor vehicles can defend themselves with a complaint that some circumstances exclude their responsibility. This includes the possibility of invoking the contribution of third parties, but the owners of the vehicles involved in the collision are not considered third parties in relation to each other. In the interest of the injured party deviated from the general rules on liability.[69]

The analogy with AI where multiple separate components have been manufactured, marketed (and sold) by virtue of the buyer's explicit choice stems from the independence of each of them. Just like the operators of motor vehicles, manufacturers of

[67] Karanikić Mirić (2016a, b), p. 193.

[68] Supreme Court of Serbia, 36/1995 od 7 February 1995, Supreme Court of Serbia, Rev. 2333/2003 22 October 2003.

[69] Radišić (1995), p. 409.

components may be independent of one another and not liable to any extent. This has been ignored, though, in the aforementioned court's interpretation. From the perspective of a victim, the law renders their independence from one another irrelevant. In fact, it can be argued that this argument is even more emphasized in the case of AI accidents. While the contribution of operators of multiple motor vehicles that caused the accident is discernable as a rule, this is not the case with AI. Its opacity might prevent victims and the court from being able to point a finger at a specific actor or to determine their contributions. The problem of specific contributions of parties who are jointly and severally liable is a matter that should be resolved in the recourse proceedings.

References

Books

Bertolini A (2020) Artificial intelligence and civil liability. Policy Department for Citizens' Rights and Constitutional Affairs

Chagal-Feferkorn K (2020) Tort law: applying a "reasonableness" standard. In: The Cambridge handbook on the law of algorithms. Cambridge University Press, p 504

Hubbard P (2014) "Sophisticated robots": balancing liability, regulation and innovation. Fla Law Rev 66:1826–1827

Karanikić Mirić M (2016a) Građanskopravni tretman životinje u štetnom događaju. In: Karanikić Mirić M, Davinić M, Vuković I (eds) Životinje i pravo. Pravni fakultet Univerziteta u Beogradu, p 161

Karanikić Mirić M (2016b) Prilog razumevanju pravila o solidarnoj odgovornosti imalaca motornih vozila. In: Lilić S (ed) Perspektive implementacije evropskih standarda u pravni sistem Srbije, vol 6

Karner E, Koch AB, Geistfeld AM (2021) Comparative law study on civil liability for artificial intelligence. European Commission

Koch AB (2011) Medical liability in Europe: comparative analysis. In: Koch AB (ed) Medical liability in Europe: a comparison of selected jurisdictions. De Gruyter

Koops B-J et al (2006) In: Koops B-J et al (eds) Starting points for ICT regulation. Deconstructing prevalent policy one-liners, it & law series, vol 9. T.M.C. Asser Press, The Hague

Martin-Casals M (2019a) Causation and scope of liability in the IoT. In: Lohsee S et al (eds) Liability for artificial intelligence and the internet of things: Münster Colloquia on EU law and the digital economy IV. Nomos, p 206

Martin-Casals M (2019b) The borderlines of tort law. Intersentia

Pasquale F (2016) The Black Box Society - the secret algorithms that control money and information. Harvard University Press

Radišić J (1995) Odgovornost proizvoľa~a neispravne robe, u: Komentar Zakona o obligacionim odnosima, glavni i odgovorni urednik Perović Slobodan, knjiga I, "Savremena uprava", Beograd

Reed C (2012) Making laws for cyberspace. Oxford University Press

Spier J (2005) In: Busnelli EF et al (eds) Principles of European tort law: text and commentary. Springer Vienna, p 46

Wagner G (2019) Robot liability. In: Lohsee S et al (eds) Liability for artificial intelligence and the internet of things: Münster Colloquia on EU law and the digital economy IV. Nomos

Articles

Hodgson G (2019) The right policy responses to the forces of disruption, The Glove and Mail, 27.11.2017. In: Savin A (ed) Rule making in the digital economy: overcoming functional equivalence as a regulatory principle in the EU. Copenhagen Business School Law Research Paper Series, No. 19-10

Jabłonowska A et al (2018) Consumer law and artificial intelligence: challenges to the EU consumer law and policy stemming from the business' use of artificial intelligence. EUI Department of Law Research Paper No. 2018/11

Karanikić Mirić M (2011) Odgovornost vlasnika motornog vozila kao preduslov odgovornosti osiguravača. Pravni život, No. 10:685–707

Petrović Tomić N (2020) Liability insurance as a (social) response to the changing regulatory framework: from prohibited to compulsory. Annals of Faculty of Law in Belgrade, 68

Povlakić M et al (2021) Mogućnost zloupotrebe prava u postupku javnog nadmetanja za prodaju nekretnina u izvršnom postupku u pravu BiH. Zbornik Pravnog fakulteta u Zagrebu 71(3–4)

Savin A (2019) Rule making in the digital economy: overcoming functional equivalence as a regulatory principle in the EU. Copenhagen Business School Law Research Paper Series, No. 19-10

Schwartz EV et al (2018) Deep pocket jurisprudence: where tort law should draw the line. Okla Law Rev 70:359

Tschider AC (2021) Legal opacity: artificial intelligence's sticky wicket. Iowa Law Rev Online 106:126

Chapter 7
Conclusion

Artificial intelligence is certainly worth our attention as users as well as the attention of those who create and apply legal rules. Individuals and societies around the world will probably attest to groundbreaking occurrences caused by this technology in the following years and decades. At the moment, it may appear that the buzz around it does not deserve to be so great. Products that are marketed as AI seem to have to catch more attention than the ones that are not. Services performed by AI have an aura of exclusivity compared to the ones where a human interacts with other humans. AI is seen as prestigious and desired by those who would like to be perceived as tech-savvy. At the same time, skepticism about the results of interaction between AI and persons is not insignificant. They range from the fear of not being able to be left alone due to the involvement of technology in our lives, as Shoshana Zuboff described in her book "The Age of Surveillance Capitalism", to our inability to live and meet our needs without dependency on technology, as Ivan Illich claimed in his book "Tools for Conviviality".

AI undermines fundamental principles of civil law. Party autonomy, i.e. its ability to render its own decision an example. The one who employs AI is likely to have a better understanding of the data analyzed by AI than the one who does not. Its ability to make an informed decision is severely impacted and its position in interactions with other persons is better. Also, there may be a different impact of AI. Due to its autonomous decision-making ability and self-learning capacity, it may make and even execute a decision that a person would not approve of had it known them before. If a person uses a self-driving drone, it may not be able to impact the exact route and how it avoids obstacles in the air. At the same time, if such a drone causes an accident, a person without control may be attributed with a duty to compensate victims. Moreover, a relationship between a person and AI opens a number of questions about the agency. While agency problems have been extensively addressed in the scholarship, both agent and principal had human cognition and incentives in those considerations. AI may operate on different principles and thus require different understanding. Party, which is likely to be in a position of a

N. Muftić, *Artificial Intelligence and Tortious Liability*, European Union and its Neighbours in a Globalized World 21, https://doi.org/10.1007/978-3-031-86453-7_7

principal in relation to AI, has its autonomy affected by the unknown behavior of its digital agent that may not be controllable by common methods.

What impacts party autonomy may also undermine the equality of parties. Again, the problem of information asymmetry, like in the case of party autonomy, may render the positions of persons who engage in a civil law relationship unequal. This is not a new problem, however. De fact inequality exists when there is a different level of information and expertise available to a single party in a relationship. In fact, as it may be widespread, AI may become a tool used to alleviate the position of those who were usually vulnerable, such as consumers. Google maps may act as an example, as a tool that empowers everyone to determine what is the most convenient route to reach the desired location. Such information is no longer reserved for parties who may afford expensive software.

All legal regimes have their specific features and ways to handle cases involving AI. At the time of writing this work, the case law is almost non-existent. However, there are many works in scholarship that develop their understanding of the potential problems in relation to a specific set of rules. The work follows this methodology and examines several traits of B&H law. In general, it can be noted that current B&H liability law is modern and flexible enough to be able to absorb most of the challenges brought by AI. This does not mean that specific sectors where the general rules of liability provide for undesirable outcomes should remain intact. It only refers to general framework of liability which is proven as flexible, future-proof and technology-neutral. As such, and given the early stages of AI, it can act as a general framework and secondary set of rules that captures all accidents to which special rules do not apply. Certain specific changes would be advisable, however, both concerning the interpretation of current law and statutory amendments.

Specific findings of this work are:

1. To define AI is a hard task. Even the existing definitions may be vague. Rather, AI characteristics should be regulated. In other words, the regulators should focus on the autonomy, opacity, and vulnerability of this technology. See Chaps. 2 and 3.
2. Regulation of liability for AI requires a vision of a complete regulatory landscape. Lawmakers should focus on establishing safety standards to encourage innovation while protecting consumers. Liability is just one aspect of a larger issue. In this context, it should not be expected to provide definitive solutions to all the problems currently associated with AI. With the development of technology as well as other pieces of the regulatory puzzle, some problems may disappear while others may change. Therefore, it is important to understand what can be regulated now and what can be left for future times. Safety standards may render some questions pointless. See Chap. 3.
3. Risk-based regulation is the desired and broadly recognised approach to regulating AI. This is a view championed by the EU. It already exists in the case of civil liability as it is prescribed in B&H. Thus, this approach should remain. The problem, however, is how to define risks. LO settles is by empowering courts to assess whether an object poses an increased danger to its environment. This

approach too should remain applicable in cases involving AI since vague and abstract legislative attempts to set generalized criteria are futile at this point. Furthermore, the problem of intermediated risks requires further attention. It is unclear how to address it properly. An approach worth pursuing is to consider the current regulation of advisors. See Chaps. 3 and 4.

4. Sector-specific rules should be adopted whenever possible. This includes not only rules of liability but also the rules of safety. It is unreasonable, however, not to have a general set of rules that would be applicable in the absence of lex specialis. Sector-specific rules allow for the specification of rules in line with risks that may be unique in a sector. In B&H, specific rules of liability can be integrated as specific cases, rendering LO's provisions to act as lex generali. Whether and when if would be possible to have a comprehensive set of liability rules depends on future of AI development as well as how we may understand it. This is not an urgent question and should be left for future. Urgent ones can be addressed with sector-specific liability regimes. See Chap. 3.
5. General rules of liability contained in LO have the capacity to act as a secondary set of liability rules whenever sector-specific rules have not been adopted or applicable. With mild adaptations compared to their current status in B&H law, they can respond to the questions raised by the application of AI in everyday life. See Chaps. 4, 5, and 6.
6. There is an increased importance of court interpretation in order to render the previous point possible. LO is permeated with ambiguous notions without any definitions provided, such as those of increased dangerousness, product, or defect. Throughout history, courts in B&H and Yugoslavia have expressed sensibility in adapting the law to new phenomena. They should be persistent with such an approach, especially given that they have leeway provided by LO. See Chaps. 4, 5, and 6.
7. Rules on liability for AI should be focused on persons around AI instead of AI itself. Persons are the ones who should be incentivized, punished, or awarded for their actions and omissions. Lawmakers should not consider designing rules that would incentivize AI as they are incapacitated to do so. Moreover, by providing rules that AI and not persons should follow, it is not clear what the impact those rules would have on persons. Persons should be bound by standards they need to follow in designing and employing AI, as well as by the duty to compensate if an accident involving AI occurs, provided that frontend operators, a victim, or a third party did not cause it. See Chap. 5.
8. Fault-based liability and strict liability will play important roles in regulating AI. They are potentially both applicable, depending on the responsible party and whether AI qualifies as increasingly dangerous. However, it is likely that strict liability is about to be expanded due to the lack of knowledge about AI risks. See Chaps. 4 and 6.
9. Standards of behavior used in the application of fault-based liability would need rethinking. Higher and lower standards of care one need to meet should correspond to the general state of play in the field. If AI is safer than the traditional product, a person who is held liable should need to meet higher standards,

provided that AI is available and affordable. However, this is mainly a discussion for some future occasions. This is so because AI is likely to be treated far more by strict liability. In a long-term perspective, fault-based liability may resurrect as AI becomes more familiar, safe, and common. See Chap. 4.

10. Strict liability is likely to play an increasingly important role compared to general accidents. This is so due to a number of reasons, such as an increased liability of manufacturers as they will remain in control of AI even after the product is owned and used by other persons. Manufacturers are always liable based on strict liability. Second, the involvement of AI in certain sectors requires strict liability due to per se increased dangerousness arising from the application of this technology. See Chap. 4.
11. A general clause on strict liability and a set of specific cases in LO should remain. Specific cases where AI is inherently dangerous should be added to the statutory text, while the general clause has a catch-all potential. A criterion of increased dangerousness used to apply strict liability has the potential to cover problems caused by AI, provided there is a proper understanding of the problems by the courts. The current structure through which LO treats strict liability allows for adjustments to AI. See Chap. 4.
12. The notion of increased dangerousness remains potent in addressing liability challenges. However, this does not mean that every AI should be treated as such. Case law concerning animals suggests that courts apply it to animals due to their autonomy. This is unusual because many other European regimes differentiate between animals and in some cases provide their holders with fault-based liability while in others with strict liability. A nuanced view should be applied in the case of AI. It should not be perceived that AI per se bears increased dangerousness for its environment. See Chap. 4.
13. Product liability plays an important role in regulating AI. Due to the change of control of AI, manufacturers are likely to be in a better position to navigate through a complex realm of the algorithmic world and interact with other persons' protected values or property. Moreover, even after it has left the factory, manufacturers are likely to be able to interact with AI through the provision of updates and similar inputs. In the case of B&H, it seems to be to a large extent able to efficiently allocate liability. Moreover, due to a lack of definitions of producer, product, and defect, courts are left with great leeway in interpreting it. See Chaps. 4 and 6.
14. There is no leeway for the application of vicarious liability to AI, according to LO. The reason lies in an exclusive recognition of humans as auxiliaries. However, case law based on LO suggests that the courts have considered animals to a certain extent to be a functional equivalent. They applied strict liability in those cases as animals are perceived to possess increased dangerousness notwithstanding whether they are wild or domesticated or whether they constitute increased dangerousness in a particular case. As it has been previously stated, while AI can be considered a functional equivalent of auxiliaries, it would be detrimental to treat it as increasingly dangerous without exceptions. See Chap. 5.

15. Victims of accidents should have equal rights regardless of whether an accident occurred within the purview of contract or tortious liability. While legal theory and case law in B&H have not dealt extensively with a distinction between the two, it is important at the outset not to discriminate between victims. The courts should take this into account when applying vague standards envisaged in LO, by having in mind fundamental principles of civil law. See Chap. 6.
16. Traditional criteria of allocation of responsibility point to a manufacturer as the person who has the ultimate control of AI. Additionally, it is the party who may be the cheapest cost avoider in most scenarios. Due to the prospect of expansion of strict liability, control is expected to play an increasingly important role, while, accordingly, objectionable behavior is expected to be less important as the application of fault-based liability may apply less commonly, at least at the beginning. Benefits from the use of technology are a justification for joint and several liability in order to ease a victim's position. See Chaps. 5 and 6.
17. Law should recognize persons who are in control to have increasined liability exposure. In the case of AI, those would likely be manufacturers and/or persons who determine and control AI's specific conduct. It would be advisable to employ concepts akin to backend operator and frontend operator, as suggested in the EU Parliament 2020 Resolution. Updates to PLD also follow this line of reasoning by providing higher liability exposure for a manufacturer. Those concepts should be implemented into B&H law. See Chaps. 5 and 6.
18. Liability of AI itself, whether as a separate legal person or with any type of halfway status, has the potential to undermine the goals of tort law. This idea should be abandoned at the moment, at least until AI changes to the extent it merits a different approach. The law should remain focused on persons as addresses of liability. There are several reasons why holding AI liable would be a bad idea. Such a radical shift in the law may provide a lack of incentives to persons who participate in manufacturing and use of AI to act responsibly. Furthermore, entirely new set of rules would be necessary to provide for funds of a newly created defendant as well as how it can represent its interests aptly. See Chap. 5.
19. The position of an injured party is likely to be deteriorated compared to traditional accidents. The reasons are manyfold and range from the specific importance of one's data to the hardship of establishing causation. Safety standards as a set of ex ante measures are the first line of protection for victims. However, until they have been established (and perhaps even after), the position of an injured party should be enhanced until it is equal to traditional accidents. The role of courts in that respect is to interpret existing broad notions in B&H in line with the principle of equality of parties. See Chap. 6.
20. A victim is likely to face increased costs related to their claim. The costs of expert witnesses may be inevitable and high. Furthermore, B&H civil procedure law does not provide a guarantee that success in the proceedings will shift the costs to the defendant, despite a different opinion of the highest national court instances. Their understanding should be implemented in order to settle this conundrum. See Chap. 6.

21. A lack of definition of standard of proof allows courts to be flexible and thus should not be changed. The burden of proof, although borne by a victim, is supplemented with the rules of adverse inference in case a defendant fails to provide data necessary for establishing causation. While the current state of play is apt, further clarification of the effects of adverse inference should be prescribed explicitly in the statute in order to provide clarity to parties in the proceedings. See Chap. 6.
22. Logging by design is desired in the regulation of liability, at least for three reasons: 1. victim's ability to prove the claim; 2. responsible party's ability to prove its innocence in the recourse proceedings; 3. insurance company's ability to monitor potentially responsible parties. Corresponding problems related to data retention require further consideration. However, implementing this feature should take into account potential risks such as data protection. This question requires to be studied separately. See Chaps. 4, 5, and 6.
23. Insurance and compensation funds play important role in achieving timely compensation in B&H liability law. They should be adopted in case of AI accidents, and mandatory insurance and/or compensation funds should be imposed in sectors where the frequency of accidents and magnitude is high. B&H has a significant experience with these devices and their extension to the new technologies should not be too problematic. See Chaps. 3 and 6.
24. Joint and several liability should be interpreted as to include all backend and frontend operators of AI. This is a significant measure whereby a position of an injured party would be enhanced. This would solve a judgment-proof problem and as well as provide a deep-pocket defendant. Recourse proceedings between potential defendants require further consideration. At the outset, it is important to have logging by design features in order to provide parties with data in order to prove their roles in the accident. Should the accident occur due to a behavior of AI that cannot be attributed to any defendant, liability should be not borne by the users as they are unable to impact modus operandi of AI to the extent as those who manufactured it can. See Chaps. 5 and 6.

Bibliography

Court Cases and Opinions

- Cantonal Court of Tuzla, 126 0 P 142724 21 Gž 2, 10.05.2021.
- Conclusion XIV Joint sessions of the Federal Court, republican and provincial supreme courts and of the Supreme Military Court of 25 and 26 March 1980.
- Court of B&H, S1 3 P 0 16700 16 Gž 2, 03.06.2016.
- Court of Sarajevo Canton, 65 0 Ps 022929 09 Pž, 23.9.2011.
- European Court of Justice, C-183/00, González Sánchez v Medicina Asturiana SA, [2002] ECR I-3901.
- European Court of Human Rights, Dorić v. Bosnia and Herzegovina, 68811/13, 2017.
- European Court of Human Rights, Škrbić and Vujičić v. Bosnia and Herzegovina, 37444/17 i 75271/17, 2019
- European Court of Human Rights, Hadžajlić v. Bosnia and Herzegovina, 10770/18, 2020.
- European Court of Justice, C-65/20, ECLI:EU:C:2021:471.
- Supreme Court of B&H, Gž. 286/78, od 11. 05. 1978., Bilten Vrhovnog suda BiH, br. 3., Sarajevo, 1978.
- Supreme Court of Croatia Rev - 2156/1991.
- Supreme Court of Croatia Rev - 985/1988.
- Supreme Court of Croatia, Rev. 405/99, 22. 4. 1999. - Izbor odluka 2/1999 – 46.
- Supreme Court of Croatia, Rev-382/85.
- Supreme Court of Croatia, Gž 596/80.
- Supreme Court of FB&H, 070-0-Rev-08-000194.
- Supreme Court of FB&H, Gvl–9/03.
- Supreme Court of Federation B&H, 070–0–Rev–06–000939, 23.08.2007.
- Supreme Court of Federation B&H, P 091661 11 Rev.
- Supreme Court of Serbia Rev. 2066/80, Bilten sudske prakse 5-6-/1981.

N. Muftić, *Artificial Intelligence and Tortious Liability*, European Union and its Neighbours in a Globalized World 21, https://doi.org/10.1007/978-3-031-86453-7

- Supreme Court of Serbia, 3393/92.
- Supreme Court of Serbia, 36/1995.
- Supreme Court of Serbia, Rev. 2333/2003.
- Supreme Court of Serbia, Rev. 535/06.
- Supreme Court of Serbia, Rev. 2875/05.
- Supreme Court of Serbia, Rev. 3454/2004.
- Supreme Court of Serbia, Rev. 368/96.
- Supreme Court of Serbia, Rev. 4115/01, 18 April 2002, Bilten sudske prakse VSS, 1/2003.
- Supreme Court of Serbia, Rev. 4206/94.
- Supreme Court of Slovenia Gž. 11/1966 and Gž. 1148/58.
- Supreme Court of Slovenia, Ips 142/1980 i 143/1980.

Legislative Materials and Studies

- A European approach to artificial intelligence, available at: https://digital-strategy.ec.europa.eu/en/policies/european-approach-artificial-intelligence
- The Alan Turing Institute (online) Data science and AI glossary, available at: https://www.turing.ac.uk/news/data-science-and-ai-glossary
- AI Act Explanatory memorandum, available at: https://eur-lex.europa.eu/legal-content/EN/TXT/?uri=CELEX%3A52021PC0206
- Andrea Bertolini, Study on artificial intelligence and civil liability (2020) European Parliament's Committee on Legal Affairs, Policy Department for Citizens' Rights and Constitutional Affairs, Study Requested by the JURI Committee https://www.europarl.europa.eu/RegData/etudes/STUD/2020/ 621926/ IPOL_STU(2020)621926_EN.pdf
- Artificial intelligence, human rights, democracy, and the rule of law - a primer, available at: https://rm.coe.int/primer-en-new-cover-pages-coe-english-compressed-2754-7186-0228-v-1/1680a2fd4a
- Artificial intelligence and human rights, available at: https://www.coe.int/en/web/artificial-intelligence/secretary-general-marija-pejcinovic-buric
- Artificial intelligence, blockchain and the future of Europe, available at: https://www.eib.org/en/products/advising/innovfin-advisory/ai-blockchain-and-future-of-europe-the Report
- Bundestag nimmt Gesetz zum au-tonomen Fahren an, available at: https://www.bundestag.de/dokumente/textarchiv/2021/kw20-de-autonomes-fahren-840196
- Christiane Wendehorst, Safety and Liability Related Aspects of Software, European Commission, 2020.
- Commission, 'Commission Staff Working Document on the free flow of data and emerging issues of the European data economy' SWD (2017) 2 final, 40ff.
- Communication from the Commission to the European Parliament, the European Council, the Council, the European Economic and Social Committee and the

Committee of the Regions on Artificial Intelligence for Europe, Brussels, 25.4.2018 COM(2018) 237 final.
- Communication from the Commission to the European Parliament, the Council, the European Economic and Social Committee and the Committee of the Regions: A Digital Single Market Strategy for Europe (COM/2015/192 final).
- Communication on Fostering a European approach to Artificial Intelligence, available at: https://digital-strategy.ec.europa.eu/en/library/communication-fostering-european-approach-artificial-intelligence
- Coordinated Plan on Artificial Intelligence 2021 Review, available at: https://digital-strategy.ec.europa.eu/en/library/coordinated-plan-artificial-intelligence-2021-review
- Council Conclusions of 16 November 2020 on regulatory sandboxes and experimentation clauses as tools for an innovation-friendly, future-proof and resilient regulatory framework that masters disruptive challenges in the digital age 12683/1/20 REV 1 (2020) 13026/20.
- Council resolution of 14 April 1975 on a preliminary programme of the European Economic Community for a consumer protection and information policy [1975] OJ C92/1.
- Council resolution of 19 May 1981 on a second programme of the European Economic Community for a consumer protection and information policy [1981] OJ C133/1.
- Department of Transportation, Comparative Studies in Automobile Accident Compensation (Washington: Dept. of Transportation, 1970), 6.
- Development strategy for Federation FB&H 2021-2027 (Strategija razvoja Federacije BiH 2021-2027), available at: https://fzzpr.gov.ba/files/Strategije/Strategija%20razvoja%20FBiH%202021.-2027..pdf
- European Commission, The Report from the Commission to the European Parliament, the Council and the European Economic and Social Committee. The Report on the safety and liability implications of Artificial Intelligence, the Internet of Things and robotics, European Commission, 2020.
- European Commission, Building a European Data Economy (Communication) COM (2017) 9 final, 13ff.
- European Commission, Communication from the Commission to the European Parliament, the Council, the
- European Commission, Proposal for a Council Directive on the liability of suppliers of services, COM (90) 482 final [1991] OJ C12/8.
- European Commission, The Report from the Expert Group on Liability and New Technologies – New Technologies Formation, Liability for Artificial Intelligence and other emerging digital technologies, pp. 39–42
- European Commission's Expert Group on Liability and New Technologies – New Technologies Formation The Report on Liability for Artificial Intelligence and other emerging technologies, 2019.
- European Convention on Compulsory Insurance against Civil Liability in respect of Motor Vehicles (ETS No. 029).

- European Economic and Social Committee and the Committee of the Region, 2021 Communication on EU Enlargement Policy, 6, available at: https://ec.europa.eu/neighbourhood-enlargement/bosnia-and-herzegovina-the Report-2021_en
- European Law Institute, Guiding Principles for Updating the Product Liability Directive for the Digital Age, 2021, available at: https://europeanlawinstitute.eu/fileadmin/user_upload/p_eli/Publications/ELI_Guiding_Principles_for_Updating_the_PLD_for_the_Digital_Age.pdf
- European Law Institute, Response to the public consultation on the White Paper: On Artificial Intelligence – A European approach to excellence and trust, COM (2020) 65 final, available at: https://www.europeanlawinstitute.eu/fileadmin/user_upload/p_eli/News_page/2020/ELI_Response_AI_White_Paper.pdf
- European Parliament, Resolution of 16 February 2017 with recommendations to the Commission on Civil Law Rules on Robotics, P8_TA-PROV(2017)0051.
- European Parliament, Resolution on a framework of ethical aspects of artificial intelligence, robotics and related technologies, 2020/2012(INL).
- European Parliament, Resolution on intellectual property rights for the development of artificial intelligence technologies 2020/2015(INI).
- Expert Group on liability and new technologies, available at: https://ec.europa.eu/transparency/expert-groups-register/screen/expert-groups/consult?do=groupDetail.groupDetail&groupID=3592
- German Data Ethics Commission, Report on Data and Algorithmic Systems, 2019.
- Global Artificial Intelligence Industry Whitepaper, available at: https://www2.deloitte.com/cn/en/pages/technology-media-and-telecommunications/articles/global-ai-development-white-paper.html
- Google, Perspectives on Issues in AI Governance, available at: https://ai.google/static/documents/perspectives-on-issues-in-ai-governance.pdf
- High-Level Expert Group on Artificial Intelligence set up by the European Commission, A definition of AI: Main capabilities and scientific disciplines, available at: https://www.aepd.es/sites/default/files/2019-12/ai-definition.pdf
- New aspects and challenges in consumer protection, available at: https://www.europarl.europa.eu/RegData/etudes/STUD/2020/648790/IPOL_STU(2020)648790_EN.pdf
- One Hundred Year Study on Artificial Intelligence, Stanford, University, September 2016, available at: http://ai100.stanford.edu/2016-the Report
- Opinion of the Dataethikommision, available at: https://www.bmj.de/DE/Themen/FokusThemen/Datenethikkommission/Datenethikkommission_EN_node.html
- PricewaterhouseCoopers Global Artificial Intelligence Study: Exploiting the AI Revolution, available at: https://www.pwc.com/gx/en/issues/data-and-analytics/publications/artificial-intelligence-study.html
- Principle 22; Conference held on the 6–8 July 1997, available at http://europa.eu.int/ISPO/bonn/Mindeclaration/ifinalen.html.

- Proposal for a Regulation of the European Parliament and of the council laying down harmonised rules on artificial intelligence (artificial intelligence act) and amending certain union legislative acts, available at: https://eur-lex.europa.eu/legal-content/EN/TXT/?qid=1623335154975&uri=CELEX%3A52021PC0206
- Proposal for a Regulation of the European Parliament and of the Council on a Single Market for Digital Services (Digital Services Act) and amending Directive 2000/31/EC (COM/2020/825 final).
- Proposal for the Dartmouth summer research project on artificial intelligence, available at: http://www-formal.stanford.edu/jmc/history/dartmouth/dartmouth.html
- Resolution with recommendations to the Commission on a civil liability regime for artificial intelligence (2020/2014(INL)).
- Response of the European Law Institute, Public Consultation on Civil Liability Adapting liability rules to the digital age and artificial intelligence, 2022, available at: https://europeanlawinstitute.eu/fileadmin/user_upload/p_eli/Publications/ELI_Response_to_Public_Consultation_on_Civil_Liability.pdf
- Road traffic injuries, available at: https://www.who.int/news-room/fact-sheets/detail/road-traffic-injuries
- The Report from the Commission to the European Parliament, the Council and the European Economic and Social Committee on the application of the Council Directive on the approximation of the laws, regulations, and administrative provisions of the Member States concerning liability for defective products (85/374/EEC).
- UNCITRAL Model Law on Electronic Commerce with Guide to Enactment 1996 with additional Article 5 bis as adopted in 1998
- United Nations General Assembly, The Report of the Special Rapporteur on extreme poverty and human rights, 2019, available at: A/74/493—E—A/74/493 -Desktop (undocs.org)
- Ursula von der Leyen, A Union that Strives for More: My Agenda for Europe, Political Guidelines for the Next European Commission 2019-2024, 2019.
- Vodič: Suđenje u razumnom roku, Constitutional Court of B&H, 2021, available at: https://www.ustavnisud.ba/uploads/documents/vodic-sudjenje-u-razumnom-roku_1611845149.pdf
- What is artificial intelligence and how is it used?, available at: https://www.europarl.europa.eu/news/en/headlines/society/20200827STO85804/what-is-artificial-intelligence-and-how-is-it-used

Legislation

- Automated and Electric Vehicles Act 2018, available at: https://www.legislation.gov.uk/ukpga/2018/18/contents/enacted
- Directive (EU) 2019/770 of the European Parliament and of the Council of 20 May 2019 on certain aspects concerning contracts for the supply of digital content and digital services (Text with EEA relevance.)

- Directive 2009/103/EC of the European Parliament and of the Council of 16 September 2009 relating to insurance against civil liability in respect of the use of motor vehicles, and the enforcement of the obligation to insure against such liability [2009] OJ L263/11.
- Directive 2014/104/EU of the European Parliament and of the Council of 26 November 2014 on certain rules governing actions for damages under national law for infringements of the competition law provisions of the Member States and of the European Union [2014] OJ L349/1.
- Directive 95/46/EC of the European Parliament and of the Council of 24 October 1995 on the protection of individuals with regard to the processing of personal data and on the free movement of such data COM (1990) 314.
- Family law of FB&H (Official Gazette FB&H 34/2005, 31/2014).
- Family law of Republika Srpska (Official Gazette Republika Srpska 54/2002, 41/2008 i 63/2014).
- Law on authorship and related rights (Official Gazette B&H 63/10).
- Law on fundamentals of traffic safety in Bosnia and Herzegovina (Official Gazette B&H 6/06, 75/06, 44/07, 84/09, 48/10, 18/13, 8/17).
- Law on inheritance of FB&H (Official Gazette FB&H 80/2014 i 32/2019).
- Law on Mandatory Traffic Insurance of Republika Srpska (Official Gazette Republika Srpska 82/15).
- Law on Mandatory Traffic Insurance of the Federation of BiH (Official Gazette Federation B&H 57/20).
- Law on the Collective Management of Copyright and Related Rights (Official Gazette B&H 63/10).
- Law on the Protection of Indications of Geographical Origin (Official Gazette B&H 53/10).
- Law on the Protection of Topographies of Integrated Circuits (Official Gazette B&H 53/10).
- Regulation (EU) 2016/679 of the European Parliament and of the Council of 27 April 2016 on the protection of natural persons with regard to the processing of personal data and on the free movement of such data, and repealing Directive 95/46/EC (General Data Protection Regulation) [2016] OJ L119/1.
- Law on notary public FB&H (Official Gazette FB&H 45/02).
- Law on Industrial Designs (Official Gazette B&H 53/10).
- Law on Obligations FB&H (Official Gazette SFRJ 29/1978, 39/1985, 45/1989 … 2/1992, 13/1993 i 13/1994; Official Gazette FB&H 29/2003 i 42/2011).
- Law on Obligations RS (Official Gazette SFRJ 29/1978, 39/1985, 45/1989 … 2/1992, 13/1993 i 13/1994; Official Gazette RS 17/1993, 3/1996, 37/2001, 39/2003 i 74/2004).
- Law on Patents (Official Gazette B&H 53/10).
- Law on Trademarks (Official Gazette B&H 53/10).
- Law on Copyright and Related Rights (Official Gazette B&H 63/10).
- Law on competition of B&H (Official Gazette B&H 48/05, 76/07 i 80/09) in Article 44 even allows for direct application of the Court of Justice of the EU case law and decision of the EU Commission.

- Council Directive 85/374/EEC of 25 July 1985 on the approximation of the laws, regulations and administrative provisions of the Member States concerning liability for defective products [1985] OJ L210/29, as amended by Directive 1999/34/EC of the European Parliament and of the Council of 10 May 1999 [1999] OJ L141/20.
- Law on notary public RS (Official Gazette Republika Srpska 86/03, 2/04, 74/05).
- Law on inheritance of Republika Srpska (Official Gazette 1/2009, 55/2009, 91/2016, 28/2019, 82/2019).
- Law on attorney profession (The Official Gazette FB&H 27/03 21/09), Law on attorney profession RS The Official Gazette Republika Srpska 80/2015).

Media Articles

- Amazon scraps secret AI recruiting tool that showed bias against women, available at: https://www.reuters.com/article/us-amazon-com-jobs-automation-insight-idUSKCN1MK08G
- Artificial Intelligence: Does Consciousness Matter?, available at: https://www.frontiersin.org/articles/10.3389/fpsyg.2019.01535/full
- Encyclopædia Britannica consciousness, available at: https://www.britannica.com/topic/consciousness
- Bias isn't the only problem with credit scores—and no, AI can't help, available at: https://www.technologyreview.com/2021/06/17/1026519/racial-bias-noisy-data-credit-scores-mortgage-loans-fairness-machine-learning/
- Comment le Code de la route s'adapte à la voiture autonome, available at: https://www.rtl.fr/actu/sciences-tech/comment-le-code-de-la-route-s-adapte-a-la-voiture-autonome-7900052176
- Fake News Is Rampant, Here Is How Artificial Intelligence Can Help, available at: https://www.forbes.com/sites/bernardmarr/2021/01/25/fake-news-is-rampant-here-is-how-artificial-intelligence-can-help/?sh=3abf5c7d48e4
- Federacija BiH namjerava razvijati umjetnu inteligenciju, available at: https://www.klix.ba/scitech/tehnologija/federacija-bih-namjerava-razvijati-umjetnu-inteligenciju/210308082
- Financial Conduct Authority, Regulatory sandbox, available at: https://www.fca.org. uk/publication/research/regulatory-sandbox.pdf
- Gender Shades: Intersectional Accuracy Disparities in Commercial Gender Classification, available at: http://proceedings.mlr.press/v81/buolamwini18a/buolamwini18a.pdf
- Google's 'Infringenovation' Secrets, Forbes, available at: www.forbes.com/sites/scottcleland/2011/10/03/googles-infringenovation-secrets/#78a3795430a6.
- Marilyn Cooper, Jewish Word | Golem, available at: https://momentmag.com/jewish-word-golem/

- Memorial ceremony for deceased tunnel workers, available at: https://web.archive.org/web/20200427001530/https://www.alptransit.ch/en/media/press-releases/detail/news/memorial-ceremony-for-deceased-tunnel-workers-977/
- Self-Driving Uber Car Kills Pedestrian in Arizona, Where Robots Roam, available at: https://www.nytimes.com/2018/03/19/technology/uber-driverless-fatality.html
- Stephen Hawking: 'Transcendence looks at the implications of artificial intelligence - but are we taking AI seriously enough?', available at: https://www.independent.co.uk/news/science/stephen-hawking-transcendence-looks-implications-artificial-intelligence-are-we-taking-ai-seriously-enough-9313474.html
- Tesla in deadly California crash was on Autopilot: Authorities, available at: https://www.aljazeera.com/economy/2021/5/14/tesla-in-deadly-california-crash-was-on-autopilot-authorities
- Tesla Model 3: Paris' largest taxi firm suspends cars after fatal crash, available at: https://www.bbc.com/news/world-europe-59647069
- Tracking AI Investment Initial Findings From the Private Markets, available at: https://cset.georgetown.edu/publication/tracking-ai-investment/
- Want Europe to have the best AI? Reform the GDPR, available at: https://iapp.org/news/a/want-europe-to-have-the-best-ai-reform-the-gdpr/
- What should we learn from past AI forecasts?, available at: https://www.openphilanthropy.org/focus/global-catastrophic-risks/potential-risks-advanced-artificial-intelligence/what-should-we-learn-past-ai-forecasts
- When a computer program keeps you in jail, available at: https://www.nytimes.com/2017/06/13/opinion/how-computers-are-harming-criminal-justice.html
- Who Is Winning the AI Race: China, the EU or the United States?, available at: https://datainnovation.org/2019/08/who-is-winning-the-ai-race-china-the-eu-or-the-united-states/
- Zaragoza Radiotherapy Accident – 1990, available at: https://devastatingdisasters.com/zaragoza-radiotherapy-accident-1990/amp/?fbclid=IwAR13ptifQovRLaexMnT0sB7NPY75wKlTUe976Ax2UNYJAPY3JJgvBKWomNA

MIX
Papier aus verantwortungsvollen Quellen
Paper from responsible sources
FSC® C105338

If you have any concerns about our products,
you can contact us on
ProductSafety@springernature.com

In case Publisher is established outside the EU,
the EU authorized representative is:
Springer Nature Customer Service Center GmbH
Europaplatz 3, 69115 Heidelberg, Germany

Printed by Libri Plureos GmbH
in Hamburg, Germany